Y0-AZH-175

INTERNATIONAL BANK FOR RECONSTRUCTION AND DEVELOPMENT

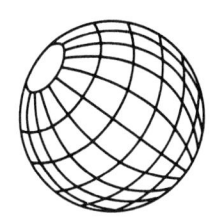

WORLD BANK STAFF OCCASIONAL PAPERS NUMBER FOURTEEN

This paper may not be quoted as representing the view of the Bank and its affiliated organizations. They do not accept responsibility for its accuracy or completeness.

Editorial Committee

Stanley Please (Chairman)
T. H. Silcock (Editor)
George Baldwin
Bela Balassa
Barend A. de Vries
Ravi Gulhati
Mahbub ul Haq
P. D. Henderson
John A. Holsen
Benjamin B. King
Shlomo Reutlinger

HANS H. THIAS AND MARTIN CARNOY

COST-BENEFIT ANALYSIS IN EDUCATION
A CASE STUDY OF KENYA

REF/ LB 2970 .K4 T45
Thias, Hans H.
Cost-benefit analysis in
education

Distributed by The Johns Hopkins Press
Baltimore and London

Copyright © 1972
by the International Bank for Reconstruction and Development
All rights reserved
Manufactured in the United States of America
Library of Congress Catalog Card Number 72-187064

ISBN 0-8018-1335-2

FOREWORD

I would like to explain *why* the World Bank Group does research work, and why it publishes it. We feel an obligation to look beyond the projects we help to finance toward the whole resource allocation of an economy, and the effectiveness of the use of those resources. Our major concern, in dealings with member countries, is that all scarce resources, including capital, skilled labor, enterprise and know-how, should be used to their best advantage. We want to see policies that encourage appropriate increases in the supply of savings, whether domestic or international. Finally, we are required by our Articles, as well as by inclination, to use objective economic criteria in all our judgments.

These are our preoccupations, and these, one way or another, are the subjects of most of our research work. Clearly, they are also the proper concern of anyone who is interested in promoting development, and so we seek to make our research papers widely available. In doing so, we have to take the risk of being misunderstood. Although these studies are published by the Bank, the views expressed and the methods explored should not necessarily be considered to represent the Bank's views or policies. Rather they are offered as a modest contribution to the great discussion on how to advance the economic development of the underdeveloped world.

ROBERT S. MCNAMARA
President
International Bank for
Reconstruction and Development

TABLE OF CONTENTS

FOREWORD	v
PREFACE	xiii
I. INTRODUCTION	1
Purpose of the Study	1
The Cost-Benefit Method Applied to Education	2
II. KENYA'S EDUCATIONAL SYSTEM	9
A Historical Survey of Education in Kenya	9
The Present Educational System	11
Education Cost and Finance	21
III. EARNINGS AND SCHOOLING, SOCIO-ECONOMIC AND OCCUPATIONAL CHARACTERISTICS	27
The Approach	27
The Data Basis	29
The Model	32
The Relationships between Education, Age, and Earnings	34
The Significance of Non-Schooling Variables—A Digression	54
Rural Incomes and Schooling	56

IV. RATES OF RETURN TO SCHOOLING 63

Types of Rates and Adjustments 63
Calculation of the Rates and the Sources of Data 67
Unadjusted Urban Rates 71
Adjusting for Taxes and Mortality 73
Adjusting for Socio-Economic Differences 75
Adjusting for Occupational Variables 75
The Question of Ability 77
Rates of Return to Education in the Rural Sector 83
Rural and Urban Unemployment 86
Final Rates, Adjustments Accumulated 90

V. POSSIBLE APPLICATIONS OF RATE-OF-RETURN ANALYSIS TO EDUCATIONAL PLANNING: An Illustration 95

The Model 95
The Supply of Educated Labor 97
Estimates of Demand for Educated Labor 100
Demand Projections and Equilibrium Estimates for Africans with Primary Schooling 108
Demand Projections and Equilibrium Estimates for Africans with Secondary Schooling 118
Demand Projections and Equilibrium Estimates for Africans with University Training 122
Results and Conclusions 125

VI. OUTCOME OF THE STUDY 127

The Specific Results 127
The General Lesson 134

ANNEXES

A. THE DETERMINANTS OF EXAMINATION PERFORMANCE AND RATES OF RETURN TO SCHOOL INPUTS: An Exploratory Analysis 143
B. SCOPE AND ORGANIZATION OF THE LABOR FORCE SAMPLE SURVEY 173
C. REGRESSION ANALYSIS, INCOME AND EDUCATION OF AFRICAN MALES: SCHOOLING AS A VARIABLE 177

D. DERIVATION OF PROCEDURES FOR ESTIMATION OF ABSOLUTE EARNINGS FROM REGRESSION DATA 181
E. CORRECTION OF RURAL LANDHOLDER INCOMES FOR ACREAGE AND FAMILY SIZE DIFFERENTIALS BETWEEN AGE GROUPS AND BETWEEN EDUCATION LEVELS FOR GIVEN AGE GROUP 184
F. SOLUTION FOR CHANGE IN WAGE LEVEL TWO FROM DISCOUNT FORMULA 189

SELECTED BIBLIOGRAPHY 191

TABLES

2.1 Enrollments in Primary and Secondary Education, 1959–68   12
2.2 Average School-Leaving Age of Urban Employees, by Ethnic Group, Sex, and Educational Achievement, 1968   15
2.3 Range of Annual Fees in Harambee Schools   20
2.4 Students from Kenya at the East African University Colleges   22
2.5 Estimated Expenditure on Primary Education, 1967   24
2.6 Estimated Education Expenditure from Domestic Sources by Main Components, 1966   26
3.1 Key for Variables Used   30
3.2 Unadjusted Age-Earnings Profiles, African Males, by Years of Schooling, 1968   32
3.3 Regression Coefficients of Independent Dummy Variables; Dependent Variable: Monthly Earnings, African Males, 1968   36
3.4 Age-Earnings Profiles of African Males by Years of Schooling, 1968: Adjusted for Parents' Literacy, Tribe, and Father's Occupation   37
3.5 Regression Coefficients of Independent Dummy Variables, Socio-Economic Variables Held Constant; Dependent Variable: Monthly Earnings, African Males, 1968   38
3.6 Means of Independent Variables, African Males, by Years of Schooling, 1968   40
3.7 Age-Earnings Profiles, African Males, by Years of Schooling, 1968, Adjusted for All Variables   43

3.8	Coefficients of Independent Variables, All Variables Held Constant, Dependent Variable Monthly Earnings, African Males, 1968	44
3.9	Unadjusted Age-Earnings Profiles, African, Asian and European Females by Years of Schooling, 1968	46
3.10	Regression Coefficients of Independent Dummy Variables; Dependent Variable: Monthly Earnings, All Sex-ethnic Groups and Means of Variables for African Males with 13 Years of Schooling, 1968	49
3.11	Regression Coefficients of Independent Dummy Variables; Dependent Variables: Monthly Earnings, All Sex-ethnic Groups with 17 Years of Schooling, 1968, and Means of Variables for African Males	51
3.12	Unadjusted Age-Earnings Profiles by Years of Schooling, All Sex-ethnic Groups, 1968	52
3.13	Unadjusted Age-Earnings Profiles for African Males, Alone and as Variable, 11, 12–13 and 14–17 Years of Schooling, 1968	53
3.14	Mean Annual Income, Farm Acreage, and Age of Household Heads by Education Level of Household Head, 1963–64, Rural Central Province	58
3.15	Total Income of Rural Head of Household by Age and Education, 1963–64, Adjusted for Acreage and Family Size Differences between Age Groups and between Education Levels	59
3.16	Mean Annual Income of Rural Landholding Heads of Household by Age and Education, 1963–64, Unadjusted for Acreage and Family Size Differences between Age Groups and between Education Levels	59
3.17	Mean Annual Gross Rural Family Income by Age and Schooling of Household Head, 1963	60
4.1	Average Delay between Leaving School and Starting Work of African Male Urban Employees by Level of Education and Year of Leaving School	68
4.2	Annual Earnings Foregone and Other Private Costs by Age and Years of Schooling, Male Africans, 1968	69
4.3	Annual Costs per Student Used in Calculating Social Rates of Return	71
4.4	Average Social and Private Rates of Return to Schooling for Africans by Years of Schooling, Adjusted for Age Only; for Age, Taxes and Mortality Only; and for Age and Socio-Economic Variables Only	72

4.5 Average Rates of Return to Different Examination Scores and Schooling Periods, Adjusted for Socio-Economic Variables, 1968   79
4.6 Distribution of African Landowners by Age, 1963–64   83
4.7 Rates of Return to Schooling, Landholding Household Heads in Rural Central Province, 1963–64, Corrected for Probability of Being Landholder   84
4.8 Rates of Return to Schooling, Landholding Household Heads in Rural Central Province, 1966 Costs and 1963–64 Benefits, Corrected for Probability of Being Landholder   85
4.9 Estimated Numbers of African Male Primary School Leavers and Estimated Urban Employment Probabilities, 1960–66   88
4.10 Urban and Rural, Weighted and Combined Private Rates of Return to Primary Education, 1960–66   89
4.11 Urban and Rural, Weighted and Combined Social Rates of Return to Primary Education, 1960–1966   89
4.12 Combined Urban and Rural Rates of Return to Primary Education, Adjusted for Socio-Economic Background, 1960–1966   90
4.13 Average Private Rates of Return to Schooling, All Adjustments, by Years of Schooling, 1968   91
4.14 Average Social Rates of Return to Schooling, All Adjustments, by Years of Schooling, 1968   92
4.15 Social Internal Rates of Return to Schooling for Males in Seven Developing Countries, Based on Urban Samples: Kenya, Uganda, India, Mexico, Chile, Colombia and Venezuela   94
5.1 Projected Annual Pupil Outflow, 1969–74   99
5.2 Average Annual Earnings, 1957–66   103
5.3 Employment by Ethnic Groups and Major Economic Sectors, 1957–66   104
5.4 Gross Domestic Product at Factor Cost by Major Economic Sectors, and Cost of Living Index, Nairobi, 1957–66   105
5.5 Projections of Demand for Teachers, 1974   109
5.6 Growth Alternatives, 1968–74: Social Rate of Return, Wages and Employment for Two Labor Force Levels   109
5.7 Growth Alternatives, 1968–74: Wages and Employment for Africans with Primary and Secondary School and University Training   110

6.1	Rates of Return to Investment in Physical Capital	130
6.2	Attitudes of East African Pupils toward Family Planning, 1965–66	138
A.1	Average Value (Mean) of Main Variables Used in Examination Performance Regressions, CSC and HSC Cycles, 1966	162
A.2	Rates of Return to Additional per Pupil Expenditure	166
A.3	Salary Scales for the Teaching Service	170
C.1	Regression Coefficients of Schooling and Independent Dummy Variables, Dependent Variable: Monthly Earnings, African Males, 1968, Schooling from 0–11 Years	178
E.1	Gross Family Farm Income and Imputed Farm and Non-Farm Income of Household Head, by Age and Education, 1963–64	187

FIGURES

2.1	Kenya: Structure of Education, 1969	13
3.1	Unadjusted Age-Earnings Profiles, African Males by Years of Schooling, 1968	35
3.2	Unadjusted Age-Earnings Profiles, African Females by Years of Schooling, 1968	47
4.1	Variants of Rates of Return to Education Developed in Kenya Case Study	64
5.1	Supply of and Demand for Educated Labor	96
A.1	Time—Path of School Output Quality as a Function of Examination Performance	145

PREFACE

This study is part of the continuing work in the Economics Department on problems of sector and project analysis, and is the second Department report dealing with problems of the economics of education. It was preceded by a paper prepared for the Bank by Mr. M. Blaug of the University of London Institute of Education and the London School of Economics, *A Cost-Benefit Approach to Educational Planning in Developing Countries* (EC-157, December 20, 1967).

Both studies originated from a growing awareness that the methods currently used in planning expenditure for education in developing countries fail to take into account important links between the educational system and the economy. On the one hand, current methods take the economic value of more education largely for granted; they do not attempt to measure the benefits of the various types of education in monetary terms, thus precluding systematic economic analysis of the benefits as well as the costs of providing additional education by type and level. On the other hand, little if any attention is being paid to the role of earnings in the demand for and supply of educated people in a country; both demand and supply are affected by earnings and are dependent on each other.

Whereas the earlier study provided a theoretical framework for a cost-benefit analysis of educational expenditure, the present report is an attempt to implement those suggestions in a case study on one country: Kenya. Although most of Mr. Blaug's proposals have been followed up successfully and some lines of thought have been developed well beyond the original suggestions, the authors did not expect the study to yield a once-and-for-all answer to the question of how to approach educational planning in developing countries. They consider it a true reflection of its experimental nature that it revealed almost as many new problems as the well-known ones it helped to answer.

The authors wish to express their appreciation for the great help they received during the various stages of the study. While it would be impossible to list all those who supported the field work in Kenya, the authors would like to mention Messrs. P. R. C. Williams, Ministry of Education; A. T. Brough, Ministry of Economic Planning and Development; D. Higgs, Ministry of Local Government, and K. Wilson, Ministry of Education, without whose contributions the study could hardly have been undertaken.

Mr. E. Rado of the Institute for Development Studies, University College, Nairobi, participated as a consultant in the early stages of the study. His assistance and wise advice, along with the knowledge and experience of Mr. D. C. Rogers, then at the Institute for Development Studies, significantly helped the authors to overcome the initial difficulties and to understand the country's economy and educational system. The hospitality the authors enjoyed from Mr. D. L. Gordon and his colleagues at the World Bank's Permanent Mission for Eastern Africa was very much appreciated.

Messrs. J. Gitua, O. C. Ntapengerwa, C. Okemo, D. Otieno, G. Owino, J. Ouma, E. K. Rotich, and J. B. Rudasingwa were intelligent and hardworking interviewers, on whose judgment the authors could always rely. The organizational skills of Miss V. Henderson, the authors' secretary in Nairobi, deserve the greatest praise.

Last but not least, the authors gratefully acknowledge the cooperation of the management and employees of the firms participating in the Kenya Labor Force Survey, on which the success of the study depended more than on anything else.

The ensuing analysis in Washington benefited greatly from the thorough work of Miss N. Abudabbeh, then a research assistant in the Economics Department. Mr. H. Schneider and Mr. J. Kim did most of the programming work efficiently and with unfailing patience. In the final stages of the study, Mr. R. C. Manning made significant contributions to the presentation of its theoretical basis; Mrs. S. Henneman proved to be a competent and considerate editor. Mrs. Amy Wang, Miss J. Nasaire, Miss C. Morales, and Mrs. D. Drabwell did a splendid job of typing the long and difficult manuscript and many tables.

From its inception, the authors' work profited from the guidance of Mr. H. G. van der Tak, whose expert advice is reflected in the study's present scope and form, and whose impartial support was on more than one occasion a genuine encouragement.

While discussions with all the above-mentioned and with colleagues in the Economics and Education Projects Department helped to clarify many difficult points, the responsibility for any remaining shortcomings and errors, of course, remains entirely with the authors.

P. D. HENDERSON
Director
Economics Department

INTERNATIONAL BANK FOR RECONSTRUCTION AND DEVELOPMENT

WORLD BANK STAFF OCCASIONAL PAPERS NUMBER FOURTEEN

I

INTRODUCTION

Purpose of the Study

This study presents a cost-benefit approach to education that attempts to take into account a number of considerations left aside by previous studies of this kind. It concentrates on the income effects of education, hence it does not claim to give guidelines for education policy, which encompasses *all* aspects of education. However, it does provide a framework for an economic evaluation. We sought to derive from these data several kinds of information which are valuable in assessing an educational system, and which so far have not been combined in cost-benefit studies of education. The most important are:

a) Private and social rates of return to investment[1] in education adjusted for differences in socio-economic background and other factors;

b) Wage/employment alternatives for the future, given projected outputs of the education system; and

c) Rates of return to increasing different kinds of expenditures per pupil, with benefits related to improvement in examination performance (in an Annex).

---

[1] Throughout the study, investment is understood to mean expenditure, whether by individuals (school fees, income foregone) or by the government, and is not restricted to capital or development expenditure.

We have followed the country case study method to illustrate empirically the approach proposed, choosing Kenya as an example. The data were based on interviews with almost 5,000 employees in three urban areas in Kenya. These were conducted in January and February of 1968 by us and a few local assistants, and the data were supplemented by other information on the economy and the education system collected from Kenya.

While the data from the study apply to the Kenyan case only, the conceptual framework and analytical methods employed in this exercise have wider applicability; it is on these concepts and methods rather than on the particular situation in one country that we focus our attention.

The Cost-Benefit Method Applied to Education

The study tries to meet the usual objections raised to applying a cost-benefit approach to expenditure on a social product such as education. Conceptually we believe that these objections have been met, though data shortcomings sometimes make it impossible to test the empirical relevance of the framework developed. Due to the fact that some of the problems of the educational system in Kenya are untypically easy to identify, this case provides a less convincing demonstration of the approach than would be possible in a country where the demand for and supply of educated manpower were more balanced.

Even so, a less sophisticated analysis of the problem would not produce figures which estimate the economic consequences of a country's educational policy, nor would it be able to build the empirical foundations for alternative policies as this study does. The usefulness of the cost-benefit approach should not therefore be judged by any shortcomings of the present study; these are rather attributable to data insufficiencies and the fact that the case chosen did not fully test the power of the approach. In less clear cases the method can provide information not available from simpler analyses, and it can be of great value in the face of major educational investment decisions.

Objections to Its Use

There are five major objections to cost-benefit analysis of investment in education. First, this type of analysis usually treats the difference between the earnings of less educated and more educated persons as the benefits due to their additional formal schooling. However, these incremental earnings are due not only to additional schooling, but also to other basic differences arising from varying socio-economic background and from other "ability" differences generally unrelated to schooling. Therefore, using additional earnings as a measure of the benefits to investment in education exaggerates these benefits.

Second, the use of earnings or wage differentials as the benefits to additional schooling overlooks the impact of unemployment. Significant unemployment may make wages or salaries invalid as the sole measure of benefits from the point of view both of the individual, who allows for the probability of unemployment in his calculations, and of society, which has a certain percentage of graduates at each level earning no wages.

Third, cost-benefit analysis assumes that wages are a valid measure of productivity. Even if there is no unemployment, distortions in the labor market may create gaps between wages and productivity. In Kenya and many other developing countries, public sector wages are higher than private sector wages, and union pressure and national manpower policies set wage and hiring guidelines that may be totally unrelated to productivity. To correct for these distortions, we should estimate "shadow wages" which would prevail in a purely competitive, distortion-free labor market.

Fourth, cost-benefit analysis derives rates of return to investment in schooling on the basis of benefits and costs at the time the data were collected. The rates may measure the return to investments already made, but they may very well not remain valid for further investment undertaken now or in the future, since both wage differentials and costs are likely to change over time. Therefore, the method should offer some theoretically sound way of calculating future rates of return which allows for changes in the benefits and costs of investment in schooling at various levels.

Fifth, cost-benefit analysis can perhaps measure the direct economic return to education investment, but education is justifiable for many other reasons: as a consumer good, enjoyable and worthwhile for both parents and children alike; or as a political good, a means of changing attitudes towards, for example, family planning, national identity, or other socio-political issues. The analysis should therefore take these potential effects of education into account.

Response to the Objections

In response to the first objection we have succeeded in adjusting the income streams of urban Africans for socio-economic background, ability, and occupational variables which may or may not be directly related to increased education. Chapter III is devoted to the calculation and adjustment of age-income profiles for urban Africans (see Tables 3.1–3.5), from which income streams are derived in Chapter IV. Rates of return calculated from the adjusted streams are therefore corrected for these factors.

The procedure used in Chapter III to arrive at the adjusted age-income profiles for urban Africans is as follows. Broadly speaking, regression analysis is used to find what differences between the average incomes of wage-earners are due to educational variables, socio-economic variables, and job-related variables. The first group of variables includes schooling and examination scores; the second, age, tribe, parents' literacy and father's occupation; and the third, size and nature of the firm employing a wage-earner, his job level, and whether he had received on-the-job training. The effect of ability defined as innate intelligence cannot satisfactorily be assessed from the survey data, but the effect of ability as reflected in examination scores can be traced by separately analyzing data for persons with the same education and socio-economic background who achieve different scores.

Specifically, the 4,742 individuals are separated into sex-ethnic groups, and within those groups into schooling subgroups by year of schooling and by primary and secondary examination performance. Three sets of regressions are then carried out, correcting earnings for differences in (i) age distribution, (ii) socio-economic characteristics, and (iii) occupational characteristics. The adjusted age-income profiles are calculated from the regression data.

In response to the second objection, an adjustment for past employment probabilities is made once the rates of return for males have been calculated in Chapter IV. A combined rate of return reflecting unemployment in both urban and rural sectors is estimated by weighting the urban and rural rates of return to investment in primary schooling by the probability that a primary school leaver would have found gainful employment in each of the two sectors over the years 1960–66. The resulting rates are only approximate, as several assumptions have to be made in the weighting process, and the rates of return in the rural sector are only crude estimates. Nevertheless, it can be seen that adjusting for unemployment can drastically reduce the return.

The third objection criticizes the rates-of-return approach for ignoring three kinds of labor market imperfections and for equating earnings with the marginal productivity of labor. The three imperfections usually dealt with in the literature are: (i) anomalies due to the employer's irrational behavior; (ii) distortions in the wage structure, for example those resulting from a colonial past; and (iii) imperfections brought about through the power of collective bargaining groups.

It has often been maintained that for prestige or other reasons, large firms will hire persons with unnecessarily high technical skills and educational qualifications even where these skills are in short supply.[2] While such "conspicuous consumption" of skills may be found in developed

---

[2] This is different from the case in which primary education is universal and secondary education so widespread that firms are forced to hire the latter for jobs which the former could do simply to insure that they find sufficiently able employees.

countries, the data of the Labor Force Survey conducted by the authors (Table 2.2) reveal no such behavior in the Kenyan labor market.

The second group of imperfections is a relic of the past, when the colonial government found it necessary to offer high salaries to attract qualified expatriates. After independence, institutional rigidity prevented a downward adjustment in the wage structure despite an increasing supply of local personnel. In Kenya average salaries of comparably qualified groups (four years of secondary schooling) are indeed higher for public employees.[3] The public sector data in the Labor Force Survey are not based on a random sample and cannot therefore yield firm conclusions; we can use them, however, to adjust the income stream of the group most affected by higher government wages—secondary school leavers—and thereby correct the rate of return to investment in secondary school for this distortion without using shadow prices. We also discuss how the adjusted and unadjusted rates all related to different concepts of the wage-productivity relationship.

Imperfections that can be traced to monopoly or monopsony behavior in specific labor markets may be relatively common, but these are probably less permanent than the other types of distortions. In this study the introduction of union membership as an explanatory variable results in a significant difference between the salaries of members and non-members with up to nine years of schooling; the differences cease to be statistically significant beyond that point, however.

When any such distortions are persistent and expected to be permanent features of the economy, it may be better simply to define productivity in terms of income at the uncorrected rate. If, for example, union pressure on wages is believed to be a permanent feature of the economic system, the social rate should reflect its effects. If tariffs or foreign exchange policy reduce farm wages, the rate of return to rural schooling may also be persistently low. For this reason, and in order to keep the scope of the study within manageable proportions, no estimates are made of shadow wages reflecting such "permanent" disturbances.

In reply to the fourth, or marginality, objection, Chapter V provides a set of rough supply and demand projections for educated labor in Kenya in 1974. The supply of labor is projected by using time-series extrapolations for primary and secondary school leavers, with some assumptions about growth of enrollment in different forms (grades) within the secondary school cycle. University student projections had to be made in a very global way because of uncertainty as to the future role of the ethnic minorities which

---

[3] For persons with university education or incomplete primary schooling the opposite holds; such employees in the private sector received significantly higher salaries than civil servants.

make up a large part of Kenya's university population. The data are inadequate to derive estimates of the supply of labor from demand functions which express the supply of labor as a function of income, fee levels, and other variables, but they are derived instead from simple extrapolations.

Demand for labor with different amounts of primary schooling is projected as a function of wages and GDP growth, using wage and GDP elasticities of demand based on 1957–66 employment, wage and GDP data. Demand for labor with secondary and university level schooling is also projected as a function of wages and GDP, but the elasticities are approximated rather than estimated. Comparisons of projected demand and supply are made in several different ways:

a) Assuming that the efficient allocation of resources in the economy implies equal monetary rates of return to all investments, and equal rates of return to investment in all levels of schooling, we ask how the wages of those who attain each level of schooling should change if the desired rate of return to all investment were 10 percent, and we ask what these wage changes imply for total employment of those at each level of schooling.

b) As real wages increased in the period 1957–66 despite increasing unemployment among primary school leavers, we ask what employment of those at each level of schooling in 1974 would be implied if real wages remained constant between 1966 and 1974.

c) Using the supply projections of skilled labor for 1974, we ask what the wages would be for those with different amounts of schooling if full employment were projected for 1974.

Rates of return based on full employment wage estimates are not projected to 1974 because, except for university graduates, full employment wages are unrealistically low. Instead, we use the more plausible 1974 employment projections from b) and compare them with projected supply to estimate unemployment of those with given levels of schooling.

The fifth objection is to the use of additional earnings as the sole measure of benefits because these do not include the many important indirect benefits of education. These spillover benefits range from personal fulfillment—a quasi-consumption item—to the promotion of national identity, the formation of an informed electorate, the transformation of a rural society, and a more equitable distribution of income. By their very nature these effects are difficult to identify and measure. The legitimacy of pursuing such benefits is beyond doubt, and they are important, if often implicit, considerations underlying a country's educational policy. However, a country with very limited resources for its development might be ill-advised to pursue these benefits if alternative investments outside education were to have much higher yields. Kenya's official policy on this subject was articulated soon after independence. "At Kenya's stage of development, education is much more an economic than a social service. It is our principal means for relieving the shortage of domestic skilled manpower and equalizing economic opportunities among all citizens."[4]

The only objection to cost-benefit analysis with which we do not directly deal and which may be important in justifying the scope of educational efforts in Kenya and elsewhere is that education is a vital force in changing attitudes (e.g. towards family planning) or economic behavior (e.g. savings habits). This topic is dealt with in the conclusion, Chapter VI.[5]

Education Process Analysis

The study's calculation of rates of return to investment in different levels of education does lead to the identification of large areas within the educational system where investment is most rewarding, and to comparisons of the relative profitability of investment in education and in physical capital. But to justify any investment in, for example, general secondary schooling on the grounds that the high overall rates of return found there would imply that each dollar of input into the secondary school system had the same effect on the quality of output would certainly be an untenable assumption. Therefore, in addition to the analysis of the overall rates of return, the study analyzes the influences of educational policy variables—size of school, pupil-teacher ratio, teachers' salaries per pupil, etc.—on students' scores on the three major examinations: the Kenya Preliminary Examination (primary school leaving examination and qualifying examination for secondary education), the Cambridge School Certificate examination (after the first four years of secondary schooling), and the Higher School Certificate (senior secondary examination). It then assesses the returns, in terms of additional earnings, to increased inputs into the school system. This analysis, which is dealt with in Annex A, is beset with significance problems and other data shortcomings, but yields some interesting results which point to new possibilities for future research.

Outline of the Study

Chapter II presents background information on Kenya and its educational system. Chapters III and IV give an in-depth analysis of the data

---

[4] Republic of Kenya, *African Socialism and its Application to Planning in Kenya*, Sessional Paper No. 10/1965, Nairobi, 1965, pp. 39–40.

[5] For a more detailed discussion of possible spillovers of education in Kenya see a previous, more extended version of this study that was published in November, 1969, as an Economics Department Staff Study (referred to hereafter as EC-173).

collected in 1968. Age-income profiles are calculated and adjusted in Chapter III, and adjusted average rates of return are derived in Chapter IV. Chapter V turns to the possible use of rates of return for planning purposes.

Chapter VI, the conclusion, briefly reviews the results of the case study and evaluates the experience gained from a practical point of view, interpreting the usefulness of the study techniques for educational research and planning. It indicates where the study has taken us and what lessons it offers for future study.

II

KENYA'S EDUCATIONAL SYSTEM

A Historical Survey of Education in Kenya
From 1900 to 1945

Formal education in Kenya is a development of this century, apart from the traditional Koran schools for the Arab population along the coast and early efforts by mission stations both there and around Lake Victoria. The first major schools—the European School established in 1904 in Nairobi and an Indian school founded by the Uganda Railway Authority in 1906—were schools for ethnic minorities. After the government established an Education Department in 1911, other European and Indian schools were started in the major towns and settlements (Mombasa, Nairobi, Kisumu, Eldoret, Nakuru), and Arab schools were set up at Mombasa (1912) and Malindi (1919). It was not until 1942 that primary education became compulsory for even a small segment of the population: European children between 7 and 15 years and Indian boys in Nairobi, Mombasa, and Kisumu of the same age group.

The organization and administration of schools along ethnic lines resulted in the creation of three[1] separate educational systems for Africans, Asians, and Europeans. These divisions persisted until independence, and

---

[1] Or even five, if one counts the Arab and the sometimes separate Goan schools.

are still reflected in present-day enrollment patterns. African education developed from a nucleus of mission schools.[2] Few records are available, but the stress on practical skills and the poor quality of teachers (who often were only more advanced pupils) suggest that the teaching provided was hardly sufficient to make pupils thoroughly literate.

After setting up the Education Department, the government began to subsidize mission schools and to operate its own system of African schools. The first non-general school (with teacher training and vocational courses) opened in 1913 at Machakos. Some 80,000–100,000 Africans had received some schooling by 1924/25.[3] In that year the Education Ordinance and the Grant-in-Aid Rules provided the administrative and financial basis for an expansion of education. These decrees were an explicit acknowledgement of the fact that the missions' educational engagements were now far beyond their financial means. Once the government had openly committed itself to supporting private educational efforts, other more extensive measures followed in close succession. Beginning in 1926, a primary examination for Africans gave official acknowledgement to pupils who had completed the primary course, and the new Grant-in-Aid Rules in 1934 shifted the financial responsibility for most primary education to the Local Native Councils. To this day Kenya's primary schools are still organized on the principle of centralized educational and decentralized financial responsibilities.

In the first quarter of the century African secondary education was limited to individual tutoring by missionaries or studies in neighboring Uganda. The opening of Alliance High School in 1926 marked the beginning of an African secondary school system, and by the outbreak of World War II there were three more schools in operation. Each of the four schools was located so as to serve one of the four major tribes (Kikuyu, Luo, Luhya, and Kamba). Their total enrollment in 1945 was just over 300 pupils, only two of them girls. Higher education did not become available for Africans until the 1930's, when a few Kenyans began to study at Makerere College

---

[2] About 1912 there were approximately 60 mission schools. E. W. Soja, *The Geography of Modernization in Kenya* (Syracuse, N.Y.: Syracuse University Press, 1968), p. 61.

[3] This is a very rough estimate based on data obtained from the Public Records Office, London. According to Volume III of the 1962 census, about 43,000 African males and 5,000 African females of age 50 and over had received one or more years of education. If the life expectancy of educated persons in the first decades of this century were the same as that calculated for the whole 1962 population, the total numbers of those who had received such an education in 1924/25 would be 138,000 and 26,000 respectively. Our figure allows for substantial overstatement of both age and education by old people. (Source: *Kenya Population Census, 1962. Vol. III: African Population*, Nairobi, 1966).

in Uganda. By the end of the war 50 students were in residence there, while at the same time other school leavers were obtaining bursaries in the U.K.

From 1945 to Independence

In the postwar period the African primary schools moved from selective to mass education. By 1963, 70 percent of the boys and 41 percent of the girls 7–10 years old were enrolled in primary schools (Standards or classes I–IV), and 58 percent of the boys and 21 percent of the girls 11–14 years old in intermediate schools (Standards V–VIII). At independence a certain plateau seemed to have been reached, for with just over a million pupils, the subsequent annual increases in enrollments did not even match the supposed population growth rate of 3 percent. However, in 1967 and again in 1968 primary enrollments increased significantly (see Table 2.1). Secondary schooling made even more spectacular advances. Pupil figures rose from 300 in 1945 to more than 30,000 in 1963, with 1,500 candidates sitting for the Cambridge School Certificate examination (CSC). In 1963 two hundred Africans sat for the Higher School Certificate (HSC), which Africans had entered for the first time only the year before. The Royal Technical College—the nucleus of today's University College—opened in Nairobi in 1956, thus giving Kenya her first institution of higher learning. Although it expanded rapidly, in 1963 it accommodated only about 100 of the country's 2,100 African students, while 200 were at Makerere and 1,800 overseas. (See Table 2.4 for data on all Kenyans—Africans and non-Africans—in the three East African colleges.)

The Present Educational System[4]

Primary Education

Enrollments. During the period 1963–66 primary education was changed from an eight-year course of two four-year cycles to a seven-year course. This reform left the total amount of primary education virtually unchanged, since Standards I and II (first and second grades) were switched from a half-day to a full-day basis. The Kenya Preliminary Examination (KPE) is given after completion of Standards I–VII. In 1968 1.2 million pupils were being taught in more than 6,000 primary schools (Table 2.1). The average enrollment ratio was about 75 percent for boys and 50 percent for girls.

---

[4] A number of changes in the educational system that took place after completion of the field work for this study have not been taken into account. This description thus refers to mid-1968. Figure 2.1 represents schematically the structure of Kenya's educational system in 1969.

TABLE 2.1: Enrollments in Primary and Secondary Education, 1959–68

('000)

	1959	1960	1961	1962	1963	1964	1965	1966	1967	1968
Standard I	179.0	179.6	190.0	170.0	137.2	180.3	195.7	193.9	228.8	250.8
Standard II	155.8	161.5	168.6	166.3	138.7	144.8	165.8	166.1	183.6	207.8
Standard III	140.9	154.4	163.3	165.0	143.9	139.7	139.3	152.9	165.6	178.5
Standard IV	135.3	156.7	171.1	165.7	140.0	145.0	135.1	130.3	146.9	158.9
Standard V	38.2	45.4	75.5	128.7	124.6	134.0	126.4	120.9	124.8	132.7
Standard VI	31.7	36.7	44.1	70.7	112.8	122.6	122.5	132.7	136.8	134.2
Standard VII	24.4	29.9	35.5	42.0	62.5	114.4	121.3	146.2	147.5	146.8
Standard VIII	14.2	17.2	22.5	27.4	31.8	33.9	36.0	0.4[b]	—	—
Total primary	719.5	781.3	870.4	935.8	891.6	1,014.7	1,042.1	1,043.4	1,133.2	1,209.7
Form 1	6.3	6.4	7.2	9.1	10.2	12.7	19.0	24.1	31.8	36.1
Form 2	5.3	5.6	5.6	6.9	8.2	9.1	12.6	18.5	26.6	28.9
Form 3	3.3	4.4	4.6	5.3	5.8	7.0	7.8	11.2	16.9	20.3
Form 4	2.6	3.2	4.0	4.3	4.8	5.6	6.8	7.1	10.8	14.7
Form 5	0.3	0.3	0.5	0.7	0.7	0.9	1.1	1.4	1.6	1.8
Form 6	0.1	0.2	0.3	0.4	0.4	0.6	0.7	0.9	1.1	1.4
Total secondary	19.2[a]	20.1	22.2	26.6	30.1	35.9	48.0	63.2	88.8	103.1

[a] Including 1,289 pupils whose Form is not recorded.
[b] 440 pupils.

Source: Ministry of Education.

FIGURE 2.1: KENYA: STRUCTURE OF EDUCATION, 1969

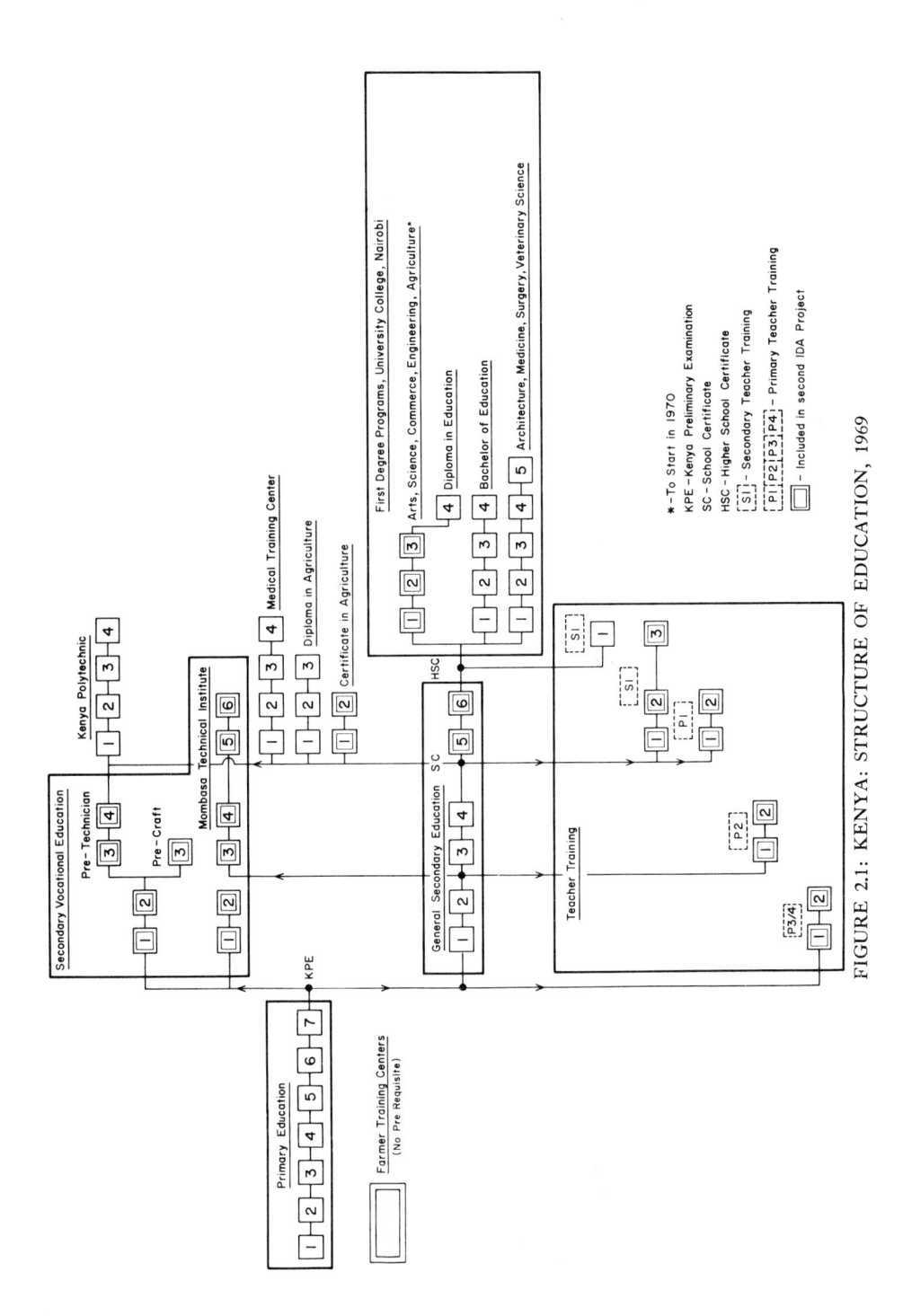

Areas with high enrollment ratios, apart from the major towns, are: Central, Nyanza and Western Provinces, Embu, Meru and Machakos Counties in the Eastern Province, Kericho in the Rift Valley Province and Taita-Taveta in the Coast Province. These counties share one or more of the following characteristics:

a) High population density;
b) Relative wealth; and
c) Long exposure to the influence of Christian missions and hence to educational efforts.

The minimum age of admission is six years at the beginning of the school year. The theoretical school leaving age would thus be 13 years. Due to repetition and temporary drop-out, however, primary school leavers are on average 14–15 years old (see Table 2.2).[5]

The teaching force. In 1968 the country's primary schools employed nearly 38,000 teachers, or about one for every 32 pupils; more than 70 percent of them were qualified (trained) in the sense of having received some specific training in teaching. Apart from the various categories of unqualified (untrained) teachers, who are paid according to their educational achievement, there are four main categories of primary school teachers, namely:

P4: Teachers having gone through the full primary course (without passing the KPE) plus two years of training,
P3: Teachers with the KPE and two years of training,[6]
P2: Teachers with two or more years of secondary education and two years of training,
P1: Teachers with a CSC (Cambridge School Certificate) and two years of training.

There are also some university graduates and S1 (secondary school) teachers working in primary schools but their number is negligible (about one percent of the teaching force).

---

[5] A figure of 14.3 years was obtained from the Muranga-Meru sample (see Annex A). School-leaving age has probably been going down in recent years: the data of the Labor Force Survey conducted by the authors in 1968 (Table 2.2) indicate that African males with only 7 years of education were on average 17.5 years old when they left school, but the average age of the population in this group is 28.8 years, which means that most of them had their education completed before independence. A separate analysis of the younger individuals in the Labor Force sample also gives a lower school-leaving age.

[6] Access to the P4 and P3 categories is also possible for unqualified teachers through special in-service courses.

TABLE 2.2: Average School-Leaving Age of Urban Employees, by Ethnic Group, Sex, and Educational Achievement, 1968

		0–2	3–5	6–7	8–9	10–11	12–13	14–16	17 and over
					Years of Education				
African Males	LA[a]	14.0	15.6	17.6	18.4	20.2	21.4	20.5	26.4
	SD	4.6	3.9	3.0	2.7	1.4	2.7	0.5	3.0
	NO	153	825	1061	167	213	31	2	28
African Females	LA	14.1	14.0	16.7	17.3	18.3	20.5	—	—
	SD	6.3	3.9	2.2	1.6	1.5	0.5	—	—
	NO	16	62	116	23	31	2		
Asian Males	LA	14.0	13.4	15.0	16.2	18.2	19.6	21.1	22.9
	SD	3.7	2.9	2.2	3.4	2.0	2.2	1.5	1.8
	NO	3	38	101	50	139	24	8	20
Asian Females	LA	—	—	14.0	15.8	17.4	19.0	20.0	23.7
	SD	—	—	0.0	1.2	1.3	1.6	0.0	0.5
	NO			1	11	77	10	2	3
European Males	LA	13.0	14.7	15.8	14.0	16.9	18.1	20.0	24.2
	SD	0.0	2.5	2.4	1.4	1.6	0.9	0.6	3.1
	NO	1	3	4	7	21	16	6	20
European Females	LA	—	—	12.0	15.0	16.9	18.0	20.5	22.0
	SD	—	—	0.0	0.0	1.4	0.7	0.5	0.0
	NO			1	2	56	22	2	1

[a] LA = Average School-Leaving Age, SD = Standard Deviation, NO = Number of Observations.

Source: Labor Force Sample Survey, January/February, 1968.

A desirable teaching establishment for a standard primary school of 200–250 pupils with one class of students in each standard is deemed to be one P1 teacher, one P2 teacher, four P3 teachers and two untrained teachers.[7] However, this goal is irrelevant for the many schools which have not yet attained full scale: more than 40 percent of all primary schools still lack Standard VII classes, and even in the more densely populated districts of Central Province, the pattern of population distribution and the demand for education result in many incomplete schools with relatively high costs.

General Secondary Education

As in other developing countries, the great majority of Kenyan pupils who continue their education beyond the primary level enter general secondary schools. These are either maintained schools, fully administered and supported by the government, assisted schools receiving government grants, or unaided schools. In the last group, the so-called Harambee schools are interesting enough to be given separate treatment.

A Kenya Junior Secondary Examination is given after Form II. At the end of Form IV, the Cambridge School Certificate (CSC) examination,[8] under the auspices of the University of Cambridge Local Examinations Syndicate, provides for a major screening process—only a small portion of those entering the CSC examination continue their education in Form V or in teacher training colleges. The CSC is thus the main entrance requirement for most of the medium-level clerical and administrative occupations. In line with the general expansion of the secondary school system, the number of schools presenting dates for this exam has increased sharply from 42 in 1956 (only 13 of which were African schools) to 144 in 1966.

Over the years a nucleus of first-rate schools has developed whose pupils consistently perform better than the average. They include most of the so-called extra-provincial schools which recruit their pupils from all over the country, as well as the great majority of the schools with an upper secondary cycle leading to the Higher School Certificate (HSC) examination.[9] Our admittedly crude comparison over time of the relative performance of individual schools in the HSC points to the existence of a rather stable qualitative hierarchy among the country's senior secondary schools.

Among secondary school pupils, 40 percent on average are boarders. However, there exist considerable differences both among types of schools—

---

[7] Republic of Kenya, *Kenya Education Commission Report, Part II*, Nairobi, 1965, p. 5.
[8] To be replaced as of 1968 by the East African School Certificate examination.
[9] Most extra-provincial schools offer the HSC.

unaided schools showing a much lower percentage (20 percent)—and between boys and girls—the latter having a higher share of boarders (47 percent) than the former (37 percent). These differences, along with the steady increase of boarders from 36 percent in Form I to 42 percent in Form IV, and to nearly two-thirds in the two senior secondary years, are inevitable consequences of widening catchment areas.

The teaching force. As in primary education, the 3,600 teachers in secondary schools can be classified as either trained or untrained, regardless of their level of education. The share of the trained group has fallen from nearly 70 percent in 1960 to 65 percent in 1967. Nearly 40 percent of all teachers are trained graduates; these are followed by untrained graduates and, in close succession, S1 teachers, (unqualified) HSC holders, and P1 teachers. The high proportion of teachers with poor qualifications is mainly due to the inferior quality of teachers in the unaided Harambee schools. This problem will be discussed in the next section. For the group of maintained and assisted secondary schools, the situation was distinctly better: in 1966 more than 80 percent of the teachers were trained, and every second teacher was a trained graduate.

About one secondary school teacher in three is a citizen of the country. However, this average is mainly due to the high proportion of citizens among P1 teachers (90 percent) and among untrained non-graduate teachers (86 percent). On the other hand nine out of ten graduates, trained or untrained, are non-citizens. These figures are an indication of the country's dependence on expatriate educators, many of whom (30 percent on average and nearly 60 percent in the key category of trained graduates) are supplied by aid schemes such as the Overseas Service Aid Scheme, the British Expatriates Supplementation Scheme, or the Peace Corps.

In spite of the introduction in early 1966 of bursaries tied to a three-year terms of duty in the public service, and the allocation of the largest share of the Science and Arts faculties bursars to the teaching service (30 and 50 percent, respectively), the situation is not likely to improve rapidly. Even after these bursars begin to swell the teaching force, a moderate increase in enrollments is anticipated, and many non-citizen teachers employed on local terms are likely to emigrate. The annual output of S1 teachers is at present only in the neighborhood of 200 (91 in 1966, 191 in 1967),[10] and even the output of P1 teachers, who are admittedly inadequate except for work in the lowest forms, is only about 300–400 per year. Furthermore, P1 teachers have to be shared with the primary school system—the P1 level being the preferred (if often unattained) qualification for headmasters.

---

[10] Including 57 P1 teachers in upgrading courses.

The qualitative shortcomings of the country's secondary school teachers have become more serious as the recent educational expansion has brought an ever increasing number of disadvantaged pupils into the system. The pupils' disadvantages include parents unable or unwilling to help with tutoring, obligation to help on the fathers' farm, long commuting distances, a poor diet, and genuine ability differences. Although the centralized marking of the CSC and HSC results does not permit the tracing of this supposed deterioration over time, its presence can be inferred from the results of the education process analysis in Annex A. Pupils of schools in educationally less developed areas of the country are at a disadvantage, but it is one which could be remedied by increased spending on specific inputs such as boarding facilities. The large-scale application of such remedial policy measures would encounter severe financial constraints, however. There may therefore be closed or nearly closed ability pools in Kenya, produced by circumstances rather than by nature.

Harambee schools. The Harambee schools, named after the nation's motto,[11] illustrate the paradox of community self-help: a willingness to sacrifice may result in remarkable achievements, but spontaneous developments often become uncontrollable. Before independence there were some schools which were Harambee schools in essence, though not in name. It was not until 1964, however, that the Harambee movement presented a serious problem to educational administrators. In the following year the Kenya Education Commission devoted an entire chapter of its report to the "Control and Planning of Harambee Schools."[12] Most of the arguments then used against uncoordinated local activities in the field of secondary education are still valid:

a) Harambee schools very often took over the permanent buildings of a local primary school, starting with the classroom vacated by the Standard VIII class (which was discontinued at about the same time). Great numbers of P1 teachers were recruited from primary schools with an inducement of about K£90–120 above their regular annual salaries. This was no small drain on the meager resources of the primary school system.

b) From the beginning Harambee schools were faced with a serious teacher deficit—both quantitatively and qualitatively—and inadequate buildings. This meant overcrowded classes subjected to the teaching of a non-science curriculum "pursued in a sterile, academic manner."[13]

---

[11] The Swahili word harambee means "let us all pull together."
[12] Republic of Kenya, *Kenya Education Commission Report, Part II*, pp. 21–26.
[13] Republic of Kenya, *Kenya Education Commission Report*, p. 23.

c) The financial odds against the continuation and expansion of these schools were overwhelming. Even after the local Harambee school committee had succeeded in collecting the initial capital installment of £2000 required by law, the operating costs of such a school were a formidable financial burden "well beyond the resources of most local communities."[14]

d) The hope of parents that some years of education beyond the primary level would permit their children to escape from rural life was defeated by the sheer logic of numbers. By 1968, 393 schools with more than 40,000 pupils were registered as Harambee schools,[15] but only a few of these provided for more than an extension of primary education. There was little if any hope of ever catching up with the aided schools, although some Harambee schools had succeeded in reaching up to Form IV by 1968.

A corollary of this development was an ever increasing flow of school leavers (mainly Form II) unrelated to the limited absorptive capacity of the urban labor markets. In order to permit merit-oriented recruitment for scarce job openings and for further training, the government in 1966 introduced the Kenya Junior Secondary Examination for pupils who had completed Form II. In the first year more than 9,000 candidates were presented (28 percent passing), in the second, nearly 19,000 (35 percent passing).[16]

The dimensions of this uncontrolled allocation of resources become clear when we examine fees and other financial data. If we assume, on the basis of the incomplete information presented in Table 2.3, that the average level of Harambee fees is about Ksh 750 per year, it follows from a comparison with Table 2.5 that the total amount of Harambee school fees paid in 1968 must have represented about half the sum total of primary school fees. The total volume of recurring expenditure during the period 1964–68 may have been of the order of K£4–5 million.

Technical Education

At the base of the system of secondary vocational and technical schools there are seven technical and trade schools enrolling KPE certificate

---

[14] The Commission expected the annual teacher salaries for a fully established (Forms I–IV) school to be of the order of K£5000 under minimum staffing assumptions.

[15] Statement by the Minister of Education in Parliament, reported in the *East African Standard*, May 29, 1968. The enrollment figure has been estimated by the authors.

[16] These figures encompass not only Form II leavers, but other candidates with comparable qualifications as well (e.g. P3 teachers).

TABLE 2.3: Range of Annual Fees in Harambee Schools

District	Annual Fees (Ksh) Boarding Schools	Annual Fees (Ksh) Day Schools	Other Sources of Finance[a]
Bungoma		700–800	
Embu		400–750	(CO)
Kakamega		500–600	(CC)
Kiambu		600–750	
Kisii	600		CO
Kitui		450–500	AL
Machakos	600	450–500	CC
Murang'a		600–800	(CC)
Nyeri	900–1,000	700–900	

[a] CO = grants from agricultural co-operatives.
CC = grants from County Council.
AL = annual levy on all taxpayers.
(parentheses indicate that financial help occurs irregularly and/or does not cover all schools.)

Source: J. E. Anderson, Report on the Conference of Harambee School Headmasters, August 10–14, 1966, Nairobi, 1966 (mimeo).

holders in either two, three, or four-year courses; their total enrollment in 1967 was more than 850 students. The technical streams of Nakuru Secondary School offer an education which leads to the HSC level. Students from the technical high schools in Nairobi and Mombasa and from the Sigalagala Technical School are accepted into the Form V and VI classes. Kenya Polytechnic and the Mombasa Technical Institute are at the top of the system of technical schools; these are junior colleges rather than secondary schools, and in 1967 had an enrollment of 1,800 and 500, respectively. They offer regular, full-time General Certificate of Education (GCE) courses at the ordinary and advanced levels, but the majority of their students attend classes on a day release and/or "sandwich" basis.

There are about 25 teacher training colleges for the primary levels and these have a total enrollment of more than 5,000 students. A number of these institutions are relatively small, and it is likely that the process of concentration which has been observed in the past may well continue. Besides training teachers of various categories, generally in two-year courses, they enroll teachers already on the force in short upgrading courses, these are mainly aimed at helping them move from an unqualified status to P4/P3.

Secondary S1 school teachers are trained at Kenyatta College and the Kenya Science Teachers College, and graduate teachers at the Faculty of Education, University College, Nairobi. There were 75 S1 passes in 1966, with cohorts about twice as large enrolled in the first and second years of the long S1 course. This course is taken after the CSC, as opposed to the short one-year course following the HSC.

Higher Education

Table 2.4 shows the development of Kenyan enrollments at the three constituent colleges of the University of East Africa—Makerere, Nairobi, and Dar es Salaam (Tanzania)—from 1960/61 to 1967/68. These figures and the development plans seem to indicate that each college (and particularly the University College, Nairobi) is moving towards the status of an autarkic multi-faculty institution. This is a departure from the original concept which envisioned common faculties at each of the three colleges and professional faculties shared by the East African countries.

Despite the availability of university training in most disciplines within East Africa, and the government's policy of not granting overseas scholarships except for specialized studies not available locally, there are still a large number of Kenyan students going overseas (3,643 in 1966/67, two-thirds of whom were staying in three countries—the U.K., the U.S.A. and the U.S.S.R.). Sixty percent of these are studying privately, and thirty percent have received foreign scholarships offered through the Kenya government. Only the country of study is known; there is no information available on the exact nature of their studies or the probable date of their return to Kenya. A fair number of them can be assumed to be non-Africans, which could mean that they have left Kenya permanently.

Education Cost and Finance

Costs of Primary and Secondary Education

In this section we discuss social cost figures and private fees. Other costs to individuals and society are discussed in Chapters III and IV where age-income-education profiles are developed and rates of return to education calculated.

Unlike the Education Ministries in many other developing countries, the Kenya authorities have at their disposal very detailed and seemingly reliable cost data. This holds in particular for the secondary school system, where data are available on a school-by-school basis. The situation is somewhat different with regard to primary education, however, where the delegation of financial responsibilities to the county councils and municipalities makes the quality of the data dependent in some degree on the competence of the local administrations. Strangely enough, cost figures are most difficult to obtain at the university level, a situation which may be explained by the complex financial arrangements between the constituent colleges of the University of East Africa and the member governments. Hence, the university cost figures used for our rate-of-return calculations in Chapter

TABLE 2.4: Students from Kenya at the East African University Colleges

	1960/61 M	1960/61 F	1961/62 M	1961/62 F	1962/63 M	1962/63 F	1963/64 M	1963/64 F	1964/65 M	1964/65 F	1965/66 M	1965/66 F	1966/67 M	1966/67 F
Undergraduate Common Faculties														
Makerere	112	7	118	8	110	6	95	8	96	17	76	20	78	25
Nairobi	—	—	13	3	31	11	57	19	96	29	179	59	249	86
Dar es Salaam	—	—	—	—	—	—	—	—	22	1	34	1	61	7
Total	112	7	131	11	141	17	152	27	214	47	289	80	388	118
Undergraduate Professional Faculties														
Makerere	61	2	68	1	75	—	81	2	95	4	116	5	144	4
Nairobi	—	—	15	—	43	—	80	—	96	—	137	—	153	—
Dar es Salaam	—	—	4	—	12	1	19	1	32	3	41	3	54	4
Total	61	2	87	1	130	1	180	3	223	7	294	8	351	8
Postgraduate														
Makerere	—	—	—	—	—	—	10	1	12	4	16	6	8	2
Nairobi[a]	—	—	—	—	—	—	3	—	25	2	31	4	40	4
Dar es Salaam	—	—	—	—	—	—	—	—	—	—	—	—	—	—
Total	—	—	—	—	—	—	13	1	37	6	47	10	48	6
Other														
Makerere	215	3	123	1	24	—	28	2	22	5	12	3	21	5
Nairobi	201[b]	—	158	45	109	49	84	46	61	40	31	38	26	43
Dar es Salaam	—	—	—	—	—	—	—	—	—	—	4	—	7	—
Total	215	3	281	46	133	49	112	48	83	45	47	41	54	48
Total														
Makerere	388	12	309	10	209	6	214	13	225	30	230	34	251	36
Nairobi	—	—	186	48	183	60	224	65	278	71	378	101	468	133
Dar es Salaam	—	—	4	—	12	1	19	1	54	4	79	4	122	11
Total	388	12	499	58	404	67	457	79	557	105	687	139	841	180

Source: Ministry of Education Triennial Survey 1964–66 and Annual Report for 1966, Nairobi, 1967.

[a] It has had to be assumed that 90 percent of these postgraduate students are men, since the breakdown by sex was not available.
[b] Royal College, Nairobi (later University College) did not attain University status until 1961.

IV are plan figures rather than actual ones. This chapter concentrates on the costs of primary and secondary education.

Primary education. Since teacher salaries constitute by far the most important cost element, the bulk of total costs can be derived relatively easily despite the occasional shortcomings of county cost data. The procedure is to multiply the national totals in each category of teachers by the respective average salary. The numbers of teachers can be assumed to be accurate, because data are centrally collected through the Teachers' Service Commission. Average salaries were derived from Annex Table A.3. Where possible the weighted averages available for two major counties (Kiambu and Nyeri) were used as giving a closer approximation than the mid-point of the salary ranges, because for most categories the average age of teachers is low. Expenditure on equipment is supposed to be in the neighborhood of the customary capitation grant of Ksh 15; finally, a lump sum of K£300,000 is entered for other expenditures, including Ministry of Education contributions. The estimates for 1967 presented in Table 2.5 are consistent with estimates for 1966 of the Ministry of Economic Planning and Development which later came to the authors' attention.[17] The latter indicate a total of K£7.2 million spent by local authorities alone on primary education in 1966.

The capital costs of primary schools can be supposed to be in the neighborhood of K£12–20 per pupil place for permanent structures and K£9–15 for semi-permanent structures.[18] A separate estimate of K£1 per pupil place is made for the traditional "mud-and-wattle" structures prevailing in most of rural Kenya. These are standard three-room buildings housing 100–120 pupils.[19]) If the duration of the various structures is assumed to be 40, 30, and 10 years, respectively, the annual undiscounted amortization charges come to Ksh 6–10, Ksh 6–10 and Ksh 2 respectively, i.e. the three types of buildings show lesser cost differences than might have appeared at first sight.

Secondary education. The cost components of secondary schools are analyzed in Annex A (for a summary of the main figures, see Annex Table

---

[17] Republic of Kenya, *Economic Survey, 1968*, Nairobi, 1968.

[18] Adapted from J. B. Knight, *The Costing and Financing of Educational Development in Tanzania*, UNESCO: International Institute of Educational Planning, Paris, 1966. The upper figures assume 30 pupils per classroom, the lower 50.

[19] Assuming expenses of K£20 for wattle poles, K£50 for corrugated iron sheets, and an imputed wage of K£50 for 1,000 hours of labor. The annual maintenance costs of these constructions may be in the neighborhood of Ksh 50. These figures emerged from discussions with Mr. D. S. Higgs, Senior Local Government Officer, and other officials from the Ministries of Local Government and Cooperatives and Social Services.

TABLE 2.5: Estimated Expenditure on Primary Education, 1967

Teacher Salaries	Numbers	Average Salaries (K£)	Total Salaries (K£'000)
Professionally qualified teachers			
Graduates	80	1257	100.6
S1	310	846	262.6
P1	1684	411	692.1
P2	3797	301	1142.9
P3	16031	204	3270.3
P4	2821	179	505.0
Others	327	150	490.5
Non-professionally qualified teachers			
Graduates	40	1257	50.2
HSC	71	325	23.1
CSC	809	240	194.2
KPE	8384	96	804.9
Others	1318	84	110.7
Total teacher salaries	35672	214	7647.1
Equipment grants			849.9
Other expenditures			300.0
Total expenditures			8797.0
(1,133,179 pupils)			or Ksh 155 p. p.

Note: Average salaries for categories P1, P2, P3, P4, UTT (KPE) and UTT (Others) derived from data on distribution of teachers over salary scale in two counties which comprise 13 percent of the country's primary school teachers. For the other categories (which count for less than 5 percent of the total teaching force) the scale mid-points were assumed to be the average salaries (which probably implies a small overestimate). Item "other expenditure" estimated from data on four counties.
Source: Ministry of Education data.

A.1). The mean costs are about K£65 for day schools and K£95 for boarding schools, but for high-cost schools the figure may be K£200 or more.[20] Schools with Form V and Form VI classes are much more expensive than lower secondary schools, not only because of the larger share of boarding pupils (particularly outside the Nairobi area) but also because of a better average qualification of teachers (the upper classes are taught by graduates only) and a lower pupil/teacher ratio (the legal maximum is 30, as compared to 40 in Forms I–IV).[21]

---

[20] Our figures yield a mean of K£87 (of which K£67 were spent on teachers' salaries) for schools with Forms I–IV only (regardless of whether they had boarding facilities or not), and of K£175 for senior secondary schools (K£144 on teacher salaries).

[21] See the Education (Education Standards) Regulations 1968, para. 3 (April 4, 1968). Due to considerable dropout in Form V, the actual average size of Form VI classes is only about 25 pupils.

Initial construction costs for lower secondary schools range from K£120 to K£400 per pupil/place, depending on whether the school has boarding facilities and on where it is located (Nairobi vs. up-country). These figures refer to schools with three streams and thus reflect certain economies of scale. The construction of senior secondary schools, particularly those with a science stream, is likely to be more expensive.[22]

The Financing of Primary and Secondary Education

The responsibility for the management and financing of primary schools is delegated to the local authorities (county councils and municipalities).[23] Recurring expenditures are met out of their regular revenue, school fees contributing about a third. The central government lends some support in the form of grants channelled through the Ministry of Local Government. The level of fees varies considerably among counties, and within counties among Standards. The national averages for fees in Standards I–VII range from Ksh 54 to Ksh 70.

Fees in the secondary school system differ widely according to the status of the individual school (maintained, assisted, or unaided) and to whether or not the pupil is a boarder. Senior secondary classes in most schools were exempted from fees in 1966.[24] In Harambee schools fees are considerably higher than in most aided schools—fees being the major source of school committee income. An estimate of fee ranges and the extent of regional variations is given in Table 2.3.

A global estimate of all educational expenditures financed from domestic sources may be found at the conclusion of this chapter (Table 2.6). The figures for the private sector contribution are subject to considerable uncertainty. Although these estimates may not be completely free of double-counting, they are still probably rather low. It is natural to ask whether this considerable investment in human capital formation will pay off. The following chapters of the study will be concerned with this question.

---

[22] Source: Ministry of Education.

[23] Only three aided primary schools are exempt from this rule.

[24] In the so-called high cost schools fees remained substantial. In 1966 fee exemption applied to 1,168 out of 2,079 students in Forms V and VI; 505 pupils paid K£10/14, 74 paid K£33/10, and 334 pupils up to K£140. It can be assumed, however, that for the great majority of African pupils fee exemption or coverage of fees by scholarships was the rule. The figures cited in this footnote were computed by Mr. P. R. C. Williams, Ministry of Education, and communicated by Dr. Daniel C. Rogers.

TABLE 2.6: Estimated Education Expenditure from Domestic Sources by Main Components, 1966

(million K£)

Central Government: recurrent expenditure	7.92
Municipal Councils: recurrent and capital expenditure	1.46
County Councils: recurrent expenditure	5.70
East African Community: General Fund Services	0.26
General Government: capital expenditure	0.91
Private Sector Contribution[a]	2.23
Miscellaneous[b]	0.14
Total	18.62
Share in 1966 GDP at market prices:	4.5%

[a] Secondary education fees and all expenditure on unaided secondary schools.
[b] Expansion, replacement, and maintenance of temporary primary school constructions.
Source: Republic of Kenya, Economic Survey, 1968, and own estimates.

III

EARNINGS AND SCHOOLING, SOCIO-ECONOMIC AND OCCUPATIONAL CHARACTERISTICS

The Approach

Studies in both developed and developing countries have established a positive relation between a person's earnings and the amount of formal schooling he has received.[1] For the most part, these studies estimate average earnings of individuals grouped by sex, age, urban and rural residency, and number of years of schooling. They attribute the differences in lifetime earnings among individuals with various schooling levels to the schooling they have had.

Other studies have shown that differences in schooling are not the only reason for two individuals' earnings to differ. Other factors such as home background and achievement motivation also affect earnings, and additional schooling contributes only a part of the difference in earnings.[2] Even

---

[1] Among others, see Gary S. Becker, "Investment in Human Capital: A Theoretical Analysis"; *Journal of Political Economy* (supplement), Vol. LXX (Oct. 1962); Theodore W. Schultz, *The Economic Value of Education* (New York: Columbia University Press, 1963); Martin Carnoy, "Earnings and Schooling in Mexico," *Economic Development and Cultural Change*, July, 1967; T. P. Schultz, "Returns to Education in Bogota, Colombia," The Rand Corporation, Memorandum RM-J645-RC/AID, September 1968, and Samuel Bowles, *Planning Education for Economic Growth* (Cambridge, Mass.: Harvard University Press, 1969).

[2] See Edward F. Denison, *The Source of Growth in the United States and the Alternatives Before Us* (New York: Committee for Economic Development, 1962). Additional earnings due to factors like background and motivation can be thought of as returns to education costs incurred outside formal schooling.

those studies which make some adjustment for non-schooling factors generally do so uniformly at every schooling level.[3] There are also other factors which may distort earnings differentials: for example, union action, government employment, tariffs, subsidies, and national employment programs, to name a few. When these effects are important, they will influence wages paid and possibly also earnings differences between schooling levels.

We have attempted to improve on earlier treatments of educational benefits by taking these factors into account. By a multiple regression analysis using detailed data collected from our 1968 Labor Force Survey, we derive earnings figures which are corrected for individuals' socio-economic and occupational characteristics, including union membership and government sector employment. Long-term distortions such as tariffs, subsidies, and national employment programs are not corrected for as they are thought to be a fairly permanent feature of the economic framework, and to belong to a set of political decisions outside the scope of this study.

The analysis of earnings is first done for urban areas. Each of the six sex-ethnic groups in Kenya is treated separately: African males and females, European males and females, and Asian males and females. Each of these six groups is broken down into sub-groups with the same amount of schooling; schooling, ethnic group, and sex are parameters, and the variation in earnings is estimated as a function of the variation in the non-schooling variables. The data basis, model, and earnings profiles are discussed in the following three sections.

In some cases lack of a sufficient number of observations limits the analysis. For this reason, no multivariate regression estimates of earnings are possible for European males at any schooling level, or for any single sex-ethnic group with more than 11 years of schooling. For the same reason we cannot correct the profiles of females, Asian males, or of persons with more than 11 years of schooling for socio-economic or other variables. Thus, African males with less than 11 years of schooling constitute the group for which information is most abundant and the most detailed analysis possible, and we start with them. African females, non-Africans, and persons with more than 11 years of schooling are dealt with afterwards.

We then digress to take a brief look at the considerable amount of detailed data available from our Labor Force Survey to see how the adjustments change earnings and what some of the specific factors explaining earnings differences in Kenya are. Unlike the earnings figures, most of the results of this digression are tentative, mere hints of sociological and occu-

---

[3] However, Denison does differentiate between secondary and university levels, assigning 60 percent of income differentials to schooling at the secondary and 66 percent at the university level.

pational phenomena in Kenya. Nevertheless, they give a feeling of the way in which education, society, and the economy interact.

Finally, we consider the effects of education on income for Kenya's large rural population. The Economic Survey of Central Province, 1963/64 provides data on gross income (total and non-farm) for families of small landholders by level of education. From these data we are able to derive the incomes of the head of household. Two sets of age-earnings profiles for landowning heads of household, each based on different assumptions, are presented in Tables 3.7 and 3.8. No correction of the rural rates of return for socio-economic background is possible.

Earnings data from the present chapter and cost data from Chapter II are used in the next chapter to calculate the rates of return to education in 1968. All earnings data used in Chapter IV are derived in this chapter, but not all the age-earnings profiles calculated here are used in Chapter IV. The figures used in Chapter IV are: the profiles for African males with 11 years of schooling or less, unadjusted except for age (Table 3.1), and adjusted for socio-economic variables (Table 3.2); the unadjusted profiles for African females with 11 years of schooling or less (Table 3.4, columns 1–5); and the unadjusted profiles for African males with 12–17 years of schooling (Table 3.5, columns 3 and 5). Rates of return in rural areas are estimated from both sets of rural profiles (Tables 3.7 and 3.8). Some of the profiles are not developed into rates of return due to problems of statistical significance and the relative unimportance of these groups in the labor force—for example, the profiles for non-African females (Table 3.4, columns 6 and 7) and for Asian males. The profile in Table 3.3, which is adjusted for both socio-economic and occupational variables, is not used to avoid overadjustment.

The Data Basis

The study makes use of cross-section urban earnings data for Kenya, collected in the Labor Force Survey we made in January/February 1968. In that period we took a sample of 4,742 wage-earners in the cities of Nairobi, Mombasa, and Nakuru.[4] The sample was stratified by size of firm, city, and sector (private and government). An effort was made to sample proportionately to total employment in each city and each size-group of firms in the private sector. The firms sampled were selected randomly from the list of firms participating in a survey with nearly complete coverage conducted in 1967 by the Ministry of Economic Planning. The wage-

---

[4] The original sample comprised 4,848 employees; however, a number of defective questionnaires had to be excluded from the analysis.

TABLE 3.1: Key for Variables Used

	Dummy Number	Name of Dummy	Meaning of Dummy
Age	2	Public Sector	Sector—public
	5	Age ≤14	14 years age group
	6	Age 15–16	15–16 years age group
	7	Age 17–19	17–19 years age group
	8	Age 20–24	20–24 years age group
	9	Age 25–29	25–29 years age group
	10	Age 30–34	30–34 years age group
	12	Age 45–54	45–54 years age group
	13	Age 54+[a]	54+ years age group
Firm Location & Size	14	Nairobi	City—Nairobi
	15	Mombasa	City—Mombasa
	17	Firm size 1–14	Firm size—1–14 employees
	18	Firm size 15–49	Firm size—15–49 employees
	20	Firm size 100+	Firm size 100+ employees
Parents' Literacy	21	Father illit.	Illiterate father
	22	Father lit.	Literate father
	24	Mother illit.	Illiterate mother
	26	Mother no ans.	Mother's literacy—no answer
Tribal Group	27	Kikuyu	Tribe—Kikuyu, Meru, Embu
	28	Kamba	Tribe—Kamba
	29	Luhya	Tribe—Luhya, Kisii, Kuria
	30	Coastal	Tribe—Mijikenda, Taita, Taveta
	31	Luo	Tribe—Luo
	32	Kalenjin	Tribe—Kalenjin-speaking tribes
Secondary Exam Score	34	CSC Division I	CSC exam score—Division I pass
	35	CSC Division II	CSC exam score—Division II pass
	36	CSC Division III	CSC exam score—Division III pass
	37	CSC GCE	CSC exam score—GCE(0) pass
Occupation	39	Farmer	Interviewee's occupation—farmer
	40	Prof. 1	Interviewee's occupation—professional (scientific and technical)
	41	Prof. 2	Interviewee's occupation—professional (other)
	42	Tech.	Interviewee's occupation—technician
	43	Foreman	Interviewee's occupation—foreman
	44	Admin.	Interviewee's's occupation—administrative, executive and managerial worker
	45	Clerk	Interviewee's occupation—clerical and sales worker
	46	Skill	Interviewee's occupation—skilled worker
	47	Occ. semi-skill	Interviewee's occupation—semi-skilled and unskilled worker
Firm Sector	48	Manufacturing	Industry—manufacturing
	50	Construction	Industry—manufacturing
	51	Commerce	Industry—commerce
	52	Services	Industry—private services

TABLE 3.1—Continued

	Dummy Number	Name of Dummy	Meaning of Dummy
Union	53	Union	Union membership
Types of Schools Attended	56	Primary public	Type of primary school—public
	57	Primary private	Type of primary school—private
	58	Primary no ans.	Type of primary school—no answer
	60	Sec. public general	Type of secondary school—public general
	61	Sec. public teacher training	Type of secondary school—public teacher training
	62	Sec. private tech.	Type of secondary school—private technical
	63	Sec. private general	Type of secondary school—private general
	64	Sec. private teacher training	Type of secondary school—private teacher training
	65	Sec. Harambee	Type of secondary school—Harambee
	66	Sec. not appli.	Type of secondary school—not applicable
	67	Sec. no answer	Type of secondary school—no answer
Father's Occupation	68	Farmer	Father's occupation—farmer
	69	Prof. 1	Father's occupation—professional (scientific and technical)
	70	Prof. 2	Father's occupation—professional (other)
	71	Tech.	Father's occupation—technician
	72	Foreman	Father's occupation—foreman and supervisor
	73	Admin.	Father's occupation—administrative, executive and managerial worker
	74	Clerk	Father's occupation—clerical and sales worker
	75	Skill	Father's occupation—skilled worker
	76	Semi-Skill	Father's occupation—semi-skilled and unskilled worker
Additional Education or Training	78	Addl. educ.	Additional education taken while working
	79	No addl. educ.	No additional education taken while working
	81	Addl. training	On-the-job training
	82	No addl. training	No on-the-job training

Variables withdrawn because of linear dependence

11	Age 35–44	35–44 years age group
16	Nakuru	City—Nakuru
19	Firm size 50–99	Firm size—50–99 employees
23	Father no ans.	Father's literacy—no answer
25	Mother lit.	Mother's literacy—mother literate
33	Other East African	Tribe—other East African tribes or not identifiable or no answer
38	CSC fail	CSC exam score—fail
48	Occ. unskill.	Occupation—unskilled worker
52a	Public services	Industry—public services
58	Primary no ans.	Type of primary school—no answer
59	Sec. pub. tech.	Type of secondary school—public technical
77	Faocc. unskill.	Father's occupation—unskilled worker
80	Addl. educ. no ans.	Additional education—no answer
83	Addl. training no ans.	On-the-job training—no answer

[a] Midpoint taken equal to 58 years of age.

TABLE 3.2: Unadjusted Age-Earnings Profiles, African Males, by Years of Schooling, 1968

(Ksh per month)

Age	0–2	3–5	7F[a]	7P[b]	7Q[c]	7 All	9	11F[d]	11 All
≤14	—	—	224*	—	—	224*	—	—	—
15–16	—	—	60*	—	—	60*	—	—	—
17–19	194	231	209	278	275	257	227	405	405
20–24	285	258	260	283	335	278	357	573	619
25–29	288	326	326	402	505	379	481	755	830
30–34	325*	367*	410*	581*	531*	495*	632	1,075*	1,182*
35–44	335	390	427	604	786	505	898	1,404	1,372
45–54	326*	367*	450*	893	181**	616	739*	140**	140**
55+	314*	353*	—	673*	—	673*	3,000**	—	—

* Coefficient of age dummy is not significantly different from zero at 5 percent level of significance. Therefore, earnings are not significantly different from those of the 35–44 years of age group.
** Significant, but represents only one case.
[a] Primary school completed, failed in KPE.
[b] Primary school completed, passed KPE.
[c] Primary school completed, qualified on KPE for entry into Form I of secondary school but did not continue.
[d] Form IV of secondary school completed, failed in CSC.
Source: Labor Force Survey, January/February, 1968; See Table 3.3.

earners in the public sector were not selected at random. They numbered less than 15 percent of the total sample.

Information was collected through a questionnaire in direct interviews with workers. The questionnaire provided data on the worker's wage or salary, sex, the number of years of schooling completed, the type of school attended, age, father's occupation, parents' literacy, ethnic origin, the number of years spent in the city where interviewed, age at finishing school and beginning work, number of years with the present employer, whether or not currently receiving formal education, whether having taken or taking on-the-job training, and, if African, his or her tribe. In addition, a worker was classified by the type of industry in which he worked (public or private sector), size of firm and the city in which it was located, and whether or not he belonged to a union. (For a more complete description of the survey and a copy of the questionnaire, see Annex B, "Scope of Labor Force Sample Survey.")

The Model[5]

Since we want to analyze the data to see how earnings vary with other wage-earner characteristics, we constructed a simple equation expressing

---

[5] This and the next section and Annex D have greatly benefited from the authors' discussions with Mr. R. C. Manning and from his written comments.

the dependency of income on all factors except years of schooling. For all those with a given level of schooling,

Income = function of (age, father's occupation . . . union membership).

A list of the factors, or variables, is given in Table 3.1. Most of them are dichotomous variables; in other words, for any given individual either they apply or they do not. They can be quantified by converting them into "dummy variables," which take a value of unity whenever the wage-earner has that particular characteristic, and zero when he does not.[6] Thus, if an interviewee is, say, a clerk, the occupational category "clerk" receives a value of unity, and the other nine categories a value of zero. Dummy variables are used even for age, a continuous variable, since it is not necessarily directly related to earnings, but rather serves as a proxy for job experience and maturity.

Using mathematical notation, the equation becomes:

$$Y = f(X_j, Z_k) \qquad \begin{array}{l} j = 1, 2, \ldots m \\ k = 1, 2, \ldots l \end{array} \qquad (3.1)$$

where X_j are age variables and the Z_k are groups of socio-economic and occupational variables. The relationship between the dependent and independent variables is assumed to be linear. The error term U_i accounts for variations in income not covered by the changes in X_j or Z_k, and is assumed to be random and to have the usual properties necessary for least squares estimation of the parameters.

$$Y_i = B_o + \sum_j B_j X_{ij} + \sum_k C_k Z_{ik} + U_i \qquad \begin{array}{l} j = 1, 2, \ldots m \\ k = 1, 2, \ldots l \\ i = 1, 2, \ldots n \end{array} \qquad (3.2)$$

X_j and Z_k are the independent variables and Y_i is the dependent one.

After the regressions are performed, one for each level-of-schooling group, the predictive form of the equation (3.2), obtained by least squares, is

---

[6] Since, for each individual, the values for a group of dummy variables covering one characteristic by definition add up to unity—the individual falls in only one age group, one occupation category, etc.—the required linear independence exists neither among the dummy variables within the group, nor between those groups and the implicit constant term. However, if we withdraw one dummy variable from each group, we can properly estimate a reduced set of parameters. The intercept term will then represent the income of the subpopulation described by the withheld dummy variables, and the individual coefficients will be estimates of the income differentials attributable to their corresponding variable. That such "reparametrization" is inevitably arbitrary can be seen from the reduced groups of dummy variables and the list of variables withdrawn, both in Table 3.1.

used to derive the education-earnings profile for each schooling group. This is given in (3.3)

$$\hat{Y}_i = b_o + \sum_j b_j X_{ij} + \sum_k c_k Z_{ik} \qquad j, k, i \text{ as above} \qquad (3.3)$$

where $\hat{Y}_i$ = predicted value of Y_i
$b_o = \hat{B}_o$, the least squares estimator of the intercept;
$b_j = \hat{B}_j$, the least squares estimator of the age coefficients;
$c_k = \hat{C}_k$, the least squares estimator of the socio-economic and occupational coefficients.

The data collected give values for Y_i, X_j, and Z_k, one complete set of values for each of the 4,742 interviewees. These sets are first divided into the three major ethnic groups (Africans, Asians, Europeans) and then subdivided into males and females to yield six data groups. Because of their preponderance in the labor force (75 percent of the total), we focus on African males. Comparative data on females and non-Africans are discussed later in the chapter.

The Relationships Between Education, Age, and Earnings

Age-adjusted Education-Earnings Profiles of Urban Males with 11 or Fewer Years of Schooling

To estimate for a given schooling group the mean earnings associated with any particular age we need to group the data by years of schooling.[7] The estimate of average monthly earnings for each age-education category would then take into account both the influence of age and education separately, and their combined (interaction) effect. The sub-samples are further divided at two levels of schooling (end of the seventh and eleventh years) according to the results obtained in the examinations that take place at these two points.

Figure 3.1 shows graphically the age-adjusted education-earnings profiles from Table 3.2 which are based on the regression estimates in Table 3.3. In this regression, only age variables were held constant. As explained in the description of the model, the intercept term for each schooling group in Table 3.3 represents the mean earnings attributable to the withdrawn dummy variable, which for the age variable is the figure for 35 to 44 years of age. Therefore, for each schooling group, one must add the coefficients of the other age groups to the intercept term in Table 3.3 to find the mean earnings for the age groups in Table 3.2.

---

[7] We also performed the regression analysis on the sample of African males using years of schooling as a continuous variable. The results are described in Annex C.

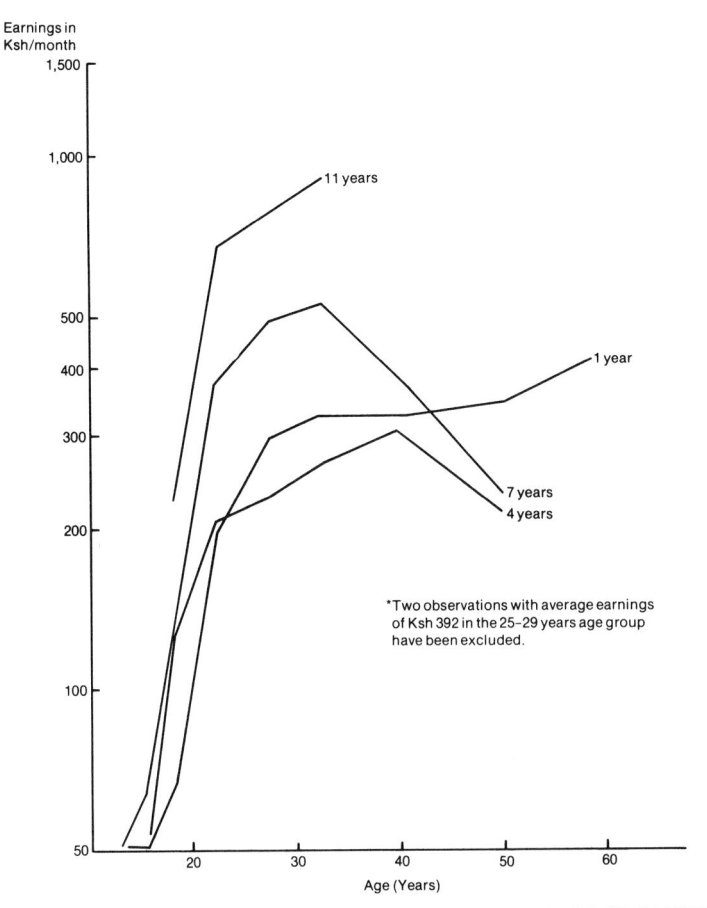

FIGURE 3.1: UNADJUSTED AGE-EARNINGS PROFILES, AFRICAN MALES BY YEARS OF SCHOOLING, 1968

Example: From column (1) of Table 3.3 we see that the intercept term for the group 0 to 2 years of schooling is 335.0. Hence, this figure appears in Table 3.2 as the earnings of the age group 35 to 44 years. Since for the same schooling level the coefficient of the 17 to 19 years of age group is given as −141.0, the earnings of this age group at this schooling level are given in Table 3.2 by

$$335.0 - 141.0 = 194.0.$$

The influence of socio-economic factors on earnings. Now that we have shown the relation of age and earnings for a given schooling level, we proceed to correct the age-earnings profile at each schooling level for the effect

TABLE 3.3: Regression Coefficients of Independent Dummy Variables; Dependent Variable: Monthly Earnings, African Males, 1968

	Independent Variable, X_i	\multicolumn{8}{c}{Years of Schooling}
		0–2	3–5	7 All	7F	7P	7Q	9	11 All	11F
5	Age ≤ 14	—	—	−281.2*	−202.9*	—	—	—	—	—
6	Age 15–16	—	—	−445.2*	−366.9*	—	—	—	—	—
7	Age 17–19	−141.0	−158.9	−248.4	−218.0	−325.7	−511.2	−671.2	−967.4	−999.3
8	Age 20–24	−50.0	−132.4	−227.2	−166.9	−320.6	−450.8	−541.2	−753.0	−831.2
9	Age 25–29	−47.1	−64.4	−125.8	−100.6	−202.3	−281.1	−417.4	−542.4	−649.2
10	Age 30–34	−9.7*	−22.6*	−9.9*	−16.9*	−22.6*	−255.2*	−266.1	−190.1*	−328.9*
12	Age 45–54	−9.2*	−23.4*	110.6	23.3	289.1	−605.2	−159.1	−1,231.7	−1,263.6
13	Age 55+	−21.0*	−36.6*	167.8*	—	69.4*	—	2,102.4	—	—
	Intercept	335.0	389.9	505.2	426.9	603.6	786.2	897.6	1,371.7	1,403.6
	R^2	0.01	0.05	0.14	0.15	0.21	0.23	0.43	0.17	0.18
	Mean Earnings (Ksh/Month)	320.6	354.7	401.3	342.1	438.5	468.8	505.2	763.8	712.0
	Mean Age (Years)	38.6	34.0	28.8	28.6	28.2	27.3	26.8	25.4	25.4

* Not significant.

Note: The exam now given at the end of the seventh year is called the Kenya Preliminary Exam (KPE). A student can either fail (7F), pass (7P) or qualify (7Q) for secondary school on this exam. The eleventh year exam is called the Cambridge School Certificate exam (CSC) on which a student can score a Division I, II, or III pass, a GCE-0 pass, or fail. (11F) covers the last three categories, plus those who did not take the exam at the end of 11 years of schooling or who did not answer the question.

Source: Labor Force Sample Survey, January/February 1968.

of socio-economic characteristics. The calculation of the adjusted profiles (Table 3.4) is based on the results (Table 3.5) of regressing both age and socio-economic variables on income. While we used the intercept term in Table 3.3 as a reference point for deriving income profiles, the intercepts in Table 3.5 cannot be used in exactly the same way because the latter intercepts include the effect of the other variables besides age in the regression. We must hold the socio-economic variables at some level to allow incomes of different schooling groups to be compared independently of socio-economic characteristics. We therefore adjusted the schooling group regressions to make each socio-economic variable equal to the average value of that variable for the whole sample of African males with 11 or fewer years of schooling.

TABLE 3.4: Age-Earnings Profiles of African Males by Years of Schooling, 1968: Adjusted for Parents' Literacy, Tribe, and Father's Occupation

(Ksh per month)

Age	0–2	3–5	7F	7P	7Q	7 All	9	11F	11 All
≤14	—	—	236*	—	—	215*	—	—	—
15–16	—	—	92*	—	—	87*	—	—	—
17–19	187	259*	218	238	230	234	276	247	226
20–24	305	266	261	275	342	270	296	563	565
25–29	312	329	345	367	438	358	427	741	757
30–34	355*	369*	412*	556*	563*	478*	547	1,066*	1,151*
35–44	356	394	436	589	727	494	884	1,449	1,337
45–54	348*	374*	477*	865	185*	620	728*	143**	88
55+	337*	367*	—	701*	—	680*	2,551**	—	—

* Not significant, see Table 3.2.
** Significant but only one observation.
a See Footnotes *a–d*, Table 3.2.
Source: Tables 3.5 and 3.6.

We did this in two stages. First we corrected the average earnings figures for the different schooling groups; we took the initial average figure given in the last rows of Tables 3.3 and 3.6 and corrected it by adding an adjustment based on the multiple regressions in Table 3.5 and the mean values in Table 3.6. For each age group the coefficient was taken from Table 3.5 and multiplied by the average value, or frequency, taken from the corresponding column of Table 3.6. The sum of all these multiplications was added to the average earnings figure mentioned above, to give an average earnings figure for the age group 35 to 44 years, corrected for socio-economic variables within the group.

This made no allowance for differences in socio-economic variables between the different schooling groups. To achieve an age profile allowing for this we took the multiple regression coefficient for each socio-economic variable from Table 3.5 and multiplied it by the difference between the

TABLE 3.5: Regression Coefficients of Independent Dummy Variables, Socio-Economic Variables Held Constant; Dependent Variable: Monthly Earnings, African Males, 1968

| | Independent Variable X_i | \multicolumn{10}{c}{Years of Schooling} |
		0–2	3–5	7 All	7F[a]	7P	7Q	9	11	11F
Age	5 Age ≤14	—	—	−278.8*	−200.3*	—	—	—	—	—
	6 Age 15–16	—	—	−407.4*	−344.3*	—	—	—	—	—
	7 Age 17–19	−168.8	−135.0*	−259.8	−218.4	−350.8	−496.8	−608.1	−1111.3	−1202.1
	8 Age 20–24	−50.6	−128.0	−224.0	−175.4	−313.7	−385.1	−588.2	−771.7	−886.1
	9 Age 25–29	−43.5	−64.9	−136.4	−91.0	−222.5	−289.0	−457.1	−579.8	−708.1
	10 Age 30–34	−0.8*	−24.9*	−16.4*	−24.5*	−33.1*	−164.2*	−337.1	−186.2*	−382.9*
	12 Age 45–54	−8.1*	−20.5*	125.0	40.6*	276.2	−542.1*	−155.5*	−1249.3	−1306.0
	13 Age 55+	−18.9*	−27.2*	185.6*		113.5*		1667.3		
Literacy	21 Father illiterate	−66.6*	134.1*	−10.8*	−49.2*	61.0*	873.5*	41.0*	644.2*	838.8*
	22 Father literate	7.7*	123.1*	33.1*	−42.8*	124.5*	974.3*	195.8*	746.5*	926.0*
	24 Mother illiterate	−44.9*	−71.3	−74.3	−24.6	−118.0	−1.2*	−15.5*	9.5*	14.5*
	26 Mother—no answer	−69.5*	87.7*	−3.6*		137.2*	865.2*	90.9*	564.6*	790.9*
Tribe	27 Kikuyu	−35.9*	−33.2*	−35.6*	−137.7	5.7*	−220.4*	−260.2	22.2*	57.9*
	28 Kamba	−58.8	−20.3*	2.2*	−101.6	64.1*	−188.6*	−312.6	−144.0*	−77.1*
	29 Luhya	−78.3	−44.7*	−14.8*	−122.7	23.0*	−150.7*	−356.3	−46.8*	−89.3*
	30 Coastal	−116.8	−43.0*	−23.1*	−97.4*	41.5*	−177.1*	27.9*	−187.5*	−119.2*
	31 Luo	−85.6	−29.0*	−16.6*	−38.5*	15.1*	−249.1*	−274.0*	11.1*	115.0*
	32 Kalenjin	85.8*	22.5*	−90.3*	−269.6	−22.7*	−16.1*	79.5*	−13.1*	5.1*
Father's Occupation	68 Farmer	24.1	24.7*	36.3*	38.3*	37.7*	83.8*	19.3*	69.0*	27.9*
	69 Professional (Scien.)	0.9*	262.9*	1.9*	23.5*	33.3*		−91.7*	−91.6*	−77.1*
	70 Professional (Other)	79.8*	91.4*	94.3*	−127.5*	110.0*	193.9*	−138.2*	−77.6*	43.9*
	71 Technician	98.4*	−27.4*	89.3*	34.1*	198.1*		−612.3*	−246.2*	−195.6*
	72 Foreman and supervisor		3.3*	6.5*	120.5*	−40.1*		394.5	80.7*	85.7*
	73 Administrator	19.4*	144.8*	117.3*	−61.4*	16.8*	342.6*	−127.5*	−115.6*	−87.4*
	74 Clerical & sales work	12.6	89.0*	42.5*	−43.1*	74.0*		102.8*	0.9*	−51.6*
	75 Skilled worker	45.9*	150.5	117.6	−70.4*	151.3	389.1*	−2.3*	93.9*	29.0*
	76 Semi-skilled	30.7*	9.6*	19.2*	65.6*	25.1*	26.5*	95.5*	319.3*	434.1
	Intercept	478.0	334.9	551.9	577.4	559.8	283.8	1034.1	644.3	502.5
	R^2	0.09	0.10	0.19	0.22	0.29	0.38	0.60	0.23	0.26

* Not significant.
[a] See Note, Table 3.3.

Source: Labor Force Sample Survey, January/February, 1968.

frequency of that variable in the schooling group in question and its frequency in the whole sample. The sum of all these corrections was then added to the corrected average above. This additional correction yielded an earnings figure for the age-group 35 to 44 years corrected for socio-economic variables not only within the schooling group but also between different schooling groups.[8]

The values for all the other years were then calculated by adding to the 35 to 44 group figure the differences in each column in the Age section of Table 3.5, in the same way as was done above with Table 3.3. When we finished these adjustments we had a set of age-earnings profiles at each education level, estimated as if all male African wage earners had the socio-economic characteristics of the "average employee," i.e. had those characteristics described by the mean values of each socio-economic variable for the whole subgroup of African males with 11 or less years of schooling. We now illustrate this procedure by reconstructing the 0 to 2 years of schooling column of Table 3.4.

Example: Column one of Table 3.5 gives the coefficients of the age categories at this schooling level (1); each is multiplied by the mean listed in column one of Table 3.6 for the corresponding age group (2), and these products are summed (3) and subtracted from the mean earnings figure for the 0 to 2 years of schooling group in the last line of Table 3.6 (4):

Age group	(1) From Table 3.5 column (1)	×	(2) From Table 3.6 column (1)	=	(3)	(4) From Table 3.6 "mean earnings"	(4) − (3)
≤14	—		0.00		—		
15–16	—		0.00		—		
17–19	−168.8		0.01		−1.69		
20–24	−50.6		0.05		−2.53		
25–29	−43.5		0.11		−4.78		
30–34	−0.8		0.20		−0.16		
45–54	−8.1		0.22		−1.78		
55+	−18.9		0.07		−1.32		
					−12.26	320.6	332.9

Therefore, mean earnings of the 0 to 2 years of schooling group corrected for socio-economic differences within the group is 332.9. Column one of Table 3.5 gives the coefficients of the categories for mother's and father's literacy, tribe, and father's occupation (1); each is multiplied by the difference (4) between the value of the mean for the

---

[8] The algebraic derivation of this procedure and an alternative form of estimation are given in Annex D.

TABLE 3.6: Means of Independent Variables, African Males, by Years of Schooling, 1968

	Independent Variables	0–2	3–5	7 All[a]	7F[b]	7P	7Q	9	11	11F	African All
	No. of Observations	1079	881	1109	302	496	60	174	220	173	3464
	Average age (years)	38.6	34.0	28.8	28.6	28.2	27.3	26.8	25.4	25.4	32.9
Age	5 Age ≤14	0.00	0.00	0.00	0.01	0.00	0.00	0.00	0.00	0.00	0.00
	6 Age 15–16	0.00	0.00	0.00	0.00	0.00	0.00	0.00	0.00	0.00	0.00
	7 Age 17–19	0.01	0.01	0.03	0.04	0.03	0.05	0.06	0.01	0.02	0.02
	8 Age 20–24	0.05	0.09	0.26	0.26	0.29	0.30	0.44	0.50	0.51	0.18
	9 Age 25–29	0.11	0.20	0.30	0.28	0.32	0.40	0.23	0.37	0.35	0.22
	10 Age 30–34	0.20	0.28	0.21	0.21	0.20	0.13	0.10	0.05	0.06	0.21
	12 Age 45–54	0.22	0.09	0.03	0.02	0.02	0.02	0.02	0.00	0.01	0.10
	13 Age 55+	0.07	0.02	0.00	0.00	0.00	0.00	0.01	0.00	0.00	0.03
Literacy	21 Father Illit.	0.90	0.75	0.56	0.57	0.54	0.57	0.40	0.30	0.34	0.69
	22 Father lit.	0.09	0.24	0.42	0.43	0.45	0.42	0.57	0.60	0.54	0.29
	24 Mother illit.	0.97	0.92	0.82	0.85	0.79	0.88	0.69	0.59	0.59	0.87
	26 Mother no ans.	0.00	0.01	0.01	0.00	0.01	0.02	0.01	0.10	0.12	0.02
Tribe	27 Kikuyu	0.27	0.27	0.35	0.37	0.36	0.38	0.36	0.49	0.43	0.32
	28 Kamba	0.27	0.23	0.16	0.18	0.15	0.15	0.10	0.13	0.14	0.21
	29 Luhya	0.14	0.21	0.17	0.16	0.20	0.22	0.24	0.13	0.15	0.17
	30 Coastal	0.10	0.05	0.06	0.07	0.04	0.03	0.03	0.03	0.03	0.07
	31 Luo	0.10	0.14	0.14	0.14	0.14	0.17	0.14	0.10	0.12	0.13
	32 Kalenjin	0.01	0.01	0.02	0.01	0.02	0.02	0.01	0.02	0.02	0.01
Father's Occupation	68 Farmer	0.44	0.46	0.49	0.48	0.52	0.53	0.47	0.53	0.50	0.47
	69 Prof. 1	0.00	0.00	0.00	0.00	0.00	0.00	0.01	0.00	0.00	0.00
	70 Prof. 2	0.00	0.01	0.02	0.01	0.02	0.03	0.03	0.03	0.02	0.01
	71 Tech.	0.00	0.00	0.00	0.00	0.01	0.00	0.01	0.00	0.01	0.00
	72 Foreman	0.00	0.01	0.02	0.01	0.02	0.02	0.01	0.00	0.02	0.01
	73 Admin.	0.01	0.01	0.01	0.01	0.02	0.00	0.01	0.02	0.02	0.01
	74 Clerk	0.01	0.01	0.03	0.03	0.03	0.00	0.05	0.04	0.04	0.02
	75 Skill	0.01	0.03	0.05	0.05	0.05	0.05	0.03	0.06	0.03	0.03
	76 Semi-skill	0.06	0.09	0.13	0.13	0.12	0.10	0.15	0.10	0.09	0.10
Firm Location and Size	14 Nairobi	0.74	0.75	0.76	0.84	0.77	0.80	0.71	0.82	0.79	0.75
	15 Mombasa	0.17	0.15	0.16	0.11	0.14	0.17	0.22	0.15	0.17	0.16
	2 Public Sector	0.02	0.04	0.12	0.11	0.14	0.25	0.18	0.51	0.46	0.10
	17 Firm size 1–14	0.00	0.01	0.01	0.01	0.00	0.07	0.00	0.00	0.00	0.01
	18 Firm size 15–49	0.07	0.12	0.09	0.11	0.06	0.10	0.13	0.06	0.06	0.09
	20 Firm size 100+	0.62	0.68	0.67	0.66	0.68	0.58	0.56	0.71	0.66	0.66

40

Occupation	39 Farmer	0.00	0.00	0.00	0.00	0.00	0.00	0.00	0.00
	40 Prof. 1	0.04	0.05	0.07	0.03	0.05	0.09	0.06	0.07	0.06
	41 Prof. 2	0.00	0.00	0.00	0.00	0.00	0.00	0.00	0.02	0.00
	42 Tech.	0.00	0.00	0.01	0.02	0.00	0.01	0.02	0.02	0.01
	43 Foreman	0.01	0.02	0.02	0.02	0.03	0.05	0.05	0.06	0.02
	44 Admin.	0.00	0.00	0.00	0.00	0.02	0.02	0.04	0.03	0.00
	45 Clerk	0.02	0.04	0.18	0.14	0.23	0.23	0.60	0.57	0.13
	46 Skill	0.11	0.18	0.25	0.25	0.25	0.27	0.12	0.11	0.18
	47 Semi-Skill	0.80	0.70	0.45	0.52	0.39	0.35	0.08	0.10	0.59
	49 Manufacturing	0.50	0.49	0.42	0.34	0.45	0.30	0.27	0.28	0.45
	50 Construction	0.07	0.09	0.07	0.06	0.07	0.13	0.01	0.01	0.07
	51 Commerce	0.14	0.15	0.18	0.25	0.17	0.20	0.11	0.14	0.16
	52 Services	0.19	0.15	0.11	0.19	0.07	0.08	0.01	0.01	0.14
	53 Union	0.73	0.75	0.67	0.66	0.69	0.69	0.44	0.49	0.70
Education	56 Primary public	0.05	0.25	0.39	0.34	0.43	0.43	0.42	0.45	0.25
	57 Primary private	0.10	0.63	0.51	0.51	0.50	0.47	0.32	0.31	0.40
	78 Addl. educ.	0.03	0.05	0.21	0.16	0.26	0.37	0.42	0.43	0.14
	79 No addl. educ.	0.96	0.95	0.78	0.84	0.73	0.62	0.49	0.46	0.85
	81 Addl. training	0.05	0.09	0.25	0.18	0.32	0.35	0.36	0.32	0.16
	82 No addl. training	0.94	0.90	0.74	0.82	0.67	0.63	0.55	0.57	0.82
	34 CSC Division I							0.05	0.00	0.00
	35 CSC Division II							0.16	0.00	0.01
	36 CSC Division III							0.20	0.26	0.01
	37 CSC GCE							0.08	0.10	0.01
	60 Sec. public general							0.55	0.49	0.05
	61 Sec. public teacher training							0.00	0.01	0.00
	62 Sec. private tech.							0.02	0.03	0.00
	63 Sec. private general							0.17	0.20	0.03
	64 Sec. private teacher training							0.00	0.01	0.00
	65 Sec. Harambee							0.01	0.01	0.00
	66 Sec. not applic.							0.01	0.02	0.62
	67 Sec. no answer							0.18	0.20	0.21
	Average earnings (Ksh/Month)	320.6	354.7	401.3	342.1	438.5	468.8	505.2	763.8	712.0	392.4

[a] The 7 All category includes 7F, 7P, 7Q, plus 251 observations who answered the KPE question "not applicable" or did not answer the question. The average income of this group is 383 shillings per month, somewhat higher than the 7F category.

[b] See Note, Table 3.3.
Source: Labor Force Sample Survey, January/February 1968.

corresponding category for the whole sample given in the last column of Table 3.6 (2) and the mean for the corresponding category for the schooling group, given in the first column of Table 3.6 (3). These products (5) are summed and added to the mean earnings figure (6) to give a new mean earnings figure (7).

Non-schooling variable	(1) From 3.5, column (1)	(2) From 3.6, last column	(3) From 3.6, column (1)	(4) = (2) − (3)	(5) = (1) × (4)
Father illit.	−66.6	0.69	0.90	−.21	13.99
Father lit.	7.7	0.29	0.09	0.20	1.54
Mother illit.	−44.9	0.87	0.97	−.10	4.49
Mother no ans.	−69.5	0.02	0.00	0.02	−1.39
Kikuya	−35.9	0.32	0.27	0.05	−1.80
Kamba	−58.8	0.21	0.27	−.06	3.53
Luhya	−78.3	0.17	0.14	0.03	−2.35
Coastal	−116.8	0.07	0.10	−.03	3.50
Luo	−85.6	0.13	0.10	0.03	−2.57
Kalenjin	85.8	0.01	0.01	0.00	0.00
Farmer	24.1	0.47	0.44	0.03	0.72
Prof. 1	—	0.00	0.00	0.00	0.00
Prof. 2	0.9	0.01	0.00	0.01	0.01
Tech.	79.8	0.00	0.00	0.00	0.00
Foreman	98.4	0.01	0.00	0.01	0.98
Admin.	19.4	0.01	0.01	0.00	0.00
Clerk	12.6	0.02	0.01	0.01	0.13
Skill	45.9	0.03	0.01	0.02	0.92
Semi-skill	30.7	0.10	0.06	0.04	1.23
					22.93

	(5) +	(6) =	(7)
	22.93	332.9	355.83

This figure represents, then, the mean earnings of African males aged 35 to 44 with 0 to 2 years of schooling, adjusted for socio-economic variables both within this schooling group, and between it and the other schooling groups; it becomes the 35 to 44 entry in the first column of Table 3.4. To it we add the coefficients for each age group from Table 3.5 to obtain the other age-earnings figures in the 0 to 2 years of schooling column. Analogous calculations yield the figures in the remaining columns of Table 3.4.

Other adjustments and summary of results. Finally, we calculate mean earnings for the 35 to 44 year age group adjusted for both socio-economic and occupational variables and from this figure age-earnings profiles (Table 3.7) in a manner completely analogous to the calculation described in the section dealing with the adjustments for socio-economic variables.[9] These calculations are based on Tables 3.6 and 3.8.

---

[9] These profiles are based on only the significant coefficient values. We opted for this simplification because of the large number of variables and the fact that the profiles are not used to derive rates of return.

TABLE 3.7: Age-Earnings Profiles, African Males, by Years of Schooling, 1968, Adjusted for All Variables

(Ksh per month)

Age	0–2	3–5	7F	7P	7 all	9	11 all
≤14	—	—	289*	—	287*	—	—
15–16	—	—	183*	—	266*	—	—
17–19	261	264	267	320	243	310	125
20–24	332	275	276	322	266	187	385
25–29	339	328	339	410	345	315	484
30–34	385*	353*	388*	558*	447*	384	791*
35–44	387	387	399	596	466	685	898
45–54	380*	383*	505*	907	633	538*	405*
55+	379*	358*	—	592*	460*	1,981**	—

Years of Schooling[a]

* See Table 3.2.
** See Table 3.4.
[a] See Footnotes, Table 3.2.
Source: Tables 3.8 and 3.9.

However, these accumulated corrections of the profiles over-adjust to some degree, because job-related characteristics such as occupational distribution, firm size, city of employment, sector of employment, industry in which employed, type of school attended, additional education and training taken, are probably closely connected with the amount and quality of schooling received, and so should not be isolated from the schooling-earnings relationship. That is, having a specific occupation or working in a certain sector, a large or small firm, or a particular city is in part a consequence having a given amount of schooling and should not be separated from the effect of schooling on earnings. Except for union affiliation, which is assumed to be exogenous to schooling,[10] the inclusion of occupational variables in Table 3.8 therefore overadjusts.[11]

As we would expect, earnings in the unadjusted age-earnings profiles rise with the level of schooling of African male employees (Table 3.2). The increase is not monotonic: different years of schooling cause income to increase by varying amounts. For example, a 35–44 year old earns an average of 170 Ksh per month more if he has 7 years of schooling instead of 0–2 years; if he has 11 years of schooling he earns 867 Ksh a month more than with 7 years.

[10] It should be noted, though, that for the subsample of African males with 11 years of schooling or less, the probability of union membership is somewhat inversely associated with the amount of education received (see Table 3.6). The difference is not very great except for the 11 years of schooling group.
[11] Only if it were assumed that the distribution of all these variables is exogenous to the schooling process—i.e. a question of, say, innate ability or chance—would these fully adjusted age-earnings profiles be a correct estimate of the increase in earnings due to more schooling. It is difficult, though, to subscribe to this hypothesis.

TABLE 3.8: Coefficients of Independent Variables, All Variables Held Constant, Dependent Variable Monthly Earnings, African Males, 1968

(Ksh per month)

Variable Group		Variable X_i	Years of Schooling						
			0–2	3–5	7F[a]	7P	7 All	9	11
Age	5	Age ≤14	—	—	−110.3*	—	−179.2*	—	—
	6	Age 15–16	—	—	−216.4*	—	−200.1*	—	—
	7	Age 17–19	−126.3	−122.8	−131.4	−275.5	−223.3	−375.2	−884.4
	8	Age 20–24	−54.8	−112.2	−123.1	−273.8	−200.8	−498.3	−540.3
	9	Age 25–29	−48.4	−59.1	−59.5	−186.3	−121.1	−370.6	−414.9
	10	Age 30–34	−2.1*	−33.9	−10.8*	−37.7*	−19.9*	−301.2	−33.8*
	12	Age 45–54	−6.8	−3.8*	105.8*	311.6	167.8	−147.9*	−516.5*
	13	Age 55+	−7.7	−28.8*	—	−3.7	−5.6*	1269.4	—
Literacy	21	Father illit.	−68.6	8.9*	−60.0*	−22.2*	−55.6*	−49.3*	421.8*
	22	Father lit.	−16.9	−2.1*	−51.4*	20.4	−27.9*	40.8*	497.9*
	24	Mother illit.	−20.4	−34.0*	18.0*	−73.8	−38.6*	28.9*	32.5*
	26	Mother no ans.	−61.8	16.4*	—	420.9*	−180.7*	470.5*	334.9*
Tribe	27	Kikuyu	−51.9	−57.8	−57.2*	27.5*	−6.6*	−270.7	−17.5*
	28	Kamba	−48.0	−42.0*	−37.9*	49.1*	8.2*	−306.1	−132.3*
	29	Luhya	−61.3	60.1	−41.4*	43.7*	15.9*	−308.3	44.4*
	30	Coastal	−66.0	−45.0*	−43.2*	−64.1*	−44.0*	−55.5*	−280.6*
	31	Luo	−37.3*	−40.7*	37.7*	11.4*	12.9	−233.8	−120.5*
	32	Kalenjin	83.7*	38.3*	−234.7	−2.3*	−61.6*	289.3*	−148.5
Father's Occupation	68	Farmer	23.2	7.5*	38.3*	24.9*	17.9*	4.6*	34.0*
	69	Profes. 1	—	168.2*	7.4*	29.7*	1.8*	96.9*	465.8*
	70	Profes. 2	−24.7*	57.5*	−57.1*	13.8*	32.0*	−189.2*	−10.3*
	71	Tech.	38.5*	−91.0*	134.1	209.8*	165.1*	−569.6*	−193.8*
	72	Foreman	7.3*	−17.8*	6.1*	−88.5*	−31.5*	225.8*	76.7*
	73	Admin.	−17.5*	105.7*	7.1*	6.3*	−122.9*	−72.8*	23.8*
	74	Clerk	−11.7*	58.4*	−25.4*	12.2*	−13.1*	4.9*	174.1*
	75	Skill.	45.3*	113.0	4.1*	108.7*	83.3	44.6*	32.0*
	76	Semi-skill.	22.5*	6.2*	70.5	29.6*	20.1*	89.1*	325.9
Firm Location and Size	14	Nairobi	18.5*	32.5*	21.6*	38.7*	39.6*	−3.1*	42.2*
	15	Mombasa	21.2*	−16.1*	3.3*	110.3*	89.4	36.3*	514.1*
	2	Public sector	−238.3	−210.3	−124.6	35.3*	36.6*	145.1*	792.6
	17	Firm size—1–14	−96.8	−28.8*	−54.1*	−277.9*	−124.7*	—	—

44

Occupation	18	Firm size—15–49		−55.9	64.6	−85.4	−99.3*	−90.2	20.1*	39.4*
	20	Firm size—100+		44.0	74.3	3.7*	−105.6	−51.9	2.6*	63.6*
	39	Farmer		—	—	—	—	—	—	—
	40	Profes. 1		7.7*	−28.7*	159.9*	134.5*	−73.1*	563.9	−155.5*
	41	Profes. 2		22.9*	—	121.8*	−375.5*	80.9*	—	−166.9*
	42	Tech.		—	220.1*	—	222.7*	−238.9*	304.0*	453.5*
	43	Foreman		160.8	23.8*	227.9*	229.9*	117.8*	738.1	182.8*
	44	Admin.		180.7*	—	524.3	364.8*	212.3	1162.7	337.8*
	45	Clerk		104.4	45.8*	—	156.3*	482.5	478.2	−183.3*
	46	Skill		52.2*	13.1*	213.9	35.7*	85.6*	399.0	−189.9*
	47	Semi-skill.		−47.1*	−64.6*	166.7*	−44.7*	−23.1*	258.1*	−212.5*
	49	Manufacturing		−69.5	−101.0	49.4*	22.6*	−115.7	132.4*	390.6
	50	Construction		−118.5	−121.4	−68.6*	43.2*	42.1*	207.2*	41.9*
	51	Commerce		−47.8*	−88.3	−102.4*	17.3*	13.9*	167.7*	401.5*
	52	Services		−73.4	−125.3	−28.4*	43.5*	−42.2*	74.8*	−253.0*
	53	Union		86.2	67.1	−138.6	80.2	−12.9*	204.5	111.7*
						60.9		111.4		
Education	56	Primary public		14.1*	14.5	−13.1*	−86.9*	−3.0*	47.9*	−184.6
	57	Primary private		−11.0*	25.8	−41.3*	−120.4	−27.9*	89.5*	−127.4*
	78	Addl. educ.		187.8	105.7	19.3*	134.7	162.4*	−201.6*	−146.2*
	79	No addl.		35.2	65.8	−27.5*	110.9*	128.2*	−259.4*	−104.3*
	81	Addl. training		−130.7	−87.2*	31.2*	433.8	−299.3*	479.7*	389.8*
	82	No addl. training		−238.3	−125.8*	—	346.6*	−365.7	493.6*	115.4*
	34	CSC—Division I								122.8*
	35	CSC—Division II								58.1*
	36	CSC—Division III								48.8*
	37	CSC—GCE								128.3*
	60	Sec. public general								−573.4
	61	Sec. public teacher tr.								−187.2*
	62	Sec. public tech.								−697.6
	63	Sec. private general								−787.8
	64	Sec. private teacher tr.								−905.0*
	65	Sec. Harambee								−568.3*
	66	Sec. not applic.								−708.8*
	67	Sec. no answer								−536.3
		Intercept		658.7	494.3	393.4	115.3	709.1	34.1	416.5
		R^2		0.32	0.26	0.56	0.44	0.39	0.78	0.55

* Not significant.
a See Note, Table 3.3.
b See note, Table 3.6.
Source: Labor Force Sample Survey, January/February 1968.

In general, differences in earnings are somewhat reduced by the adjustment for socio-economic variables, especially for lower age brackets and lower levels of schooling. The reduction of differences is much more pronounced, however, when occupational variables are taken into account. As we have already pointed out, this last adjustment is an obvious overcorrection of the age-earnings profiles. Therefore, in our estimates of rates of return, we prefer to use the unadjusted profiles (Table 3.2) and those adjusted for socio-economic variables (Table 3.4). In addition, in Chapter IV corrections are made on the rates of return for ability differences and for two occupational variables, union affiliation and the public sector, which may affect earnings in a way which is not related to certain quantities of schooling.

Age-Adjusted Education-Earnings Profiles of African Females and Non-Africans

Lack of data prevents as detailed a discussion of age-earnings profiles for the other five sex-ethnic groups as has been possible for African males. Earnings estimates for European males have not been feasible at all. The earnings profiles for females are given in Table 3.9 and in Figure 3.2 (African females only). This table is analogous to Table 3.2, the unadjusted profile for African males. While this profile is not adjusted for any variables but age, the data still give us some valuable clues.

The results on African females are the most complete and cover all schooling groups up to the 11-year level. African females with two years of schooling or less earn about the same as African males with the same education, but the gap between males' and females' earnings widens as the

TABLE 3.9: **Unadjusted Age-Earnings Profiles, African, Asian and European Females by Years of Schooling, 1968**

(*Ksh per month*)

	Years of Schooling					Asian Females	European Females
	African Females						
Age	0–2	3–5	7	9[a]	11	11	11
≤14	50	—	50	—	—	—	—
15–16	50	53	64	—	—	—	—
17–19	67	124	138*	—	228	643	986
20–24	198	205	369*	—	673*	863	1106
25–29	294*	229*	490*	—	392	1090*	1452*
30–34	326*	262*	523*	—	909	1259*	1471*
35–44	325	306	383	—	—	1359	1649
45–54	345*	215*	234*	—	—	—	1797*
55+	415	—	—	—	—	—	1475*

* See Table 3.2.
[a] There are no significant coefficients in the 9-year schooling category estimates.
Source: Labor Force Sample Survey, January/February 1968.

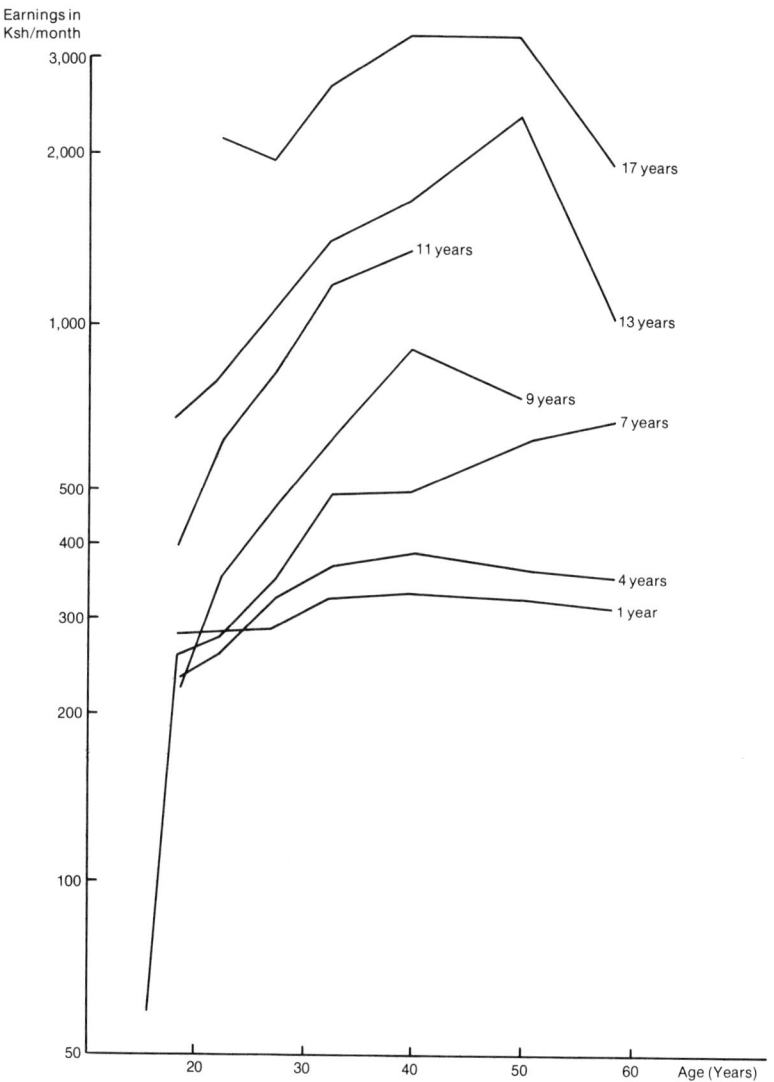

FIGURE 3.2: UNADJUSTED AGE-EARNINGS PROFILES, AFRICAN FEMALES BY YEARS OF SCHOOLING, 1968

level of schooling rises. Information on Asian males permits comparison with African males in the 7 to 11 year range only: Asians with equal schooling earn more but the difference in earnings decreases as the amount of schooling increases. At the 11-year level the difference is still apparent but small; the Asian salaries are 27 percent higher in the 17 to 19 age group, 14 percent higher in the 20 to 24 age group, and only 7 percent higher in the 35 to 44 age group. This convergence is probably due to the increasing fraction of African males in higher-paying government positions as the level of schooling increases.

Comparisons of non-African females' earnings with those of other sex-ethnic groups are possible only at the 11-year level. European females earn more than any other group at this level, and are followed by Asian males, Asian females, African males, and African females.

Age-Adjusted Education-Earnings Profiles for Persons with Higher Secondary Schooling and University Education

The small number of interviewees with more than 11 years of schooling (239 observations, or 5 percent of the total) considerably restricts the regression analysis at this level. There are not enough data to permit a separate analysis for each sex-ethnic group, as was done for those interviewees with up to 11 years of schooling. Therefore, the only distinction made is between those with 12 to 13 and those with 14 to 17 years of schooling; a regression analysis is carried out for each of the two education groups. A portion of the results is shown in Tables 3.10 and 3.11. Ethnic group, sex and age are regressed on earnings (Equation 1), then parents' literacy and father's occupation are added to the variables (Equation 2), and thereafter, occupational characteristics, citizenship status, and type of schools attended (Equation 3). In the last equation, number of principal subjects passed is included as a variable for the 12 to 13 years of schooling group, and field of university study for the 14 to 17 years group. The age-earnings profile derived from these regressions is shown in Table 3.12.

An attempt is made to construct a separate profile for the 66 African males with post-secondary schooling, but this produces few significant results (see Table 3.13, columns 1, 2, and 4). Therefore figures for African males are derived by assuming that the dummy variable for African males equals unity and that for other ethnic groups, zero. The coefficient thus obtained for African males is added to the intercept to get the earnings for the 35 to 44-year-old African males (Table 3.13, columns 3 and 5). These figures are used in the next chapter to estimate rates of return.

While most of the regression coefficients presented in Tables 3.10 and 3.11 are insignificant, and the few significant ones so dispersed that individually they add little to our understanding, a few results are worth mentioning. The age and sex-ethnic variables as a group account for nearly two-thirds of earnings variation in the 12 to 13 years of schooling group, and for almost one-half in the 14 to 17 years category. Adding all the other variables brings the value of the coefficient of determination (R^2) to 0.77 (0.89 for 17 years of schooling). These are much higher values than those obtained for primary and secondary schooling.

TABLE 3.10: Regression Coefficients of Independent Dummy Variables; Dependent Variable: Monthly Earnings, All Sex-ethnic Groups and Means of Variables for African Males with 13 Years of Schooling, 1968

	Independent Variables X_i	Equation (1)	Equation (2)	Equation (3)	Means of Variables, African Males
	Age (years)				27.9
	Monthly earnings (Ksh)				1121.9
Sex-Ethnic	Male Asian	251.8*	68.1*	275.3*	—
	Male European	2793.7	2783.0	3098.7	—
	Female African	205.7*	447.7*	−121.9*	—
	Female Asian	−383.1*	−681.2*	−119.1*	—
	Female European	354.7*	355.8*	1012.0*	—
Age	Age 17–19	−978.8*	−1019.6*	−91.9*	0.00
	Age 20–24	−859.4	−1108.1	−1055.1	0.47
	Age 25–29	−602.3	−693.9	−698.9	0.22
	Age 30–34	−275.9*	−223.8*	308.0*	0.11
	Age 45–54	664.6	500.8*	553.4*	0.06
	Age 55+	−638.1*	−807.3	−395.4*	0.00
Literacy	Father lit.		−176.8*	−342.0*	0.69
	Father no ans.		216.8*	449.5*	0.25
	Mother lit.		33.2*	−22.5*	0.44
	Mother no ans.		0.0*	0.0*	0.25
Father's Occupation	Farmer		−189.3*	91.8*	0.33
	Prof. 1		258.8*	103.9*	0.00
	Prof. 2		238.0*	447.9*	0.11
	Tech.		1646.1	518.9*	0.03
	Foreman		851.9*	209.6*	0.06
	Admin.		435.6*	633.6*	0.06
	Clerk		727.2*	451.9*	0.03
	Skill		306.7*	435.7*	0.06
	Semi-skill		1139.2	860.6*	0.08
HSC	Princ. subj. passed—1			−118.3*	0.08
	Princ. subj. passed—2			−207.9	0.06
	Princ. subj. passed—3			—	0.00
	Princ. subj. passed 4+			−83.8*	0.06
Firm Location and Size	Public Sector			1112.6*	0.69
	Mombasa			1108.8*	0.17
	Nakuru			−577.0*	0.00
	Firm size 1–14			—	0.00
	Firm size 15–49			321.6*	0.06
	Firm size 100+			−205.0*	0.80
Occupation	Manufacturing			1009.2*	0.22
	Construction			1014.9*	0.00
	Commerce			159.0*	0.03
	Services			227.5*	0.00
	Farmer			—	—
	Prof. 1			−58.6*	0.11
	Prof. 2			−684.4*	0.17
	Tech.			527.8	—
	Foreman			107.7*	—
	Admin.			198.8*	0.06

49

TABLE 3.10—Continued

	Independent variables X_i	Equation (1)	Equation (2)	Equation (3)	Means of Variables, African Males
	Skill.			14.4*	0.06
	Semi-skill.			40.3*	—
	Unskill.			−2211.2*	—
	Union			−138.3	0.25
Education	Primary public			−143.3*	0.44
	Primary private			−587.9	0.22
	Sec. public general			377.3*	0.53
	Sec. public teacher training			−515.1*	—
	Sec. private tech.			—	—
	Sec. private general			518.5*	0.11
	Sec. Private teach training			462.6*	—
	Sec. Harambee			—	—
	Sec. not applic.			72.1	—
	Sec. no answer			398.5*	0.33
	Addl. education			369.8*	0.36
	No addl. educ.			548.3*	0.36
	Addl. training			−59.1*	0.25
	No addl. training			−360.6*	0.47
Citizenship	Citizen other E.A.			—	—
	Citizen non-African			−320.5*	—
	Applied Kenya			−495.4*	—
	Citizen no answer			−69.3*	—
	Intercept	1655.3	1637.5	384.3	—
	R^2	0.64	0.69	0.77	—
	Number of observations	135	—	—	36

* Not significant
Source: Labor Force Sample Survey, January/February 1968.

In comparing the percentage of African males with higher education in each cluster of variables with the comparable percentages for all Africans in Table 3.6, we learn that more than half of the highly educated Africans' fathers are literate, as compared to only 30 percent for all Africans; a similar difference exists as regards the literacy of mothers. Likewise, somewhat fewer higher educated Africans had fathers who were farmers than the average (33 and 40 percent vs. 50 percent), and fewer had fathers who were skilled, semi-skilled or unskilled workers (33 and 37 vs. 48 percent). A higher percentage of highly educated workers are in firms with 100 or more employees, and their occupations are predominantly clerical in the 12 to 13 year category, and technical and professional at the 14 plus level. Very high proportions—69 and 90 percent respectively—of Africans with higher secondary or university education work in the public sector, compared to 10 percent for all Africans in our sample.

TABLE 3.11: Regression Coefficients of Independent Dummy Variables; Dependent Variables: Monthly Earnings, All Sex-ethnic Groups with 17 Years of Schooling, 1968, and Means of Variables for African Males

	Independent Variables X_i	Equation (1)	Equation (2)	Equation (3)	Means of Variables, African Males
	Age (years)				30.4
	Monthly Earnings (Ksh)				2429.4
Sex-Ethnic	Male Asian	−936.2*	−946.2*	−785.0*	—
	Male European	3409.0	2842.0	2576.8	—
	Female African	—	—	—	—
	Female Asian	−1907.1*	−1951.6*	−577.9*	—
	Female European	737.2*	−801.0*	−388.0*	—
Age	Age 17–19	—	—	—	0.00
	Age 20–24	−1303.1*	−1313.0*	−1615.9*	0.33
	Age 25–29	−1472.5	−1412.6*	−482.8*	0.40
	Age 30–34	−791.0*	−750.7*	−285.4*	0.43
	Age 45–54	5.2*	394.1*	829.9*	0.00
	Age 55+	−1495.3*	−2410.1	−18.9*	0.00
Literacy	Father lit.		−78.8*	−296.8*	0.50
	Father no ans.		4815.7*	5240.1*	0.30
	Mother lit.		−505.6*	−728.7*	0.40
	Mother no ans.		−5383.8*	−8065.6*	0.30
Father's Occupation	Farmer		−1755.0	−1094.6*	0.40
	Prof. 1		1501.6*	803.4*	0.00
	Prof. 2		48.6*	−1384.1*	0.07
	Tech.		—	—	0.00
	Foreman		−1601.6*	−2215.5*	0.03
	Admin.		−1241.1*	−1254.8*	0.03
	Clerk		−1625.3*	−1301.4*	0.07
	Skill		−846.6*	−2424.4	0.07
	Semi-skill.		−497.6*	−1446.2*	0.13*
Firm Location and Size	Public sector			8096.2*	0.90*
	Mombasa			932.8*	0.07
	Nakuru			−937.6*	0.00
	Firm size 1–14			−4430.9*	0.00
	Firm size 15–45			−5842.0	0.07
	Firm size 100+			−6604.7	0.87
Occupation	Manufacturing			4915.8	0.07
	Construction			6334.8	0.00
	Commerce			6235.7	0.03
	Services			9642.7	0.00
	Farmer			—	0.00
	Prof. 1			−1634.5*	0.17
	Prof. 2			383.7*	0.50
	Tech.			148.1*	0.00
	Foreman			5199.6	0.00
	Admin.			2439.6	0.10
	Skill.			—	0.00
	Semi-skill.			—	0.00
	Unskill.			—	0.00
	Union			1181.0*	0.10

TABLE 3.11—Continued

	Independent Variables X_i	Equation (1)	Equation (2)	Equation (3)	Means of Variables, African Males
Education	Primary public			1321.6*	0.30
	Primary private			−1855.7	0.37
	Sec. public general			1315.9*	0.50
	Sec. public teacher training			782.0*	0.00
	Sec. private tech.			−1412.7*	0.00
	Sec. private general			2063.9*	0.13
	Sec. private teacher training			—	0.00
	Sec. Harambee			—	0.00
	Sec. not applic.			3163.44*	0.00
	Sec. no answer			493.28*	0.37
Citizenship	Citizen other E.A.			—	—
	Citizen non-African			−1174.08*	—
	Applied Kenya			−982.63*	—
	Citizen no ans.			−761.77*	—
University	University Nairobi			2588.52*	0.07
	University other E.A.			143.22*	0.13
	University no ans.			−1630.20*	0.07
	Faculty soc. sci.			1430.10*	0.67
	Faculty medicine			2495.76*	0.00
	Faculty engineering			3305.49	0.10
	Faculty agric.			—	—
	Faculty arts			−664.09*	—
	Faculty other			1450.80*	—
	Faculty other			−4427.78*	—
	Faculty other			3429.88	0.17
	Intercept	3404.7	4746.2	1044.5	
	R^2	0.44	0.56	0.89	
	Number of observations	104			30

* Not significant.
Source: Labor Force Sample Survey, January/February 1968.

TABLE 3.12: Unadjusted Age-Earnings Profiles by Years of Schooling, All Sex-ethnic Groups, 1968

(Ksh per month)

| | Years of Schooling ||
Age	12–13	14–17
17–19	1,353*	—
20–24	1,473	2,836*
25–29	1,730	2,667
30–34	2,056*	3,348*
35–44	2,332	4,139
45–54	2,997	4,144
55+	1,694*	2,644

* Not significant.
Source: Labor Force Sample Survey, January/February 1968.

TABLE 3.13: Unadjusted Age-Earnings Profiles for African Males, Alone and as Variable, 11, 12–13 and 14–17 Years of Schooling, 1968

(Ksh per month)

	Years of Schooling				
	11 years	12–13 years		14–17 years	
Age	African Males Alone	African Males Alone	African Male as Variable	African Males Alone	African Male as Variable
17–19	405	—	675*	—	—
20–24	619	714*	796	1100*	2102*
25–29	830	1326	1053	2205*	1932
30–34	1182*	1325	1379*	2661*	2614*
35–44	1372	1259	1655	2679*	3405
45–54	—	3020**	2320	—	3410
55+	—	—	1017*	—	1909*

* Not statistically significant at the 95 percent level.
** Statistically significant but represents only one observation.

Africans with 12 to 13 years of schooling earn nearly three times as much as Africans with five years of schooling, and 40 percent more than the average of Africans with 11 years. An African with 14 to 17 years of schooling makes, in turn, twice as much as one with 12 to 13 years. Average earnings of highly educated African males (13 or more years of schooling) remain below those for the overall sample of all sex-ethnic groups with this amount of education, and are considerably below the salaries of similarly educated European males:

Average Monthly Income (Ksh)

	Years of Schooling	
Ethnic group	12–13	14–17
African male	1,122	2,429
European male	2,794	3,409
All sex-ethnic age groups (Table 3.12)	1,473–2,997	2,667–4,144

In conclusion it can be said that data on urban African male employees with 11 years of schooling or less have permitted very detailed adjustments for socio-economic and occupational characteristics. The profiles obtained when occupational characteristics are held constant are considered to be over-corrected for the effect of schooling on earnings. However, the profiles derived from the regressions which include socio-economic variables are adjusted for factors largely exogenous to schooling and can be considered more appropriate measures of the true benefits from education than the initial unadjusted age-earnings profiles.

The sample size of African males for upper secondary and university schooling was too small to estimate in any meaningful way the effects of the corrections for other variables on the age-earnings profiles. At these highest levels of education, age-earnings profiles could be estimated in the broadest terms only by aggregating all sex-ethnic groups.

The Significance of Non-Schooling Variables—A Digression

Before considering data on rural incomes and schooling and the relationship between these and the urban data we have examined so far, we make a brief digression on the effect which each of the 57 non-age, non-schooling variables has on earnings. Our observations will be limited to the group of African males.

From the vast amount of basic data in Tables 3.3, 3.5, and 3.8, on which the profiles in Tables 3.2, 3.4, and 3.7 are based, we can identify the few individual variables which seem to be the main sources of income variance among African males. Table 3.3 gives the coefficients for the age groups without adjustments for other variables. Mean earnings and age are also found for each schooling group. The latter figures reveal three facts:

a) Earnings not only increase with years of schooling, but the absolute and relative size of the increments also increase;

b) Scores on the seven- and eleven-year examinations have a marked effect on mean earnings: while average earnings for the "qualify" or "pass" group in the seven-year category are 32 percent higher than earnings for the group with three to five years of schooling, a "fail" on the examination results in earnings differing little from those of the lower schooling group; and

c) Since older African men are less educated than younger ones, the average ages associated with the average earnings at each schooling level decrease as education increases. Thus the average age of an African man with two years of schooling or less is 39, while the average age of a man with 11 years is 25. The data imply that the African male labor force over 34 years of age has on the average about 1.5 years less education (3.9 years versus 5.4 years) than the African male labor force under 34 years old.

Tables 3.5 and 3.8 show the results of adjusting for socio-economic variables, and socio-economic and occupational variables together, respectively. Among the variables with insignificant coefficients, i.e., variables which seem not to have any statistically relevant effect on earnings in themselves when other variables are held constant are: father's occupation (with scattered exceptions), father's literacy, city of employment, and score on the CSC (11th year) examination. Variables which do seem to be significant when other variables are constant have to do with tribe, mother's literacy, firm size, occupational category, union membership, and (particularly for five and fewer years of schooling) sector of employment.

The figures for the first two years of secondary school show that the difference in earnings between those with nine years of school and those who pass the KPE is increased by adjusting for socio-economic variables, and essentially eliminated by the correction for employment characteristics. In fact, this latter correction causes earnings of the 9-year group to fall substantially below those for the 7-year group at all ages below the 35 to 44 bracket. Since we consider that employment characteristics are related to the amount of schooling received, the results of the adjustment for occupational characteristics imply that the main "return" to the first two years of secondary schooling lies in an ability to secure different sorts of jobs than those available to primary school leavers.

Table 3.6, which we have already used in the profile calculations, is a further display of the detail of the data analyzed. It gives, by schooling group, the percentage of individuals characterized by each of the variables, the average age and earnings, and the number of observations for each schooling group. It shows, for example, that 75 percent of African males with three to five years of schooling have illiterate fathers and 92 percent illiterate mothers, compared with 30 percent and 59 percent respectively for those with 11 years of schooling. More interestingly, while four-fifths of those in the least educated group are semi-skilled workers, and two-thirds of those with the most education work as clerks, administrators, or foremen, roughly the same proportion of these two education groups have fathers who were farmers (44 vs. 53 percent).

Some of the more notable trends which show up as we move from lower to higher levels of schooling, are:

a) The increase in parents' literacy;

b) The steadily increasing share of members of the Kikuyu tribe and the decreasing share of Kamba tribe members;

c) The increase of fathers in semi-skilled occupations of interviewees with up to nine years of schooling;

d) The rapid increase in the share of white-collar workers (Occ. Clerk), from 2 to 60 percent of the sample, as we move from the 0 to 2 to the 11 years of schooling category, the parabolic increase and decrease of skilled workers, and the rapid decrease of semi-skilled workers;

e) The decreasing number employed in manufacturing and services, and the corresponding increase in the public sector;

f) The increase in the percentage of those who went to public rather than private primary schools;

g) The increase in the percentage of those taking extra-mural schooling and on-the-job training, and

h) The decreasing share of union members.

The data in Table 3.6 could be only partially exploited in this study. However, some of the facts it contains are used in interpreting the differences between adjusted and unadjusted age-earnings profiles.

Rural Incomes and Schooling

Because of the gap between urban and rural incomes and the limitations of urban employment opportunities compared to the annual additions to the labor force, an analysis of the rates of return to education in Kenya should not be based on urban wage employment alone. However, our Labor Force Survey includes only urban workers. Consequently, the conclusions and data of the foregoing part of this chapter, which are based on the survey data, are relevant only to the quarter of wage-employed Africans who work in Kenya's urban areas. The other three-quarters of the workers in the monetary sector, not to speak of those in the non-monetary sector, are not covered. We therefore need to know whether for the rural majority of the population there is any return to investment in education such as we observed among urban employees.

Education brings little or no monetary return to two large segments of the country's male labor force: the unemployed, and farm laborers. Farm laborers' earnings are a function of age rather than schooling. Their wages range from about Ksh 2 to 3 per day; they are generally supplemented by rations valued at Ksh 25 or so per month, by housing, and by a small plot of land to be operated by the farm workers and their families for their own needs. There is no indication that persons who went to school have a better chance of finding this kind of employment than have illiterate people. On the contrary, African and non-African employers alike seem at present to be somewhat skeptical as to the suitability of educated persons for farm labor, quoting their unrealistic job expectations as a major drawback.[12]

On the other hand, the largest segment of the labor force—self-employed small landowners—definitely seem to earn more when they have had more education. These men operate small farms, cultivate some cash crops, and

---

[12] Communicated by R. Posner, University of Michigan, Ann Arbor, Mich., who is at present completing a study on the rural labor force in Kenya.

commonly derive income from occasional or regular non-farm employment as well. The total number of households headed by small landowners may be anywhere between 900,000 and one million. In some cases, the head of household or other family members may be pursuing urban employment while the family stays in the village and works on the small farm; food and other commodities are sent to town from time to time, and cash remittances flow back to the village.[13] For the vast majority of African families, however, their farm and the village are their only sources of income.

Table 3.14, based on data collected by the Kenyan government from some 800 rural households in the Central Province in 1963/64, shows that total earnings of such small landowning families clearly increase with the education of the head of household.[14] In this table we derive figures for head of household income from gross family income figures. We first subtract from gross family farm income the average implicit value of family farm labor other than the family head and the implicit value of hired labor (Ksh 165 per acre annually);[15] we also subtract a minimum rental value of land (Ksh 10 per acre annually). This farm income to the family head—that is, farm income net of family labor, hired labor, and land inputs—is negative or very low.

We then estimate non-farm head of household income (Table 3.14) by assuming that an average of 0.4 men other than the family head and 1.5 women (0.2 in man-equivalents),[16] or 0.6 men other than the family head, are available to work outside the farm. It is further assumed that family members other than the family head have about the same "effective school-

---

[13] This system seems to be gradually disappearing, however, the African "target laborer" of former times being replaced by a permanent urban worker.

[14] These data are based on the Economic Survey of the Central Province, 1963/64, undertaken by the Statistics Division of the Ministry of Economic Planning and Development, and communicated by Dr. B. F. Massell, Stanford Food Research Institute. Although it is not specified in this sample whether the rural household head is a landowner, we have assumed here that he is. It is believed that all but three or four in the sample did own land.

[15] Data from the Ministry of Economic Planning and Development, *Economic Survey of Central Province, 1963–64*, Nairobi, 1964, indicate that the average number of family man-days put in on the average 3.9 acre farm is 154 days for men, 188 days for women, and 26 days for children. There are 1.2 men, 1.5 women, and 2.8 children in the average farm family. Average wages are 2.19 shillings/day for men and 1.60 for women. It is assumed that children earn 1.00 shillings daily. The average implicit family labor cost, other than for the family head (assumed to be one of the men in the family) is therefore 152 shillings/acre. 13 shillings/acre is the average cost of hired labor.

[16] Women have a probability of 0.2 relative to men of finding work off the farm and receive about 0.73 the wages of men (2.19 Ksh for men vs. 1.60 Ksh for women), so a woman is weighted as 0.146 of a man-equivalent.

TABLE 3.14: Mean Annual Income, Farm Acreage, and Age of Household Heads by Education Level of Household Head, 1963–64, Rural Central Province

	Illiterate no schooling	Literate, no schooling	1–3 years schooling	4–8 years schooling	9 or more years schooling
Gross Family Income (Ksh/yr.)	1709 (1566)	2553 (4539)	3341 (4234)	4116 (4377)	6284 (5916)
Non-Farm Family Income (Ksh/yr.)	804 (812)	1528 (3700)	2050 (3791)	2635 (3508)	4352 (4702)
Age of Household Head (Years)	51 (15)	48 (14)	45 (14)	35 (10)	39 (11)
Number of Observations	408	130	80	149	21
Average Farm Size (acres)	6.3 (13.1)	6.7 (5.9)	9.2 (9.5)	7.2 (8.8)	9.5 (9.7)
Farm Income of Household Head (Ksh/yr.)[a]	−196 (1779)	−147 (1407)	−312 (1746)	228 (1664)	263 (2216)
Non-Farm Income of Household Head (Ksh/yr.)[b]	502	955	1281	1647	2720
Gross Income of Household Head (Ksh/yr.)	306	818	969	1875	2983

[a] Estimated as gross income minus non-farm income minus [(165 Ksh/acre imputed labor cost + 10 Ksh/acre imputed land rent) times average number of acres].
[b] Assumes that 0.6 family members (in male equivalent terms) besides the head of household, having same schooling as household head, earn non-farm income.

Note: Standard deviations are in parentheses.
Source: *Economic Survey of Central Province*, Statistics Division of Ministry of Economic Planning and Development. Data communicated by B. F. Massell, Stanford Food Research Institute.

ing."[17] Hence, 0.6/1.6, or a share of ⅜, is subtracted from a household's non-farm income to yield the part that can be attributed to its head.

The figures in Table 3.14 show that while the increase in farm income which goes with additional education of the household head is significant, much of the pay-off to more education is in higher non-farm income. The profitability of education in rural Kenya therefore depends to a large extent on the supply of off-farm jobs.

TABLE 3.15: Total Income of Rural Head of Household by Age and Education, 1963–64, Adjusted for Acreage and Family Size Differences between Age Groups and between Education Levels

(Ksh per year)

Age	Years of Schooling					
	0 Illit.	0 Lit.	1–3	4–8	9+
17	521	956	−292	1236	—
20	497	902	−71	1375	3287
30	489	798	716	2086	2874
40	577	807	1490	2461	3119
50	742	905	2167	2975	3663
60	782	1178	2873	3765	3995

Source: See Annex E.

TABLE 3.16: Mean Annual Income of Rural Landholding Heads of Household by Age and Education, 1963–64, Unadjusted for Acreage and Family Size Differences between Age Groups and between Education Levels

(Ksh per year)

Age	Years of Schooling				
	0 Illit.	0 Lit.	1–3	4–8	9+
<20	150	270	251	375	388
20–29	217	376	348	1406	2028
30–39	269	571	608	1500	2923
40–49	309	614	833	3056	2356
50–59	336	1260	1163	2625	4594
60–69	321	607	2926	1706	4594

Source: Table 3.17 and Annex Table 5.10 in EC-173.

From the data in Table 3.14 we make two estimates of the gross income of head of household by education level, one which is corrected for acreage and family size differentials between age groups and between education levels for a given age group (Table 3.15), and one which is not (Table 3.16).

In order to arrive at the Table 3.16 profiles, the implicit mean earnings of the head of household shown in Table 3.14 must first be distributed by

---

[17] We thus imply—for want of data—that the scope and composition of a rural family's economic activities is determined by the education of the head of household rather than by that of its individual members.

age. Mean income of the head of household is distributed by age and education level in the same way that total family earnings are distributed by age and education level in the rural sample. Table 3.17 shows mean family income by level of education and age, from which we derive the age-earnings profiles for household heads shown in Table 3.16. These profiles are used to estimate one set of rates of return to investment in schooling for rural landowners in the next chapter.

TABLE 3.17: Mean Annual Gross Rural Family Income by Age and Schooling of Household Head, 1963

Income in Ksh
Years of Schooling

Age	0 Illit.	0 Lit.	1–3	4–8	9+
19[a]	833	833	833	833	833
10–29	1201	1182	1168	3069	4297
30–39	1414	1820	2111	3311	6162
40–49	1724	1980	2904	6721	4971
50–59	1876	3922	4014	5784⎫	
60–69	1791	2364	8820⎫	3733⎭	9692
70+	1901	2054	4142⎭		

Income as Percent of Mean Schooling Group Income[b]
Years of Schooling

Age	0 Illit.	0 Lit.	1–3	4–8	9+
19	0.49	0.33	0.25	0.20	0.13
20–29	0.71	0.46	0.35	0.75	0.68
30–39	0.88	0.71	0.63	0.80	0.98
40–49	1.01	0.78	0.87	1.63	0.79
50–59	1.10	1.54	1.20	1.40⎫	
60–69	1.05	0.93	2.64⎫	0.91⎭	1.54
70+	1.11	0.80	1.24⎭		

[a] The means at all education levels taken equal to the mean of age 19 of those in the sample with 4–8 years of schooling.

[b] Mean incomes in this table taken as a ratio of "gross family income" for the same level of schooling shown in Table 5.6.

Source: Survey of Central Province.

Since the estimates of Table 3.16 are uncorrected for acreage differences for different age groups within a given education level, they probably underestimate, for a given age group, the earnings net of land rent of those with less education relative to those with more education. We would also expect that the amount of land owned by older farmers is greater than the amount owned by younger farmers, and so should also correct for acreage differences between age groups. In the estimate we develop for Table 3.15 we attempt to correct for these sources of bias. We also correct for differential family size among households (by age and education of household head) which affects the imputed family labor costs. These profiles are used to calculate the second set of estimates of rural rates of return in the following chapter.

The estimates of rural landholder incomes corrected for acreage and family size (Table 3.15) require a more intricate process of calculation than did those in the previous table, since we must separate the age-land and age-family size correlations. This is done in eight steps. The first four steps derive adjusted farm income profiles of the household head by age and education, and the last four derive the corresponding non-farm income profiles.

Within each schooling category, size of farm as a function of age is combined with gross farm income per acre as a function of farm size to yield farm income as a function of age, by schooling category. Family size as a function of farm size, assumptions about family composition, data on man, woman and child-days worked by farm size, and wage rates are combined to give estimates of total cost per acre for farms of different sizes. For each education group, costs per acre times acreage by age gives total costs as a function of age by education category. This is deducted from gross income by age and education to give the adjusted farm income of the household head by age and education. A similar procedure is followed in calculating an adjusted profile for non-farm income of the rural household head. (See Annex E for details).

Allowance for acreage differences eliminates from income the value of product due to land. However, information on land ownership could not be disaggregated by the form of land acquisition (inheritance, marriage, purchase). Otherwise, inheritance data could have been used as a proxy for socio-economic background. According to the capital expenditure data in the Economy Survey of Central Province, 1963–64, a surprisingly small amount of money was spent on land purchases. Even after allowing for substantially lower prices in the survey year and for extended payment periods, only a small fraction of the total available land seems to change hands through purchase. Most landowners therefore probably acquire land through family ties, and socio-economic background probably has much influence on rural earnings.[18]

The absolute level of incomes adjusted for acreage and family size in Table 3.15 is generally somewhat higher than the level of those in Table 3.16, especially at higher ages. The incomes at lower education levels have been raised considerably relative to those at higher levels, however, and

---

[18] This throws new light on the age-education-land ownership profiles in the first step of Annex E. Education should probably be interpreted not as a determining but a concomitant factor in the pattern of land acquisition.

the incomes of those with little education who are also young have been raised relative to those who are older and/or have more education. In general, they compare favorably with the unadjusted profiles for urban African males (Table 3.2), but we hold comparison of urban and rural sectors until we have calculated the rates of return in the next chapter.

IV

RATES OF RETURN TO SCHOOLING

We are now able to combine the information on benefits and costs of education in Kenya to calculate the internal rates of return to the different levels of schooling. We subject these rates to a series of successive adjustments to see how they are influenced by factors either unrelated or only indirectly linked to education. Rather than simply listing the data inputs and producing the final rates of return, we undertake the adjustment of the rates step by step. When compared among themselves, the finally adjusted rates will show at which levels of education expansion is economically best justified from the family and government points of view in present circumstances.

Because they are based on 1968 data, these rates reflect circumstances which in turn result from past investment decisions regarding private and public education. Rates calculated from 1969 data would perhaps not be very different, but the rates in this chapter describe only what past investment has produced. A discussion of the future of education investment in Kenya will be postponed until Chapter V.

Types of Rates and Adjustments

The analysis here is restricted to African males and females, although the sample covers other groups. Both private and social rates are calculated for each schooling level. Rates for landowning rural heads of house-

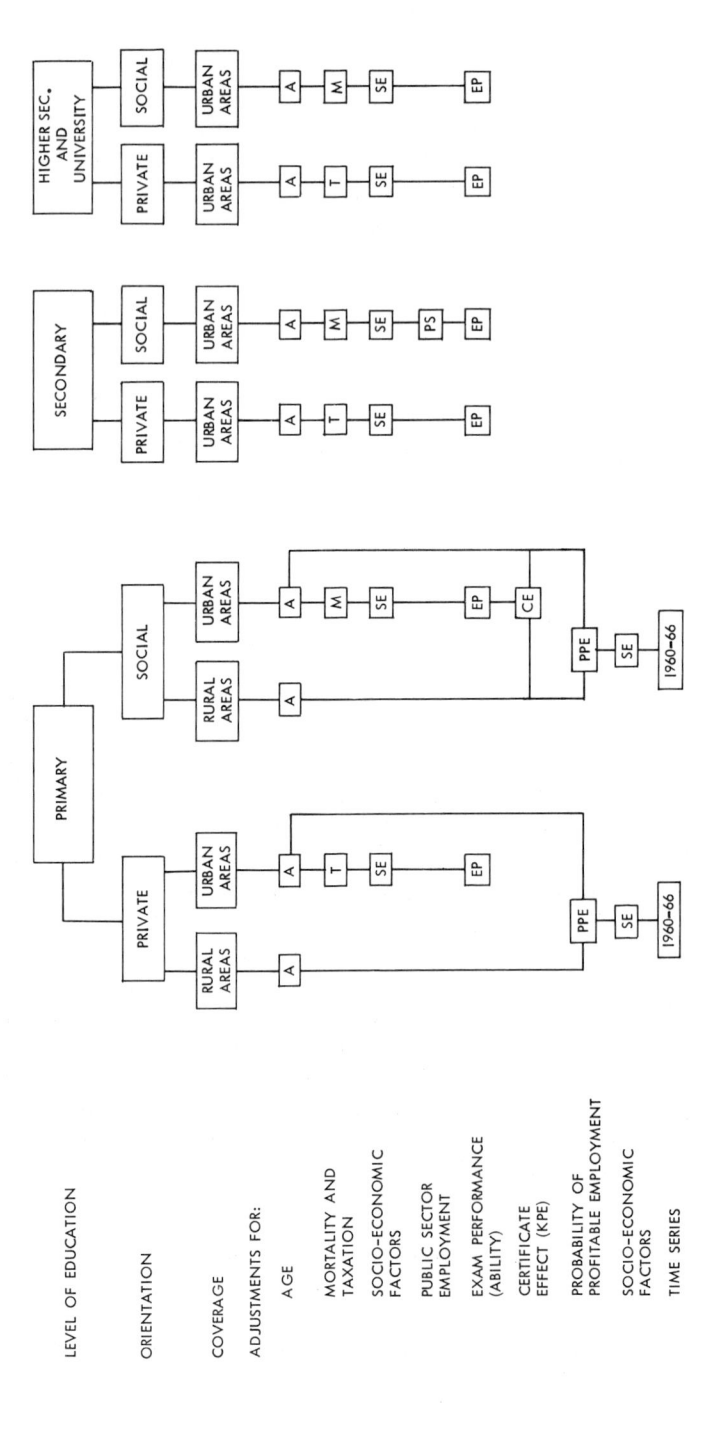

FIGURE 4.1: VARIANTS OF RATES OF RETURN TO EDUCATION DEVELOPED IN KENYA CASE STUDY

holds are also derived for the primary level. These rates are diagrammed in the top three lines of Figure 4.1.

The series, initially calculated from unadjusted benefit and cost data, undergoes a number of adjustments to make the final set of rates more realistic and comparable with real rates of return to alternative investments outside education. Figure 4.1 summarizes these adjustments. Private rates are corrected for the effect of taxes on earnings, and social rates for the effect of death on the labor force. Individuals deciding whether to invest in more schooling assume they will be able to work until retirement and do not allow for the possibility of premature death. But since the social rates reflect the return to society as a whole, they must account for mortality.

Urban rates adjusted for the effect of socio-economic differences on earnings are computed by using the appropriately adjusted age-earnings profiles from Chapter III. Corrections are also made for public sector employment and union affiliation. Rates of return to those who fail the two major examinations (KPE and CSC) are compared to rates for all students in order to separate the return to schooling alone from the return to ability. Neither of these corrections is applied to the rates for higher secondary and university education. There are insufficient data for comparing examination scores at these higher levels and no data to use for socio-economic corrections; however, it is felt that at the higher levels of education such background differences are no longer a significant determinant of earnings. Rates of return to primary schooling are also calculated for rural male Africans. These rates are based on the estimated earnings profiles of rural heads of household with different levels of education presented in Chapter III, and are not corrected for socio-economic background, taxes, or mortality.

We also calculate a combined urban and rural rate adjusted for employment probabilities in the two sectors. To estimate this combined rate, we need to separately adjust the rural and urban rates for the probabilities of employment in the corresponding sector. Because of the way in which we calculate them, the initial rural rates are already weighted by the probabilities that a primary leaver would have owned land in 1963. They are not corrected for rural unemployment, but only for the probability in each age group of owning a farm, i.e. of having rural earnings positively influenced by schooling.

These rural rates are combined with weighted urban rates to yield combined rates for 1960–66. The urban rates are based on the overall probability[1] that a primary leaver would have found urban employment during

---

[1] The data are not corrected for employment differences by age, as the data would have permitted no more than a rough age-adjusted estimate.

this period; we assume that the urban rate of return does not change over this period but that the probability of urban employment does. Since we have no time series data for the rural component, we assume that landholding probabilities and income differentials remained unchanged during this period, but that higher schooling costs brought down the rural rates after 1963. At the end of the section on combined rates we make a rough estimate of the combined rate adjusted for socio-economic variables.

Whether the separate urban and rural rates are more relevant than the combined rates depends among other things on conditions in the labor market. If there is little mobility from rural to urban areas, or if there are other reasons why the labor markets for urban and rural dwellers should be separate, then it is relevant in economic terms to compare the private urban and rural rates. If, on the other hand, mobility between rural and urban areas is good and wage-earners with the same amount of schooling are interchangeable wherever trained, it is then more meaningful to use a combined private rate of return to investment in primary schooling which allows for the employment probabilities in each sector.

From the standpoint of social investment we can consider urban and rural rates as returns to separate investment alternatives, despite the fact that the urban and rural shares of funds are not always allocated on economic grounds but are often modified by political considerations such as equity. The combined social rate of return adjusted for employment probabilities can be taken as the overall yield to total investment in primary schooling. It can be argued that the overall marginal yield to investment in primary schooling should be the rural rate adjusted for rural employment probability whenever urban employment probabilities for a given group of graduates are very low. In Kenya, however, the combined social rates differ little from the rate of return to rural schooling alone.

The combined rural and urban rate adjusted for unemployment is not calculated for the post-primary schooling levels. At these levels the urban rates of return can be taken as the overall rates to schooling in Kenya, since only a negligible proportion of Africans with more than primary schooling are rural workers.[2] These rates are not adjusted for unemployment because there was apparently no significant unemployment for Africans at these levels of education during 1960–66.

After describing the method of calculating the rates of return and the data sources, we present all unadjusted urban rates—the starting points of the analysis. We then consider each set of adjustments on the urban

---

[2] For the purposes of this study government employees in rural areas, such as primary school teachers, may be considered part of urban employment since their remuneration follows the same rules as urban government employees.

rates and its effect on the rates separately, derive the rural rates, calculate the combined rates, and present a summary of all rates. The comparison of these rates with alternative investment rates is reversed for Chapter VI.

Calculation of the Rates and the Sources of Data

The general procedure for calculating a rate of return to an investment is to find that rate which sets the discounted value of the time stream of its costs equal to that of the time stream of the benefits accruing to it. In equation form:

$$\sum_{i=1}^{n} \frac{Y_i}{(1+r)^i} = 0 \qquad (4.1)$$

where Y_i = the difference in year (i) between the net costs and the net benefits of additional schooling
r = the internal rate of return
n = the length of the prospective work life in years.

This method of relating costs and benefits was chosen because, unlike cost-benefit ratios, the internal rate of return to education investment is comparable to rates of return on alternative kinds of investment. We are also following a well-established practice, since the great majority of similar studies in other countries use the rate of return, and only a few the present value or the cost-benefit ratio criteria (see Table 4.15).

Benefits

To convert the Chapter III earnings profiles, taken as the total benefits of a given amount of schooling, into the net benefits of taking the marginal amount of schooling needed to reach that level, we calculate the difference between the earnings streams with and without the marginal schooling. Linear interpolations are made between midpoints of age groups in the profile tables to obtain continuous earnings profiles. Where an earnings figure in the profile table is statistically insignificant, a linear interpolation is made between the figures for the next higher and next lower age groups; where there is no significant figure in the highest age group, it is assigned the income of the next lower group.

The first step is the calculation of unadjusted rates. Unadjusted net benefit data are derived from Table 3.2 (unadjusted age-earnings profile for African males, 0–11 years of schooling), and Table 3.13, columns 3 and 5 (unadjusted profile for African males, 12–17 years of schooling). The other tables of Chapter III are cited as they become relevant to the discussion.

Costs

The costs of schooling borne by the private individual are different from those borne by the larger social unit. Both include earnings foregone while attending school, but private costs add only school fees paid, whereas public costs add the entire operating and capital costs incurred by the schooling system.

Earnings foregone can be estimated for each age and schooling group from the earnings profiles in Tables 3.2, 3.4, 3.7, 3.9, and 3.13. The timing of earnings foregone can be determined by adding to average school-leaving age in Table 2.2 the average delay in finding work for school leavers, given in Table 4.1. The starting point for work life is found to be 16 to 18 years of age.[3]

TABLE 4.1: Average Delay (in Years) between Leaving School and Starting Work of African Male Urban Employees by Level of Education and Year of Leaving School

Year of Leaving School	\multicolumn{7}{c}{Years of Education}
	0–2	3–5	6–7	8–9	10–11	12–13	14 and more
1966	—	1.0 (3)	1.4 (37)	1.1 (24)	0.9 (56)	0.7 (6)	0.1 (7)
1965	—	1.0 (1)	1.7 (64)	1.1 (18)	1.0 (33)	1.0 (1)	0.0 (1)
1964	2.0 (2)[a]	3.1 (11)	1.9 (70)	1.4 (11)	1.3 (23)	0.0 (2)	0.0 (2)
1963	2.0 (1)	1.9 (7)	2.2 (61)	2.1 (9)	1.2 (14)	1.0 (2)	0.0 (2)
1962	3.0 (4)	1.4 (8)	1.9 (57)	1.3 (15)	1.4 (11)	1.0 (1)	0.0 (2)
1961	—	2.9 (18)	2.7 (51)	1.7 (10)	1.4 (15)	0.0 (1)	0.0 (1)
1960	4.7 (3)	3.0 (20)	2.4 (55)	1.8 (10)	1.5 (15)	—	—
1955–59	5.6 (9)	3.0 (148)	2.6 (291)	2.3 (16)	1.8 (16)	2.3 (3)	0.3 (3)
before 1955	4.1 (134)	3.4 (583)	2.7 (346)	2.1 (40)	1.8 (12)	2.7 (3)	0.3 (3)

[a] Number of cases appears in parentheses.
Source: Labor Force Sample Survey, January/February 1968.

---

[3] We assume that no one under 17 is employed in the urban sector; only one African male and 26 African females in our survey were younger than 17 (less than 1 percent of the African observations). In some developing countries which have had long periods of rapid growth, c.f. in Latin America, children can find work in many urban services such as selling newspapers, shining shoes, working as house-boys. However, in Kenya such positions are filled by adults.

Because very few children work,[4] private costs up to the end of primary school consist of school fees only. Though the primary school course runs seven years, students need on the average eight years to complete it; half of the cost of this extra year is assigned to the cost of the first four years, and half to that of the last three. Starting at age 17, earnings foregone become an important part of private costs.

Private costs for Africans by age, sex, and educational level are shown in Table 4.2. Since higher secondary and university students generally do not pay fees, their private costs are limited to earnings foregone, which are shown in the last two columns.

TABLE 4.2: Annual Earnings Foregone and Other Private Costs by Age and Years of Schooling, Male Africans, 1968

(Ksh)

Age	M & F 1-4	M & F 4-7	Males 7Q-9	Males 7 All-9	Males 9-11	Males 11-13	Males 13-17
9	53						
10	56						
11	59						
12	29	35					
13		69					
14		69					
15		70					
16			494	494			
17			1701 + 494	1602 + 494			
18					2043 + 307		
19					2331 + 307		
20						4,617	
21						5,094	
22							7,164
23							7,623
24							8,082
25							8,541

Source: Primary school fees: Ministry of Education data on fees by district, 1966. 13–17 years of education: Table 3.13 monthly incomes are multiplied by nine to obtain annual income foregone. Secondary school fees: In 1966, 33,000 students in maintained and assisted schools paid an average of 307 Ksh/yr.; about 30,000 Harambee school students paid 700 Ksh/yr., or an average of 494 Ksh for these 63,000 students. No attempt is made to allow for bursaries or fee remissions. Earnings foregone are estimated by taking monthly earnings from Table 3.2 and Table 3.5 and multiplying by nine. For lack of data, it is assumed that a negligible number work while attending school, so these earnings foregone are not adjusted for those who do not forego them when going to school.

Information on the operating and capital costs necessary to calculate the social rates of return is not quite as complete as data on fees and income foregone. Dependable information on primary teacher salaries is available by school for only two counties. Non-teacher expenditures are only a small

---

[4] Children constituted only 0.2 percent of urban employment in 1966.

fraction (about 10–15 percent) of total operating costs at the primary level and they are derived on a per pupil basis from the county council budgets of four Central and Eastern Province counties. A random selection of schools in those counties is used as the basis for the operating cost estimates.

These figures do not permit a differentiation by year; the same estimated total cost per year has been used throughout the primary course. This is in obvious contradiction to the general rule that the more qualified and hence better paid teachers tend to instruct the higher grades, and that therefore more of the cost should be distributed to higher grades. Distributing the cost equally will distort the social rate-of-return structure, favoring the 6–7 years of schooling group at the expense of the 3–5 years category, and the latter at the expense of the 0–2 years group.

How important is this distortion? Let us assume, for example, that fees always cover a constant proportion of the cost of primary education. Fees rise from Ksh 53 in Standard I to Ksh 70 in Standard VII. This would imply that total costs per pupil use in the same proportion—from Ksh 132 in Standard I to Ksh 174 in Standard VII, a rise of Ksh 30 instead of the constant cost we assume. Even this example may be too favorable. The local authorities may, deliberately or unconsciously, give a higher proportional subsidy to the older children. If so, our error could be serious.[5] However, Column I of Table 4.4 shows that the difference between the 5–7 year schooling group and the 2–4 year one is proportionally much the same for social and for private rates of return. This suggests that there is no major distortion.

Information on secondary operating costs is more complete than that on primary costs: estimates of teaching and non-teaching expenditures are available by school for all assisted and maintained secondary schools in Kenya. University operating costs are taken from the University of East Africa Triennial Development Plan 1967–70. The Plan figure used is for 1969, when the university will be operating much closer to capacity.

Approximate capital cost data for primary and secondary schools were derived from discussions with Ministry of Education officials and from construction and equipment cost figures for several recently built secondary schools. University capital costs were taken from the Triennial Plan. At every level, the value of buildings and equipment was estimated and the capital cost reckoned equal to depreciation plus 10 percent, our assumed

---

[5] Data from a rural area in neighboring Uganda, where per-pupil costs for the seventh were more than twice those for the first grade, suggest that this is more than a theoretical consideration. (Source: P. Foster and L. Yost, "Population Growth and Rural Development in Buganda, A Simulation of a Micro-Socio-Economic System," Miscellaneous Publication No. 621, Agricultural Experiment Station, University of Maryland, College Park, Md., 1968.)

alternative cost of capital in the economy. We assumed a lifetime of 40–50 years for most school structures.[6] Capital costs for primary schools prove negligible, however, when compared to current operating costs; nor are they important for secondary schools. At the university level, however, capital costs amount to about 50 percent of total costs. The operating and capital cost figures used are shown in Table 4.3.

TABLE 4.3: Annual Costs per Student Used in Calculating Social Rates of Return

Level of Schooling	Operating Costs	Capital Costs[a]
Primary	7.7	0.1–0.5[b]
Lower Secondary	87.0[c]	3.0–10.0[d]
Higher Secondary	175.0[c]	...[e]
University	690.0[f]	625.0

[a] Undiscounted annual amortization charges per pupil place.
[b] The primary range encompasses both the usual mud-and-wattle structure and the more costly semi-permanent and permanent structures. Lifetimes of these structures are assumed to be 10, 30, and 40 years, respectively.
[c] Current cost plus Ksh 250 per student annually for the 8th and 9th years, and 500 Ksh in 10th and 11th years for rent and depreciation on school buildings.
[d] The lower figure refers to a day school located in Nairobi, the upper to a predominantly boarding school upcountry; both schools have three streams. The assumed lifetime of the buildings is 40 years.
[e] No data available; figure is probably in the neighborhood of 10–15 K£.
[f] The costs per student at the University College of Nairobi have been falling steadily over time as the College begins to reach capacity. The total cost figure of K£ 1,315 may therefore be an overestimate in two or three years. See University of East Africa, *University Development Plan*, 1967.

Unadjusted Urban Rates

The unadjusted private and social rates of return to various levels of schooling for African males, based on the costs and benefits just described, are given in column one of Table 4.4. The private rates vary among educational levels, but are all very high and favor the completion of as much education as possible. These rates are highest for lower secondary schooling as a whole (36 percent); primary comes next with 33 percent, university with 27 percent and higher secondary with 24 percent. The social rates are lower at each level because the socially incurred costs of running the schooling system are much higher than private fees. The social rates are roughly one-third lower than the private rates through higher secondary and two-thirds lower for university; the highest social rate is 24 percent to secondary schooling, then primary with 22 percent, higher secondary with 15 percent and university with 9 percent.

---

[6] The exceptions were semi-permanent and temporary mud-and-wattle structures used for primary schools. See Chapter II, page 23.

TABLE 4.4: Average Social and Private Rates of Return to Schooling for Africans by Years of Schooling, Adjusted for Age Only; for Age, Taxes and Mortality Only; and for Age and Socio-Economic Variables Only

	(1) Adjusted for Age Only				(2) Adjusted for Age, Taxes, and Mortality Only		(3) Adjusted for Age and Socio-Economic Variables Only	
	Males		Females		Males		Males	
Years of Schooling[a]	Private	Social	Private	Social	Tax-Adjusted Private	Mortality-Adjusted Social	Private	Social
Primary								
2–4	25.6	16.4	n.a.	n.a.	25.6	15.1	30.8	16.7
5–7	55.1	38.4	7.1	6.6	55.1	37.7	21.7	18.0
2–7	32.7	21.7	9.5	7.1	32.7	20.9	26.0	17.9
Secondary								
8–9	23.6	16.3	n.a.	n.a.	23.6	14.8	20.6	13.7
10–11	52.2	33.5	n.a.	n.a.	40.2	33.5	36.1	25.8
8–11	36.1	23.6	33.6	19.5	31.6	24.0	32.0	21.0[b]
Higher Secondary								
12–13	23.8	14.7	n.a.	n.a.	22.9	14.7	23.8	14.7
University								
14–17	27.4	8.8	n.a.	n.a.	19.9	8.8	27.4	8.8

[a] Investment in the schooling periods in this column yields the rates of return listed in the other columns. For example, the private return to males for investing in the second through fourth years of schooling—i.e. of taking four years instead of only one year—is 25.6 percent, adjusted for age only.

[b] The adjustment for public sector employment brings this down to 17.2.

Sources: Column (1): Tables 3.1 (males), 3.9 (females), and 4.2 and 4.3 (both). Column (2): Tables 3.1, 4.2 and 4.3 and Annex Tables 6.4, 6.5, and 6.7 in EC.173. Column (3): Tables 3.4, 4.2 and 4.3.

A note on African females. Our survey data on African female wage earners permitted estimation of unadjusted rates for only three educational levels: the whole primary course, the last three years of primary, and the first four years of secondary school. The primary rates are much lower than the corresponding rates for African males, but the secondary ones are very similar (see Table 4.4, column one).

It is possible that the unadjusted rates would be higher if we were able to include as benefits the non-marketable but economically relevant contributions made at home by educated females, such as a more efficient management of the household, superior tutoring of children and improved family health.[7] The significance of mother's literacy as shown in Table 3.6 suggests that education of females may have a positive effect on children's earnings. However, proper evaluation of the returns to education of females not reflected in the wages they earn is outside the scope of this study.

The insufficient survey data available for females means that we have no satisfactory returns estimate for a group which absorbs a large part of public and private investment in education (40 percent of primary pupils are girls) without a comparable contribution to overall benefits as measured by earnings (only 11 percent of total urban employees are females). In Chapter V some allowance is made in the employment projections for low female participation in the labor force. But leaving out African females and considering African males alone (as we have done throughout this chapter) probably results in higher estimates of the social and private rates of return (as defined in this study rather than in the above mentioned wider sense) than would apply to all Africans, males and females together.

Adjusting for Taxes and Mortality

Since individuals exclude direct taxes when evaluating their earnings benefits, the benefits used in determining private rates of return must also be corrected for taxes. From information on tax rates in Kenya by range of income, family status, and number of children, on the average number of children for African males in our sample, and earnings data from the profiles of Chapter III, we calculate average taxes for African males by age and level of education for the first 11 years of schooling and for 12 to 17 years of schooling.

---

[7] It should be noted that even traditional marriage practices, for these or other reasons such as prestige, place a definite value on education. A recent newspaper item (*New York Times*, May 21, 1969, p. 30) reported on local efforts in one African country to establish a standard bride price depending on the bride's education. The reported price ratio of 1/1.6/3 for uneducated, primary educated and secondary educated brides, respectively, without a doubt implies an assessment of the costs undergone by the family which sends a daughter to school.

Differences in taxes paid between schooling levels are so small that they do not affect the rates of return up to the 10 to 11 years of schooling level (Table 4.4, column (2)). For the latter two years, the tax adjustment cuts the rate of return by one-fifth (from 52.2 to 40.2 percent). The tax effect is negligible for the higher secondary cycle (12 to 13 years of schooling), since the additional average taxes paid by persons with 11 years of schooling differ little from those paid by persons with 13 years. The tax effect is most marked over the four years of university, where the unadjusted rate of return is reduced by a quarter (27.4 to 19.9 percent).[8]

In contrast to the considerable reduction of private rates brought about by the correction for taxes, the social rates are affected hardly at all by mortality.[9] We used mortality rates assumed to be representative for Africans in Kenya in the recent past. They show that a 15-year-old has a better than even chance (62 percent) of living to the age of 50 but a less than even chance (45 percent) of living to be 60. Linear interpolations are made between the five-year intervals to permit earnings differences to be adjusted for mortality on an annual basis, so that the earnings profiles are continuous. The resulting adjusted social rates (shown in Table 4.4, column (2)) are equal to the unadjusted rates for those with 10 or more years of schooling and are 5–10 percent less than the unadjusted rates for the lower schooling groups.

---

[8] The figure of 19.9 percent is slightly lower than the private tax-adjusted rate of return of 21.4 percent estimated by Daniel C. Rogers for university educated teachers. See "Student Loan Programs and the Returns to Investment in Higher Levels of Education in Kenya," Teachers College, Columbia University, New York, March 1969, Table 3, p. 9. (To be published in *Economic Development and Cultural Change*, 1971). The lower rate estimated by Rogers is probably the result of both the lower incomes for HSC holders used by him as compared with those used in this study as well as his somewhat higher cost figures. He therefore would have estimated lower income foregone by university students than we do.

Rogers also estimates that the tax-adjusted private rate of return to the difference between 6 and 4 years of secondary schooling (or 13 vs. 11 years total schooling) is negative, while the present study shows a 22.9 percent rate of return. The difference is probably also due to the difference in the estimate of incomes and costs at the 13-year level. Rogers' 12.2 percent estimate for the social rate to university training is 3 percent more than our estimate, but this is because he applies a much lower annual operating cost for university education: K£872 where we use K£1,315. He does not include capital costs and uses a 1967 operating cost per student rather than our lower 1969 figure.

[9] High overall mortality rates in less developed countries are usually the result of high infant mortality and higher mortality at ages over 40–45. Infant mortality does not enter into the return to schooling, and higher mortality at later ages is heavily discounted.

Adjusting for Socio-Economic Differences

The age-earnings profiles used in calculating the unadjusted rates of return in the first column of Table 4.4 lump together the returns to schooling and to a host of other inputs which may have little connection with additional schooling. To isolate the effect of schooling, we must use net benefit figures adjusted for factors which are exogenous to schooling and yet influence earnings in ways which do not depend on the amount of schooling a person has (e.g. factors such as better home training, tribal affiliation and other socio-economic differences, and union membership). The age-earnings profiles adjusted for socio-economic variables (Table 3.4) are therefore the appropriate figures to use in calculating rates of return adjusted for socio-economic differences (see Table 4.4, column (3)); the effect of union membership and another occupational variable, government employment, are discussed in the next section.

Column (3) of Table 4.4 shows that adjusting income for tribe, parents' literacy and father's occupation substantially increases the private rate of return to the first years of primary education, but cuts both the private and social rates of return to the later years by more than half. For lower secondary education the adjustment reduces the rate of return to the first two years slightly, but the main reduction falls on the second two years, where the private rate of return is cut by a third and the social rate by a quarter.

Adjusting for Occupational Variables

As discussed in Chapter III, adjusting the age-earnings profiles for both socio-economic and occupational variables tends to overadjust the earnings, because most of the occupational variables are closely related to schooling. Likewise, using such profiles for rates of return is likely to overcorrect the rates and underestimate the returns to additional schooling. Nevertheless, two of the occupational variables (as with the socio-economic variables) are not the result of additional schooling and should be considered separately for their partial effects on the social rate: union membership and public sector employment. These factors do not change the flow of benefits as perceived by the private individual, but they do change those relevant to society as a whole; thus their effects bear only on the social rates.

Union Membership

Union membership was included in our questionnaire and used as a variable in the regression analysis in Chapter III. We determined that the percentage of wage-earners who are union members decreases somewhat with decreased schooling, but among schooling levels the variation is not substantial (see Table 3.6); therefore union membership as a variable has no noticeable effect on age-earnings profiles. The one exception is the lower proportion of union members in the 11 years of schooling group; however the relevant regression coefficient is not significant (Table 3.8), and thus even in this case the effect on earnings is not important. Therefore we may safely conclude that in our particular case union membership does not change the rates of return to schooling.[10]

Public Sector Employment

Government wages for Kenyans with CSC or higher educational achievement are higher than wages for similarly trained Kenyans in the private sector. If we believe that the higher wages reflect the higher productivity of secondary-school and university graduates employed by the government then no adjustment is necessary. This belief would be consistent with the view that because the government offers higher wages, it can attract the most productive graduates, leaving their less capable classmates to find jobs in the private sector.

However, in order to account for the possibility that government wages are arbitrarily high and do not reflect the marginal productivity of secondary school and university-educated Kenyans, we have examined the earnings data of persons with this level of education to identify and correct for any earnings differentials which can be assigned to government sector employment.

Table 3.6 shows that in our sample an unusually large proportion of KPE qualifiers (25 percent), persons with two years of secondary schooling (18 percent), with full secondary schooling (51 percent) and university training (69 percent) work for the government. These groups then are the ones whose profiles would most likely contain some benefits from working at higher government wages. However, only the 11 years of schooling group shows a significant regression coefficient for public sector employment (see Table 3.8)—and a numerically large one at that. We therefore recalculated the age-correcting profile for the 11-year group, correcting for both socio-economic variables and government sector employment. When combined with the earnings profile for the 7-year group and the social cost of taking the four extra years of schooling, this profile yields a social rate of return of 17.2 percent (see Table 4.14). The comparable rate of return for the four years of secondary school not corrected for government employment is 21.0 percent (see Table 4.4, column (3)).

---

[10] There is a separate argument that exogenous constraints such as union activity, tariffs, corporate taxes, subsidies, and minimum wage laws may cause wages to be different from those in equilibrium. It is, however, more accurate to use rates biased in this way for planning purposes if the distortions are expected to persist.

Which of the two rates we choose as the marginal rate of return to 11 years of schooling depends on whether we believe that the government is paying its employees more because they are superior to their counterparts in the private sector, or whether we believe that CSC graduates in the two sectors are about equally productive but that the government overpays. If public sector salaries accurately reflect marginal productivities, the higher rate, which represents the average rate to both private and public sectors, should be used. However, if public sector salaries are unnecessarily higher than both the marginal productivity public and private sector productivity levels, then they clearly exaggerate the social benefits from investing in the first four years of secondary schooling and the corrected, lower rate should be used.[11]

The Question of Ability

By using the profiles adjusted for socio-economic variables, we have been able to separate the earnings effect of different socio-economic backgrounds from that of different amounts of schooling. Such differences in background are often considered to be closely connected with a child's overall ability, a term which we use here to include a child's preparation for learning as well as non-schooling inputs such as self-esteem; our adjusting for them eliminates to some extent the differences in the loosely defined ability factor. However, we have no information about the returns to ability as defined in terms of innate qualities or as measured by some objective intelligence test. The role of this more precisely defined characteristic is impossible to determine without gathering data on two groups of children with the same test-defined ability and ages, one of which is sent to school and the other not.[12]

Examination Success and Rates of Return

However, if we were not able to adjust for ability at all, our rates of return would probably be overestimated. Among urban African males, for example, those who fail the KPE are probably much closer in ability to those who stop after four years of school than to those who pass and qualify on the KPE.[13] Additional schooling seems to contribute little towards

---

[11] Actually, the higher salaries in government may exert a "pull" on private sector salaries so that even the lower rate may not accurately estimate the marginal social rate of return to investing in this level of schooling.

[12] This assumes that a test identifying and measuring ability in a culturally "neutral" way can be devised. See Thorsten Husen, "Talent, Opportunity, and Career: A 26-year Follow-up," *School Review* 76(2) (June 1968), pp. 190–209.

[13] Obviously, this is not true for those older persons who went to school at a time when there were few primary schooling facilities beyond the first four years in rural areas, nor those whose education was interrupted by the emergency in the 1950's.

raising the earnings of those with low ability. Individuals with greater gifts or stronger motivation are likely to earn more even if they do not receive formal schooling, since they are better equipped to handle themselves in a modernizing society. We observed in Chapter III that those who pass the KPE do in fact earn more than those who fail; the additional return they receive over that of their failing comrades is largely a return to their ability and should not be attributed to their schooling.

Although we have no data on the returns to tested ability which would enable us to properly adjust the benefits streams for ability, we can use examination scores as an estimated measure of ability. While examination scores are not an infallible measure of an individual's ability, they are the best available to us. We are able to compare the rates of return adjusted for socio-economic differences covering all students who have seven years of schooling with comparable rates for the subgroups of students who pass, fail, and qualify on the KPE. Similarly, the rates for 11-year students are compared with the rates for students with different CSC passes (see Table 4.5). We can detect and eliminate that part of the difference in earning which is due to the ability to pass an examination by comparing the earnings profiles of those with a lower level of education and those who fail each of these two examinations with the earnings of those who pass the examinations.

The ability corrected rates are approximated by the rates of return to those who fail the KPE and to CSC holders with Division III pass or below. The differences between the rates of those who fail and those of all students are small at the secondary level (28.5 percent vs. 32.0 percent for the first four years of secondary schooling), probably because our survey included very few who achieved a Division I or II pass on the CSC. But for those with only primary education the differences are very great. Failing the examination cuts by more than one-third the average rates to the whole primary course adjusted for socio-economic variables, while passing increases the rates by roughly the same amount. Qualifying for secondary school (7Q on the KPE) leads to a rate more than 50 percent higher than that for all interviewees with seven years of schooling. These observations hold true for both social and private rates (see Table 4.5).

Looking at the figures in another way, we find that the 13.0 percent social return to the investment in primary school by KPE failers is equivalent to nearly three-fourths of the rate applying to all those who complete seven years of primary schooling (17.9 percent). The latter rate can be considered the average measured return to schooling, including ability and the interaction between ability and socio-economic factors, and excluding socio-economic factors alone. The former rate measures the return to schooling including neither ability nor the interaction effect. It appears that some-

TABLE 4.5: **Average Rates of Return to Different Examination Scores and Schooling Periods, Adjusted for Socio-Economic Variables, 1968**

Years of Schooling and Exam Score[a]	Private	Social
Primary Level		
All Students		
2nd–4th year (not affected by exam score)	30.8	16.7
5th–7th year	21.7	18.0
2nd–7th year	26.0	17.9
Students who fail KPE		
5th–7th year	12.6	10.8
2nd–7th year	17.7	13.0
Students who pass KPE		
5th–7th year	27.7	22.7
Students who qualify on KPE		
5th–7th year	34.3	28.4
Secondary Level		
All Students		
8th–11th year	32.0	21.0
8th–9th year	20.6	13.7
10th–11th year	36.1	25.8
Students who take 8th and 9th years versus students who qualify on KPE without continuing schooling		
8th–9th year	9.2	6.3
Students with Division III or lower pass on CSC versus students who qualify on KPE without continuing schooling		
8th–11th year	28.5	18.5
Students with Division III or lower pass on CSC versus students with nine years of schooling		
10th–11th year	36.4	26.1

[a] Investment in the additional schooling indicated in this column yields the rates of return listed in the other columns. This means, for example, that the private return to the second through the fourth years of schooling—i.e. to taking four years instead of only one year—is 15.6 percent, and that the private return to taking seven years rather than four is 6.1 percent if at the end of the seventh year the student fails on the KPE and 27.7 percent if he passes.

Source: Annex Tables 6.8 and 6.9 (Column (2) in each) in EC-173.

what more than a quarter of the overall measured return to primary schooling is due to ability and the interaction of ability and socio-economic factors. Only 60 percent of the return to investment in the last three years of primary schooling for all 7-year graduates corrected for socio-economic factors (18.0 percent) may be due to schooling, because the social rate to failers is 10.8 percent which is 60 percent of the rate for all students.

If we compare the social rates corrected for ability and socio-economic variables in Table 4.5 with the unadjusted rates in Table 4.4, column one, the effect of these two adjustments on urban rates is striking. The adjusted social rate to the investment in primary schooling (13.0 percent) is 60 percent of the unadjusted social rate (21.7 percent), which implies that schooling itself is responsible for only 60 percent of the return to investment in primary schooling. The adjusted social rate to the last three years of primary schooling (10.8 percent) is only 28 percent of the unadjusted rate (38.4 percent). When this adjusted rate is corrected for a possible KPE certificate effect,[14] its share of the unadjusted rate rises to from 28 to 36 percent.

For investment in the first two years of secondary schooling (8 to 9 years), the adjusted social rate (6.3 percent) is 39 percent of the unadjusted rate (16.3 percent), an even lower share than for primary schooling. Since the adjusted and unadjusted rates are almost the same for the last two years of the CSC cycle, the adjusted social rate for the whole CSC cycle (18.5 percent) is nearly 80 percent of the unadjusted rate (23.6 percent). Only 7 percent of the male Africans interviewed had reached the last two years of the CSC cycle. If we assume that schooling explains almost fully the social rate of return to investment in higher secondary and university education (12 or more years of schooling), the adjusted social rates to those levels would be unchanged, but even fewer African males attain this level of education.

Biases in the Ability Effect Estimate

Our estimates of the share of rates of return attributable to schooling may reflect a bias in the instruction of students with different abilities. More able individuals may be favored by an elitist schooling system.[15] In such a system the spread of examination performances will exaggerate the spread of the students' abilities, and the ability correction made above leads us to attribute too large a part of the rate of return for all the students to ability and not enough to schooling. Likewise, if the system is egalitarian in the sense of working in favor of disadvantaged pupils, examination scores will not reveal students' ability differences, resulting in an overvaluation of the portion of the rate of return due to schooling. But if we find that the schooling system is neutral to ability in the sense that it treats all students equally regardless of ability, then those individuals either passing or failing an examination can be said to have both received the same amount and quality of schooling.

In fact there is some indication that Kenyan schools as a group may be ability-neutral, though this may not be true of individual schools. This impression is derived from an analysis of the KPE performance data from Muranga and Meru Counties in which we sought to determine the ability

---

[14] See below.

[15] It should be stressed that the word "elitist" and "egalitarian" in this case are not meant to connote social or political intentions but only to describe the possible ability/performance patterns (which more often than not will have come about by circumstances rather than by design).

neutrality or ability bias of inputs into the education process. We find that average teacher salaries are positively and significantly related to the average examination performance of a school (see Annex A). We do not know, however, whether an improved average performance means that the below-average candidates catch up, or that the above-average candidates increase their lead, or that everybody improves proportionately.

In the first case, one would expect the dispersion of individual results, measured by the standard deviation of the candidates' examination scores from the school's mean, to increase less than the mean; in the second case, more than the mean, and in the third case, by the same amount as the mean. This would correspond to an egalitarian, elitist and ability-neutral school system, respectively.[16] Calculating the regression of standard deviations on average examination scores, we would thus envision the slope of the regression line to be less than unity in the egalitarian model (and possibly negative if the convergence of individual results is due to a deliberate effort rather than a concurring feature of quality improvements mainly directed to weaker students), greater than unity in the elitist model, and equal to unity in the case of ability neutrality.

Where increased expenditure on teachers could cause any one of these three results in an individual school (depending on such factors as the quality and dedication of the staff or the headmaster) one would expect to find the correlation coefficient to be close to zero and the t-values of the regression coefficient not to be statistically significant. This is what actually happened in our first regression including all the 89 schools which yielded an R^2 of 0.004 and a t-value of -0.59.

However, when considering the data of the two counties separately, it turned out that the group of schools in Muranga County showed an insignificant positive correlation between average examination scores and their standard deviations ($R^2 = 0.00$, $t = 0.14$), while the other sample from Meru County showed a significant negative correlation ($R^2 = 0.13$, $t = -2.75$), suggesting the presence of rather strong egalitarian features.[17] Unfortunately, the available data did not permit any conclusion about the underlying reasons. These results warrant further studies on a broader geographical basis and including additional variables.

The return to education for KPE failers may be biased downward be-

---

[16] It is assumed that ability-neutral teaching will increase all marks in the same proportion.

[17] This interpretation disregards the possibility of rigged examination results in individual schools. Since a teacher's success is quite often evaluated only in terms of the number of his pupils who qualify for secondary education, there is a certain temptation to manipulate the examination results. In such a case, one would naturally expect both a high average score and a reduced range of individual results.

cause of the certificate effect: the lower incomes of KPE failers as compared to KPE passers may be largely due to lack of a certificate, not to lower ability. Possession of a certificate is in itself an advantage in obtaining a better job.

To assess this certificate effect, we want to know what part of the difference in mean earnings of the 7F and 7P groups (Ksh 96) is attributable to the advantage the 7P group has in choosing an occupation. To make an estimate, we weight the differences in occupational structure between the 7F and 7P categories by the difference in wages between the occupational groups which characterize the 7F and 7P categories. Table 3.6 shows two major differences in occupational structure between the 7F and 7P groups. Nine percent fewer wage earners with a KPE failure record are clerks than those with a KPE pass (14 vs. 23 percent), while 13 percent more KPE failers are semi-skilled workers. When we weight these differences by Ksh 201, the amount by which earnings of semi-skilled workers with 7 years of schooling differ from those of clerks with 7 years of schooling (Table 3.8, 7-All column), we find that about Ksh 26 (0.13 times 201) of the Ksh 96 difference between the 7F and 7P mean earnings is attributable to the certificate effect. Thus, the fraction of the difference in adjusted rates of return to KPE failers (social rate = 10.8 percent) and KPE passers (social rate = 22.7) which can be explained by the certificate effect is approximately 27 percent.[18] This effect would raise the ability adjusted social rate of return to completing primary schooling to about 14.0 percent. (See Table 4.14, column (5)).

The correction for examination scores may also neglect the differential effectiveness of teachers. In other words, students who pass an examination may have better teachers than those who do not, and we would be underestimating the contribution of schooling if we corrected for examination score differences. Even if we had a differential schooling cost by student, we might not pick up the contribution of better teachers if they were not paid more. This is an unknown factor in Kenya, but even a 50 percent upward adjustment to the rates for those who fail as a compensation for poorer teachers would leave both social and private rates to the last three years of primary school for failers well below the rates for all students.

---

[18] Failure in the KPE may also be treated as evidence of low ability on the job even when there is no other evidence; this could mean that the 27 percent figure is downward biased. Occupational distribution is also probably influenced by "ability," defined in this context as any inputs not accounted for by schooling and socio-economic factors, including "innate ability" if it is believed to have economic returns. If we assume that this kind of ability plays a role in occupational distribution, then the 27 percent figure is probably upward biased.

Rates of Return to Education in the Rural Sector

The private and social rates we have used thus far apply only to the urban labor force. In this section we estimate rates of return to primary education in the rural sector. To calculate the rural rates of return we use as benefits the two sets of 1963 earnings profiles estimated in Chapter III for small landholders (Tables 3.16 and 3.15). Table 3.15 is corrected for differences in acreage and farm size between age groups and between education levels for a given age group; Table 3.16 is not. The final rates for the rural sector, shown in Tables 4.7 and 4.8, have been adjusted in Table 4.6 for the probability in each age group of becoming an owner of farm land—i.e. a man who can experience a concrete positive return to investment in schooling. The rural rates are therefore corrected for the probability of being involved in an activity yielding a positive return, as opposed to being a hired rural laborer for whom additional schooling seems to have little if any pay-off. They are not corrected for unemployment in the rural population as a whole.

TABLE 4.6: Distribution of African Landowners by Age, 1963–64

Age Group	Average Age[a]	Estimated Percentage of Landowners[b]
15–19	17.0	0.4
20–24	22.0	6.5
25–29	27.0	25.4
30–34	32.0	34.0
35–44	39.5	44.3
45–54	49.5	72.5
55 and over	63.3	95.4
Average for all age groups	46.6	51.6

[a] Midpoints of age-groups except last figure, which is mean.
[b] Assuming that the sample population was representative of Kenya's small farm sector which comprised 0.9 million small farms.
Source: *Economic Survey of Central Province, 1963–64*.

Table 4.7 uses as cost figures the average annual schooling costs per pupil in 1963: Ksh 54 in Standards 1–4, Ksh 78 in Standards 5–8, and Ksh 1,243 in secondary schools. Fees were Ksh 45, 60, and 250, respectively.[19] Income foregone for those taking 7 to 10 years of schooling is estimated as three quarters (9/12 months) of the income of those with 4 to 8 years of schooling in the 18 and 19 year age group. Table 4.8 is based on the same

---

[19] All figures refer to the former African schools and are calculated from budget figures published in the Ministry of Education's *Triennial Survey, 1961–1963*, Nairobi 1964. The secondary fee figures are for day pupils in general secondary schools. Fees in technical secondary schools were considerably higher.

TABLE 4.7: Rates of Return to Schooling, Landholding Household Heads in Rural Central Province, 1963–64, Corrected for Probability of Being Landholder

	Rural				Urban	
	Income Unadjusted for Acreage and Family Size		Income Adjusted for Acreage and Family Size		Income Adjusted for Age Only	
Difference in Education	Private	Social	Private	Social	Private	Social
Illiterate, 0–2 years	14.5	13.8	15.6	15.0	n.a.	n.a.
Literate, 0–2 years	10.3	9.9	12.5	12.1	n.a.	n.a.
All, 0–2 years[a]	13.5	12.9	14.8	14.3	n.a.	n.a.
2–6 years	20.0	18.7	23.8	22.0	n.a.	n.a.
2–4 years	n.a.	n.a.	n.a.	n.a.	25.6	16.4
6–10 years	8.8	6.2	7.9	4.4	n.a.	n.a.
8–9 years	n.a.	n.a.	n.a.	n.a.	23.6	16.3

[a] Weighted average estimated using number sampled in literate and illiterate categories.
Source: Rural: Tables 3.15 and 3.16 and 1963 cost figures in text. Urban: Table 4.4, Column one.

1963 earnings profiles but on 1966 schooling costs and fees. These are the same schooling costs and fees as were used for the urban rates.

The correction for the percentage of those who own farms at a given age is made by weighting the income differentials from Tables 3.16 and 3.15 by the probability that a male of a given age will own a farm. This requires that we estimate the total number of heads of households in each age group who are small landholders. Assuming that the Central Province Survey figures are representative of the whole of rural Kenya, that there is a total of 900,000 small farms in the country, that the age composition of the African male urban population is the same as that of the 1962 census, and that the urban African male population has increased 8 percent annually since 1962, it is possible to derive from the age-breakdown of the Survey population the absolute number of owners of small farms in each age-group. When this distribution of landowners by age is divided by the corresponding distribution of African males by age, the age-specific percentages of landowners among all African males in Kenya are obtained.[20] These are shown in Table 4.6. The table shows that a youngster who leaves primary school at the age of 15 has somewhat less than a 10 percent probability of becoming a landowner and thus of realizing the differential income of Tables 3.15 and 3.16 by the time he is 22 years old; at the age of 27 he has a more than 30 percent probability, etc.

[20] Whether the rural rates should be adjusted for the probability of any African male being a small landholder or for that of a rural African male holding land depends on one's hypothesis about possible remigration from the urban areas to the countryside. In any case, there is little difference between the two sets of probabilities, since almost 90 percent of Africans live in rural areas. Thus, the rural rates in Table 4.7 are very close to being the overall rural sector rates.

We multiply the benefits from Tables 3.15 and 3.16 by the probability of receiving these benefits in Table 4.6, and discount the streams of costs and benefits to get the rural rates of return shown in Table 4.7.[21] The private rural rates to investment in primary schooling are considerably lower than the unadjusted urban rate, shown in the last column for comparison. At the lower secondary level, the rural social rates are much lower than unadjusted urban social rates. Rates corrected for differences in acreage and family size between age groups and between educational levels for a given age group are higher than the rates unadjusted for these biases, except for those with 6 to 10 years of schooling. Table 4.8 shows rural rates

TABLE 4.8: **Rates of Return to Schooling, Landholding Household Heads in Rural Central Province, 1966 Costs and 1963–64 Benefits, Corrected for Probability of Being Landholder**

	Rural				Urban	
	Income Unadjusted for Acreage and Family Size		Income Adjusted for Acreage and Family Size		Income Adjusted for Age Only	
Difference in Education	Private	Social	Private	Social	Private	Social
Illiterate, 0–2 years	13.7	10.4	14.9	11.5	n.a.	n.a.
Literate, 0–2 years	9.8	7.5	12.1	9.6	n.a.	n.a.
All, 0–2 years[a]	12.4	9.7	14.2	11.0	n.a.	n.a.
2–6 years	18.9	13.6	22.3	15.4	n.a.	n.a.
2–4 years	n.a.	n.a.	n.a.	n.a.	25.6	16.4
6–10 years	7.6	4.6	6.3	2.3	n.a.	n.a.
8–9 years	n.a.	n.a.	n.a.	n.a.	23.6	16.3

[a] Same as in Table 4.7.

Source: Rural: Tables 3.15 and 3.16; Costs from Table 4.3, and Tables 3.15 and 3.16 in EC-173. Urban: Table 4.4, Column one.

of return based on 1963 income streams and 1966 costs. These rates are relevant if it is assumed that absolute income differences between educational categories did not change from 1963 to 1966 but that the costs of schooling did. They are very similar to the rates found in Table 4.7 but are slightly lower. All the rural rates tend to be biased upward because income foregone is included as a cost beginning only at age 17 though it may be important in rural areas at lower ages.[22]

---

[21] If we did not adjust for landowning probabilities by age the rates for the first three years of primary schooling would be much lower than those presented here, since income for both 0-illiterates and 0-literate groups are much higher up to 25 to 30 years of age than incomes of those with 1 to 3 years of schooling. However, the return to investment in the 4 to 8 and 9 plus years of schooling would be much higher without the adjustment for the likelihood of owning a farm.

[22] P. Foster and L. Yost, "Population Growth and Rural Development in Buganda . . ."

Three immediate conclusions can be drawn from these figures.

a) These rates for the rural sector are low in comparison with those for the urban labor force, expecially in view of the upward biases described above.

b) From a comparison of the first two education groups, it appears that a sizable fraction of the rate of return which persons with one to three years of primary education receive when their incomes are confronted with those of illiterates cannot be attributed to formal schooling.[23]

c) The rates to investment in the first years of secondary school in rural areas are much lower than for urban labor.

Rural and Urban Unemployment

The rates of return presented thus far for the urban and rural sectors fail to reflect the fact that the earnings profiles on which they are based are relevant only for those who work. When unemployment is widespread the rates of return must be adjusted downward to account for the fact that the marginal productivity of any cohort of school leavers is not reflected by the wages of those who work.[24] In this section we develop a series of combined urban-rural social rates weighted for employment probabilities in 1960–66.

The rural rates have already been adjusted for the probability of an African male being employed in the kind of rural work in which education yields a positive return. To combine these rates with the urban rates, we must weight the latter by the probability of urban employment.

A global way of dealing with this problem is to correct the rate of return (p) to a given amount of education (i) by multiplying it by the respective probability (e_i) that a given cohort of school leavers (marginal view), or all persons with this educational qualification (average view), will find employment which yields them differential earnings corresponding to their education. The resulting rate p_i would thus be:

$$p_i = p_{r(i)} \cdot e_{r(i)} + p_{u(i)} \cdot e_{u(i)}$$

---

[23] Since a person's becoming literate by his or her own efforts is obviously much more a question of individual ability than of the socio-economic factors dealt with in the earlier sections of this chapter, the rates for the first two education groups may have very different ability and background components and thus may not be strictly comparable.

[24] In times of heavy unemployment, estimated wages may also differ from the competitive equilibrium wage even if they have been corrected for visible unemployment. However, for planning purposes the rates should not be corrected for this bias if the distortion is expected to persist.

the subscripts (r) and (u) referring to the rural and urban segments of employment, respectively.[25] This adjustment, while an acceptable approximation for social and private rates of return, may fail to give adequate results for a social rate if only a small fraction of a given cohort of school-leavers succeeds in obtaining profitable employment. The discounted costs of educating the cohort may well outweigh the total discounted differential earnings of those who find profitable employment, so that the social rate of return becomes negative. A similar argument applies to the private rates, except that the rates of return are somewhat less sensitive to changes in the prospects for earnings and employment because schooling costs are partly subsidized by public funds. The marginal rate of return to investment in primary schooling may thus be negative in Kenya, since, as we show below, a high proportion of persons now leaving primary school are unemployed or underemployed.

The probability of obtaining urban employment is estimated below on an annual basis for 1960-66. Table 4.1 indicates the average number of years which passed between a person's leaving the school and his taking up his first job. This information is given for the urban African male employees in the survey, cross-classified by level of education and year of leaving school. The figures show that the waiting time is shorter the higher the educational level, and that it has tended to increase in recent years.[26] This observation is meaningless by itself, however, since it gives no indication of the probability that a person leaving the educational system in, say, 1965 at Form II level will find an urban job. To answer this question, we make two assumptions: first, that the Labor Force Survey results are representative of all Africans in non-agricultural occupations; second, that the enrollment differences between consecutive years and grades correspond to the numbers of school-leavers from the various levels of the educational system (see Table 2.1).[27] The results are given in Table 4.9 (for

---

[25] This refers to profitable employment only, i.e. employment in which a more educated person will receive a positive income differential in comparison with less educated persons. Unemployment and non-profitable employment are equivalent in the sense that they both result in negative rates of return.

[26] However, some of the 1966 school-leavers who did find jobs were not yet recruited by the time of the Labor Force Survey. Another observation to be taken into account is the decrease we observed in the standard deviations in the last years. This suggests that nowadays young Kenyans find an urban job either soon after leaving school or not at all.

[27] For the actual calculations, Ministry of Education statistics referring to boys' enrollments were used. Whenever negative differences resulted from fluctuations in the enrollment pattern, an average for several years was used. A fixed sum for non-African primary enrollments was deducted. Secondary level enrollments referred to general secondary schools only. However, allowing for all forms of secondary education was considered a spurious refinement in view of the very crude nature of the estimates.

TABLE 4.9: **Estimated Numbers of African Male Primary School Leavers and Estimated Urban Employment Probabilities 1960–66**

	1960	1961	1962	1963	1964	1965	1966
School Leavers (thousands)							
Standards I–V	52.4	26.0	49.5	a	43.2	20.5	7.5
Standards VI–VII (VIII)	11.7	23.5	28.4	33.0	68.6	66.7	68.8
Employment Probabilities (percent)							
Standards I–V Leavers	6	9	5	a	4	2	b
Standards VI–VII (VIII)	42	20	18	16	10	9	5

a Contained in 1962 estimate.
b Contained in 1965 estimate.
Source: Calculated from enrollment statistics and Table 4.1 as indicated in the text.

incomplete and complete primary education only).[28] By dividing year-by-year recruitment figures for persons with given amounts of education (derived from the Labor Force Survey data and Table 4.1) by the corresponding numbers of apparent entries from the school system into the labor market, we arrive at estimates of employment probabilities for the two lowest education categories for the period 1960–66. The private rates of return to the 1960–66 cohorts of African males with incomplete and complete primary education weighted by these employment probabilities but not otherwise adjusted are given in Table 4.10 and the comparable social rates in Table 4.11.

These adjusted rates reflect returns to much more than schooling alone, as the socio-economic and other adjustments of the urban rates have shown. If we estimate a correction for socio-economic background on the composite unadjusted rates of Tables 4.10 and 4.11, we can expect them to fall substantially. The estimation requires us to assume that the proportional effect of socio-economic background on the increase in income associated with more schooling is the same in rural areas as in urban, and that it has not changed between 1960 and 1968.[29] We find that the 1968 private rates adjusted for socio-economic background from Table 4.4, column (3) are 120 percent of the private unadjusted rates in Table 4.4, column (1) for incomplete primary education (2 to 4 years of schooling), and 39 percent for complete primary education (5 to 7 years of schooling). The social rates in 1968 adjusted for socio-economic background are 100 and 47 percent of

---

[28] The data for persons with 10 and more years of education suggested a complete absorption of the 1960–66 cohorts into urban employment. For persons with 8 to 9 years of education, the employment probability apparently dropped to about 90 percent in 1965 and 75 percent in 1966.

[29] Since African primary school students probably were much more heterogeneous socially and economically in 1968 than than in 1960, the effect of a correction for socio-economic background probably would have been smaller in 1960. The rates in the earlier years of the series would thus be biased downward relative to the later rates.

TABLE 4.10: **Urban and Rural, Weighted and Combined Private Rates of Return to Primary Education, 1960–66**

	1960	1961	1962	1963	1964	1965	1966
Incomplete Primary Education							
Urban Component[a]	1.5	2.3	1.3	1.3[e]	1.0	0.5	0.5[e]
Rural Component[b]	19.3	19.3	19.3	19.3	19.0	18.6	18.3
Total	20.8	21.6	20.6	20.6	20.0	19.1	18.8
Complete Primary Education							
Urban Component[c]	23.2	11.0	9.9	8.8	5.5	5.0	2.8
Rural Component[d]	15.8	15.8	15.8	15.8	15.3	14.8	14.3
Total	39.0	26.8	25.7	24.6	20.8	19.8	17.1

Note: No adjustments made for socio-economic and ability factors.

[a] Differential rate 2–4 from Annex Table 6.8 (EC-173) multiplied by probabilities in Table 4.9.

[b] Average of rates for 0–2 and 2–6 from Tables 4.7 and 4.8 corrected for acreage and family size. Rates between 1963 and 1966 interpolated linearly.

[c] Differential rate 5–7 from Annex Table 6.8 (EC-173) multiplied by probabilities in Table 4.9.

[d] Average of rates for 2–6 and 6–10 from Tables 4.7 and 4.8 corrected for acreage and family size. Rates between 1963 and 1966 interpolated linearly.

[e] 1963/62 and 1966/65 urban employment probabilities for persons with incomplete primary education assumed to be equal.

Source: Annex Table 6.8 (EC-173) and Tables 4.7, 4.8, and 4.9.

TABLE 4.11: **Urban and Rural, Weighted and Combined Social Rates of Return to Primary Education, 1960–66**

	1960	1961	1962	1963	1964	1965	1966
Incomplete Primary Education							
Urban Component[a]	1.0	1.5	0.8	0.6[e]	0.3	0.3	0.3[e]
Rural Component[b]	18.2	18.2	18.2	18.2	16.6	14.9	13.2
Total	19.2	19.7	19.0	18.8	16.9	15.2	13.5
Complete Primary Education							
Urban Component[c]	16.1	7.7	6.9	6.1	3.8	3.4	1.9
Rural Component[d]	13.2	13.2	13.2	13.2	11.7	10.2	8.8
Total	29.3	20.9	20.1	19.3	15.5	13.6	10.7

Note: No adjustments made for socio-economic or ability factors.

[a] Differential rate 2–4 from Annex Table 6.9 (EC-173) multiplied by probabilities in Table 4.9.

[b] Average of rates for 0–2 and 2–6 from Table 4.7 and 4.8 corrected for acreage and family size. Rates between 1963 and 1966 interpreted linearly.

[c] Differential rate 5–7 from Annex Table 6.9 (EC-173) multiplied by probabilities in Table 4.9.

[d] Average of rates for 2–6 and 6–10 from Tables 4.7 and 4.8 corrected for acreage and family size. Rates between 1963 and 1966 interpreted linearly.

[e] 1963/62 and 1966/65 urban employment probabilities for persons with incomplete primary education assumed to be equal.

Sources: Annex Table 6.9 (EC-173) and Tables 4.7, 4.8 and 4.9.

unadjusted rates for these two levels, respectively. Applying these percentages to the combined rates in Tables 4.10 and 4.11, we get an approximation of the rates adjusted for both employment probabilities and socioeconomic background (Table 4.12). These adjusted rates more correctly reflect the contribution of investment in schooling alone as distinct from the combined contributions of investment in schooling and extra-schooling qualities.

TABLE 4.12: Combined Urban and Rural Rates of Return to Primary Education, Adjusted for Socio-Economic Background, 1960–66

	1960	1961	1962	1963	1964	1965	1966
Incomplete Primary Education							
Private	25.0	25.9	24.7	24.7	24.0	22.9	22.6
Social	19.2	19.7	19.0	18.8	16.9	15.2	13.5
Complete Primary Education							
Private	15.2	10.4	10.0	9.6	8.1	7.7	6.7
Social	14.1	10.2	9.4	9.1	7.2	6.4	5.0

Source: Tables 4.10 and 4.11 total figures, multiplied by percentages derived in text.

Final Rates, Adjustments Accumulated

Tables 4.13 and 4.14 present the final social and private rates of return, showing each step of adjustment which we have made in previous sections of this chapter. These rates are recalculated using corrected benefit data. The crude internal rates to urban Africans, derived by relating the net additional earnings associated with additional schooling to the cost of that schooling, are seen to vary considerably among educational levels, but are generally high, ranging from 9 percent for university to 24 percent for secondary schooling. When the rates are corrected for taxes (private rates) and mortality (social rates), at least some are still acceptable investments. But the adjustment for the influence of socio-economic variables, including the correction for ability based on examination results, leads to a marked reduction in both the private and social rates of return.

At the primary school level we then combine the unadjusted urban rates, weighted for the probability of urban employment, and the rural rates, adjusted for the probability of being a small landholder, to yield overall combined rates to investment. As we noted at the beginning of the chapter, the combined urban–rural rate is a suitable yardstick for social investment decisions only if the dividing line between the two sectors is thought to be easily permeable. If this is not the case, the rural and urban rates should be considered separately from one another. Rural rates would appear to be more relevant for policy decisions given the population weight of the countryside and its lag in educational development.

TABLE 4.13: Average Private Rates of Return to Schooling, All Adjustments, by Years of Schooling, 1968

Years of Schooling[a]	Urban Rates Corrected for:			Rural Rates Based on Head of Hshld. incl., Corrected for:	Combined Urban–Rural Corrected for:	
	Age Only	Age and Taxes	Age, Taxes, Soc.-Ec. Var. and Exam Score	Prob. of Holding Land, Acreage, and Family Size	Employment Probabilities Only	Employment Probabilities and Soc.-Ec. Var.
Primary						
2–4	26	26	31	14[b]	19[e]	23[e]
5–7	55	55	13	22[c]	17[f]	7[f]
2–7	33	33	18			
Secondary						
8–9	24	24	9	6[d]		
10–11	52	40	30			
8–11	36	32	19			
Higher Secondary						
12–13	24	23	23			
University						
14–17	27	20	20			

Note: For each set of adjustments, each rate is recalculated using adjusted costs and benefits.
[a] See footnote *a*, Table 4.4.
[b] 1–2 years of schooling, 1966.
[c] 3–6 years of schooling, 1966.
[d] 7–10 years of schooling, 1966.
[e] Incomplete primary schooling, 1966.
[f] Complete primary schooling, 1966.
Source: Column 1: Table 4.4, Column 1. Column 2: Table 4.4, Column 2. Column 3: Based on Table 4.4, Column 3, and Table 4.5. Column 4: Table 4.8, Column 3. Column 5: Table 4.10. Column 6: Table 4.12.

TABLE 4.14: Average Social Rates of Return to Schooling, All Adjustments, by Years of Schooling, 1968

Years of Schooling[a]	Age Only	Age and Mortality	Urban Rates Corrected for: Age, Mortality and Soc.-Ec. Var.	Age, Mortality, Soc.-Ec. Var. and Exam Score	Age, Mortality, Soc.-Ec. Var., Ability, and KPE Cert. Effect	Age, Mortality, Soc.-Ec. Var., Ability, KPE Cert. and Gov't Empl. Effects	Rural Rates Based on Head of Hshld. incl. Corrected for: Prob. of Holding Land. Acreage, and Family Size	Combined Urban-Rural Corrected for: Employment Probabilities Only	Employment Probabilities and Soc.-Ec. Var.
Primary									
2–4	16	15	11	15	15	15	11[b]	14[e]	14[e]
5–7	38	38	17	10	14	14	15[c]	11[f]	5[f]
2–7	22	21	14	13	14	14			
Secondary									
8–9	16	15	19	6	6	6	2[d]		
10–11	34	34	28	26	26	21			
8–11	24	24	23	18	18	15			
Higher Secondary									
12–13	15	15	15	15	15	15			
University									
14–17	9	9	9	9	9	9			

Note: For each set of adjustments, each rate is recalculated using adjusted costs and benefits.
[a] See footnote *a*, Table 4.4.
[b] 1–2 years of schooling, 1966.
[c] 3–6 years of schooling, 1966.
[d] 7–10 years of schooling, 1966.
[e] Applies to incomplete primary schooling, 1966.
[f] Applies to complete primary schooling, 1966.

Sources: Column 1: Table 4.4, Column 1. Column 2: Table 4.4, Column 2. Column 3: Based on Table 4.4, Columns 2 and 3. Column 4: Based on Table 4.4, Columns 2 and 3, and Table 4.5. Column 5: Same as Column 4, plus text on KPE certificate effect. Column 6: Same as Column 5, plus text on government employment effect. Column 7: Table 4.8, Column 4. Column 8: Table 4.11.

We have shown that the unadjusted rates to investment in primary schooling, which have led the authors of some earlier cost-benefit studies to assign high priority to public investment in primary education, are probably overestimated. The social rates to primary schooling in Kenya and six other countries in Table 4.15, most of them unadjusted,[30] are relatively high, and most of the rates to university training are relatively low, compared to investment both in other education levels and in other forms of capital. The exceptions are Mexico and Venezuela, which have high rates to investment in university training; these countries had sustained rapid growth over a long period preceding the date of the estimates.

In the light of our experience, much of what has been attributed to primary schooling is more likely the result of non-schooling inputs, and therefore the rate of return to investment in primary schooling is probably much lower than the estimates indicate when these other factors are constant. Furthermore, since in some countries significant numbers of primary school graduates remain in the rural sector or are unemployed, the rates based on urban earnings data uncorrected for either of these factors clearly overestimate the returns. Once the most pressing demands for medium-level personnel have been met, a similar situation might well develop at the secondary education level. Last but not least, the omission of females from the estimates of overall returns gives them a considerable upward bias.[31]

Helpful as it may be to see the average rates of return at a given point in time as we have presented them, the education planner is more interested in what the rates are at the margin and how they will change in the future. The steady decline in the combined urban–rural rates over the period 1960–66 (Table 4.12) vividly shows that rapid changes in the returns to education have already occurred in Kenya. The essentially static exercise of Chapters III and IV is an indispensable point of departure; the next chapter will use different tools to extend the analysis into the future.

---

[30] Some studies do correct for ability or unemployment in estimating rates of return to schooling. M. Blaug's work contains a correction for ability, but the rates are adjusted uniformly by the same percentage at all schooling levels, and the rate to investment in primary schooling remains relatively high compared to those to other levels. M. Selowsky's estimates of rates of return for Colombia do not adjust for ability but do correct for unemployment and labor force participation rates. Possibly because the rates are estimated only for Bogota, the unemployment correction does not result in great changes in the estimates.

[31] The unadjusted rate of return to primary schooling for urban African females is 7.1 percent, compared to 21.7 for urban African males; for secondary schools it is 19.5 percent as compared to 23.6 percent for males. The employment probability for urban African females is of the order of 0.2 and for rural African females, 0.05 (off-farm employment; see Annex E, Step 6).

TABLE 4.15: Social Internal Rates of Return to Schooling for Males in Seven Developing Countries, Based on Urban Samples: Kenya, Uganda, India, Mexico, Chile, Colombia and Venezuela

Years of Schooling	(1) Kenya 1968	(2) Uganda 1965	Years of Schooling	(3) India 1966	Years of Schooling	(4) Mexico 1963	Years of Schooling	(5) Chile[a] 1959	Years of Schooling	(6) Colombia 1965	Years of Schooling	(7) Venezuela 1957
2–4	16	66	1–5	20	2–4	17	1–6[b]	24	1–3	35	1–6	82
5–7	38		6–8	17	5–6	38	7–9[c]	29	4–5	30	7–11	17
8–9	16	22	9–11	16	9–11	14	7–12[d]	17	6–8	18	12–15	23
10–11	34		12–15[e]	13	12–13	12	13–17	12	9–11	29		
12–13	15	78	12–15[f]	17	14–16	30			12–14	7		
14–17	9	12							15–16	negative		

[a] Rates are for males and females. Carnoy-corrected rates for Chile (see "Rates of Return to Schooling in Latin America," p. 369) are 12 percent to primary school instead of 24 percent and 12 percent to general secondary school instead of 17 percent. The other two rates were not corrected.
[b] Average schooling = 5.5 years.
[c] "Special" secondary schooling (average = 8.5 years).
[d] General secondary schooling (average = 11.5 years).
[e] First degree over matriculation.
[f] Engineering degree over matriculation.

Sources: Kenya—Table 4.10. Column (1). Uganda—John Smyth and Nicholas Bennett, "Rates of Return on Investment in Education: A Tool for Short-Term Educational Planning, Illustrated with Uganda Data," in George Bereday and Joseph Lauwerys, *World Year Book of Education*, 1967, London, 1968, pp. 299–323. India—M. Blaug, P. R. G. Layard, and M. Woodhall, *The Causes of Educated Unemployment in India*, manuscript to be published in 1969, Table 9.1. Mexico, Chile, Venezuela—for complete reference, see Martin Carnoy, "Rates of Return to Schooling in Latin America," *Journal of Human Resources*, Vol. II, No. 3 (Summer, 1967), pp. 359–374. Colombia—Marcelo Selowsky, *The Effect of Unemployment and Growth on the Rate of Return to Education: The Case of Colombia*, Harvard University, Center for International Affairs, 1968.

V

POSSIBLE APPLICATIONS OF RATE-OF-RETURN ANALYSIS TO EDUCATIONAL PLANNING
An Illustration

The Model

We move now from an estimate of rates of return at a given point in time to a model of educational planning which relies neither on a set of fixed relations between production, occupational structure, and education (i.e., perfectly inelastic demand curves for labor with different amounts of schooling), nor on the assumption of perfectly elastic demand curves for labor (i.e., fixed real wages). Instead, we attempt to account for substitutability in production of labor with different skills while assuming the elasticity of substitution to be finite.

The model begins with the premise that there is no unique mix of skills which will fulfill the needs of the economy, but that the equilibrium quantity of educated labor at any point in time is rather a function of the price of that labor relative to the price of other competitive inputs. Because labor and capital are substitutes and because different kinds of labor are substitutes for each other, relative prices are an important determinant both of the total demand for labor and of the amount of the various levels of skills the economy will absorb at a future date. Since it can also be assumed that the supply of skills is responsive to wage rate changes, specifically in the absolute differences between wages of different skill levels, the market for a given type of educated labor, x, can be described as in Figure 5.1. D and D' are the demand curves for x at the present time and some future date, respectively, and S and S' are the supply curves at

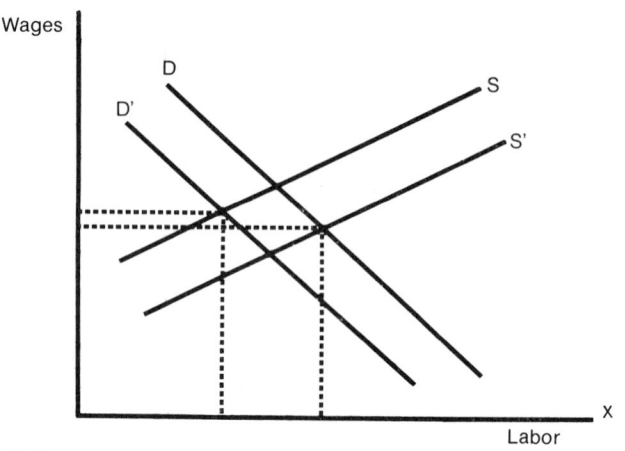

FIGURE 5.1: SUPPLY OF AND DEMAND FOR EDUCATED LABOR

those two dates. Taken by itself, Figure 5.1 merely illustrates the concepts of equilibrium employment and equilibrium wage. The analysis of demand and supply of labor (of which this figure is an abstract), repeated for various levels of qualification, can convey a picture of the future wage structure. Or, given demand projections, the model could estimate the supply of each level of educated labor which would produce a desired wage structure; given supply projections, it could estimate the growth of demand needed to produce such a wage structure.

The desired structure of wages at a future date may be related to economic or political aims in a society, or to both. To estimate the impact of a future wage pattern, the economic and political implications of the present pattern of wages have to be assessed. If on the one hand education is regarded purely as an investment in man, then wage differentials are a measure of the return to that investment, and the structure of wages directly influences the rate of return to investment in education. On the other hand, the primary aim of the society may be rather the optimum allocation of resources in the whole economy, including the allocation of resources to the formation of human capital as one element. In this case the present and future structure of rates of return to investment in various levels of education is a direct measure of the efficiency of resource allocation. Changes in the wage structure, as reflected in rates of return, are a measure of changes in that efficiency. The present structure of wages and the related rates of return to schooling present a starting point from which to gauge future wage structures as they relate to the optimum allocation of resources to education. If, for example, present wages yield very unequal rates of return to various levels of schooling, wages may have to change in order to maximize the efficiency of investment.

The application of this model can be divided into five steps:

a) Estimation of the present rate of return to different levels of education, which compares the yield to investment at each level with investment at the other levels and with the yield to physical capital;

b) Projection of the supply of the types of labor by education or wage levels;

c) Estimation of the demand curve for these types of labor;

d) Projection of the demand for these types of labor;

e) Estimation of future wages and future rates of return from demand and supply projections. Estimation of full employment equilibria for labor with various amounts of schooling from demand and wage projections ("desired" or predicted wages).

The starting point of the analysis is an estimate of the present structure of the rates of return to education; this was done in the previous chapter. The analysis here concentrates on the last three steps of the model which provide the focus and methodological interest for the present chapter.[1]

The Supply of Educated Labor

The supply curve of a given type of skilled labor represents the number of workers with a certain amount of education in the existing labor force willing to work at alternative wage rates. Shifts in the supply curve of skills stem from increased or decreased net flows into the labor force of individuals with given amounts of schooling of constant quality, assuming constant real wages. An increase in these flows may result from increased public expenditure on schooling, lower private costs of schooling, increased efficiency of a given amount of expenditures on schooling, large age cohorts, improved health which extends workers' productive life, or increased non-pecuniary returns to given levels of schooling. A decrease in flows may correspondingly arise from decreased public expenditures, higher private costs, decreased efficiency of given expenditures, smaller age cohorts, worsened health conditions, and decreased non-pecuniary returns to—or conversely, increased non-pecuniary costs of—schooling.

---

[1] The second step, namely, the supply estimates, was dealt with in detail in Chapter VIII of EC-173. We are using the previous estimates without presenting the various steps that led to them. (For lack of data, simple trend extrapolation was applied in most cases.)

Planners have invariably viewed supply shifts as a quasi-automatic outcome of shifts in the demand for education, assuming constant efficiency of the school system in "processing" pupils and in turning out graduates. Rarely do projections examine the relationship between different kinds of expenditures or the ways in which these might change the rate of output of the school system (of constant quality); hardly ever do studies examine the effect on supply shifts of changes in the proportion of schooling costs borne directly by individuals. If taxes are used to pay entirely for schooling, families would have to pay for schools whether they had children who attended or not. They would therefore be induced to take more schooling than if the costs of schooling were payable directly to the school, and depended on whether their children attended or not. In Kenya the role of private costs is especially important since families must bear about one third of the total cost of schooling at the primary level but none of the cost (other than income foregone) in the last two years of secondary school or at university. Changes in, say, primary school fees may thus have a significant effect on primary enrollment, at least in the short run.

It should also be recognized that increased public expenditures on schooling may reduce private costs without reducing fees: for example, opening additional schools in a region would tend to shorten the distances children have to travel to attend school, hence reducing private transport costs (or avoiding boarding costs). Also, increasing public expenditures per pupil in schools may reduce the non-pecuniary private cost of schooling for a child and may increase his willingness to stay in school.

The quality of education is also important in projecting supply. Increased total expenditures may increase flows of graduates, but may at the same time reduce the quality of graduates. Shifts in the supply curve must therefore be described in constant quality terms, and if the increases in supply are not homogeneous they should be adjusted accordingly. As the education "plant" is expanded and the number of graduates of a given level of schooling increases, the quality of graduates in the short-run may tend to fall. In the short run, enrollment ratios can probably be increased only by educating children from progressively weaker socio-economic groups. These children have less and less of the outside training (say, in the family) which could help them succeed in school. An increasing amount of resources per pupil, or possibly different *kinds* of resources, will have to be used therefore in order to produce a "constant quality marginal graduate." On the other hand, in the longer run non-institutional education inputs rise as parents become, on the average, better educated. This would tend to reduce the resources required per pupil to maintain homogeneity of output. Alternatively, if resources per pupil remained constant, the quality of output would rise.

Quality of output may be measured by standard examination scores at different levels of schooling. Cross-section data on average examination scores by school at the primary, lower secondary, and higher secondary levels could be related to inputs per pupil in the schools. The relation of expenditure per pupil to examination score, holding other variables constant, can show how much expenditures per pupil would have to be increased to maintain a constant quality of output (as measured by examination score) if the average quality of the school's intake varied over time. The average expenditure might rise because a higher percentage of the population in school could imply that students are drawn from a less favorable environment, e.g. with less educated parents. By the same token, the average expenditure might fall in the long run with a rising average level of education of parents over time. From this we could judge the increase or decrease in costs per student required to maintain constant quality output.

Some of these issues are treated empirically in Annex A, but the analysis does not yield estimates which can be used to project supply as a function of rates of return to schooling, or to project the quality of graduates as a function of school inputs, changes in enrollment ratios, and parents' education. Thus, while the model would ideally provide a simultaneous equation solution for the demand and quality-adjusted supply at every schooling level, the illustration given below, as far as it refers to supply projections, uses the exogenously determined, perfectly inelastic, quality uncorrected estimates shown in Table 5.1.

TABLE 5.1: Projected Annual Pupil Outflow, 1969–74

(thousands of pupils)

	1969	1970	1971	1972	1973	1974
Primary						
Standards I–V:	74	83	76	76	74	77
Standards VI–VIII:	141	131	139	140	160	180
Students who continue their education	37	38	39	41	42	44
Net outflow, VI–VII	104	93	100	99	118	136
Total Primary	178	176	176	175	192	213
Secondary						
Forms I–IV	24	30	33	33	34	34
Forms V–VI	2	2	2	3	3	4
Total Secondary	26	32	35	36	37	38
University or other Post-Secondary	0.7	0.8	1.0	1.3	1.5	1.8

Source: Tables 8.2 and 8.3 in EC-173.

Estimates of Demand for Educated Labor

As mentioned before, our aim is to estimate the demand for specific skills by relating the quantity of each skill demanded to its relative price, i.e. to the wages of workers with the amount and type of education that is associated with this skill. This can be done in two ways. When time series data are available on relative wages and the number of workers with a given amount of education in the labor force, demand can be estimated directly from such data. Otherwise demand must be derived from (cross-section) production function estimates of some kind for the economy as a whole or sector by sector. The first of these approaches can be described by the following equation:

$$q_{x(t)} = a + bw_{x(t)} + c\,\text{GDP}_{(t)} + d\frac{w_{x(t)}}{w_{y(t)}} + e\frac{w_{x(t)}}{w_{z(t)}} \quad (5.1)$$

where $q_{x(t)}$ = the quantity of workers with x education in the labor force in year t,

$w_{x(t)}$ = real wages or salary paid to workers with x education in the labor force in year t,

$w_{y(t)}$ = real wages or salary paid to workers with next highest level of education, y, in the labor force in year t,

$w_{z(t)}$ = real wages or salary paid to workers with next lowest level of education, z, in the labor force in year t,

and $\text{GDP}_{(t)}$ = real gross domestic product in year t.

The coefficient b is an estimate for the slope of the demand curve for labor as a function of real wages, with domestic product and relative wages held constant. If the regression is run as a log equation, b represents the price elasticity of demand and c the income elasticity of demand for labor with x education.[2] The coefficients d and e relate to the wage structure.

The second method is more complex. It requires cross-section estimates of production functions in which labor is no longer treated as a single input

---

[2] Since the supply function $S = f(W/P)$ is not specified and the demand and supply equations are not solved simultaneously, the absolute value of b would be a downward biased estimate of the price elasticity of demand. The higher the price elasticity of supply, the greater the bias in b. We would therefore expect that the estimates of b for labor with primary schooling would be more biased than the approximations for secondary school or university educated labor, since the elasticities of supply of the two latter categories are lower than that of the first group. Our 1974 employment estimates for a given wage level of primary school leavers are thus underestimated. Correspondingly, to bring about a drop in the rate of return, the increase in the output of the education system by 1974 would have to be greater than estimated below. However, there is no bias in the estimates which we make of unemployment in 1974 under the assumption of constant real wages.

but rather as a collection of different kinds of labor, each characterized by different amounts of education, and each considered as a separate input in the production process. Using a Cobb-Douglas production function as an example, the demand for a given type of labor can be derived in the following way.

$$V_{(i)} = A[L_{1(i)}]^\alpha \cdot [L_{2(i)}]^\beta \cdot [L_{3(i)}]^\gamma \cdot K_{(i)}^\delta \qquad (5.2)$$

Equation (5.2) is the production function for a given industry, for example, where $L_{1(i)}$, $L_{2(i)}$, and $L_{3(i)}$ are different skill levels of labor, $K_{(i)}$ is capital, and $V_{(i)}$ is value added in the industry.

$$\frac{\partial V_{(i)}}{\partial L_{1(i)}} = A\alpha[L_{1(i)}]^{\alpha-1} \cdot [L_{2(i)}]^\beta \cdot [L_{3(i)}]^\gamma \cdot K_{(i)}^\delta \qquad (5.3)$$

$$= \frac{\alpha V_{(i)}}{L_{1(i)}}$$

where $\frac{\partial V_{(i)}}{\partial L_{1(i)}}$ is the marginal productivity of $L_{1(i)}$, or, in a perfectly competitive situation, wages of $L_{1(i)}$. Similarly, the demand curves for other types of labor as functions of output of the industry and of wages can be derived. Other kinds of functions besides the Cobb-Douglas, such as the CES (constant elasticity of substitution) function, can also be used to assess demand for labor.

Our attempt to estimate demand for labor using the above production functions was unsuccessful for two reasons, both connected with data problems.[3] First, we have to use two groups of cross-section data on Kenyan firms to obtain all the necessary information:

a) Value of output by firm (1966), replacement value of capital by firm (1963), total number of employees by firm (1963, 1966, 1967) for all 126 manufacturing firms participating in the Kenyan Government Manufacturing Surveys; and

b) Wage and employment data for the 20 participating firms which employed persons in the three labor categories we decided to use in our Labor Force Survey (Jan.–Feb. 1968).

However, the confidential nature of the government employment/output data required that we use it without being able to identify individual firms; therefore we could not match these data with the individual firm employment/salary figures from our survey. Secondly, the firms in both samples are too heterogeneous for successful cross-section analysis, and data were not available for a longitudinal analysis using time-series for one firm or a group of similar firms.

---

[3] See EC-173, pp. 186–191 for details.

The Demand for Labor Estimated Directly from Wages and Employment Data

Although the time series data on employment and wages of workers by years of education which are specified in equation (5.1) are not available for Kenya, we use as proxies time series on salaries and employment of Kenyan males by ethnic group and economic sector. Our data cover three ethnic groups (African, Asian, European) and three sectors (commercial agriculture and forestry, private industry and commerce, public sector), which can be combined into nine ethnic-sector groups (see Table 5.2). We then use these groups as proxies for education groups by assuming that Africans in commercial agriculture and forestry have an average of one year of schooling; that Africans in private industry and commerce have an average of four years of schooling; that Asians in all three sectors have an average of seven years, and that Europeans in all sectors have nine years. This enables us to develop nine equations of the form of equation (5.1), some of which are used in the later sections to make projections to 1974.

The nominal earnings data for the ethnic-sector groups from 1957 to 1966 are shown in Table 5.2 and the employment figures for the same period in Table 5.3. In both commercial agriculture and private industry and commerce, nominal salaries have grown steadily during the ten-year period and employment has fallen. In the public sector, Africans' earnings have risen as has their employment, particularly since independence.

Throughout the ten-year period, gross domestic product (GDP) and prices have also been increasing. GDP and the cost-of-living index for Nairobi are shown in Table 5.4. The Nairobi cost of living index is used to deflate all salaries and GDP, so that both are expressed in 1957 prices. Since prices probably rose more during this period in Nairobi than in other towns and the countryside, the index tends to give a downward bias to real wages and GDP. The estimated coefficients relating employment to real wages and real GDP therefore are probably biased upward.

Adapting equation (5.1) to these data, we use equations of the following form.[4]

$$\log N_{i,j,k} = a_{i,j} + b_{i,j} \log(W_{i,j,k}/P_k) + c_{i,j} \log(GDP_{j,k}/P_k) \quad (5.4)$$

where N = employment (in thousands),
W/P = nominal salaries (in K£) deflated by the Nairobi consumer price index to 1957 prices, and
GDP/P = gross domestic product (in million K£), deflated by the Nairobi consumer price index to 1957 prices.

---
[4] The inclusion of the variable W_i/W_j, which relates the wages of Africans in one sector to those of the same group in another sector, showed little success and is therefore not described here.

TABLE 5.2: Average Annual Earnings, 1957–66

(K£)

	1957	1958	1959	1960	1961	1962	1963	1964	1965	1966	Index (1966) 1957 = 100	Index (1966) 1963 = 100
Agriculture and Forestry												
African	34	35	35	37	39	39	46	51	52	54	159	117
Asian	400	400	500	500	667	667	571	571	714	624	156	109
European	1111	1111	1176	1105	1313	1214	1143	1417	1545	1583	142	138
Weighted Average	42	43	43	46	49	47	55	61	62	65	155	118
Private Industry and Commerce												
African	80	83	86	92	104	110	132	124	138	148	185	112
Asian	446	452	454	457	460	485	514	523	569	628	141	122
European	1105	1147	1150	1179	1265	1321	1422	1480	1594	1779	161	125
Weighted Average	189	198	205	212	235	239	276	244	263	287	152	104
Public Service												
African	85	91	94	102	113	121	138	172	196	212	249	154
Asian	560	566	559	559	607	608	658	756	810	892	159	136
European	1196	1228	1256	1270	1506	1538	1574	1638	1667	2405	201	153
Weighted Average	177	189	192	200	223	222	232	239	259	289	163	125
All Employment												
African	60	63	64	68	76	80	95	103	124	133	222	140
Asian	478	485	486	488	511	529	561	575	622	680	142	121
European	1143	1177	1194	1213	1365	1399	1452	1516	1612	1940	170	134
Total Average	125	131	133	136	152	153	172	178	192	212	170	123

Note: Extreme fluctuations in the annual earnings of Asians and Europeans are mainly due to rounding of small absolute amounts.

Source: Calculated from data of the *Statistical Abstract, 1967*, Nairobi, 1967, pp. 150–151.

103

TABLE 5.3: Employment by Ethnic Groups and Major Economic Sectors, 1957-66

('000)

	1957	1958	1959	1960	1961	1962	1963	1964	1965	1966
Agriculture and Forestry										
African	251.1	247.2	249.4	269.1	249.8	243.5	217.6	206.8	202.8	204.4
Asian	0.5	0.5	0.6	0.8	0.6	0.6	0.7	0.7	0.7	0.8
European	1.8	1.8	1.7	1.9	1.6	1.4	1.4	1.2	1.1	1.2
Total	253.4	249.5	251.7	271.8	252.0	245.5	219.7	208.7	204.6	206.4
Private Industry and Commerce										
African	156.8	149.6	148.0	151.1	134.1	133.2	121.8	169.2	169.0	173.4
Asian	25.8	24.8	25.1	25.6	25.0	23.5	24.3	28.3	27.6	29.0
European	11.4	11.6	12.0	12.3	11.7	10.6	10.2	10.2	9.6	9.5
Total	194.0	186.0	185.1	189.0	170.8	167.3	156.3	208.3	206.6	211.5
Public Service										
African	146.9	137.0	140.0	140.7	145.9	147.2	139.5	161.8	167.2	173.6
Asian	10.9	10.6	11.1	11.8	12.2	12.0	11.7	8.2	7.9	7.4
European	9.2	9.2	9.0	8.9	8.9	7.8	6.1	4.7	4.5	4.2
Total	167.0	157.7	160.1	161.4	167.0	167.0	157.3	174.7	179.6	185.2
All Employment										
African	554.8	534.7	537.4	560.9	529.8	523.9	478.9	538.4	539.4	551.0
Asian	37.2	35.9	36.8	38.3	37.8	36.1	36.7	37.2	36.2	37.2
European	22.4	22.6	22.7	23.0	22.2	19.8	17.7	16.1	15.2	14.9
Total	614.4	593.2	596.9	622.2	589.8	579.8	533.3	591.7	590.8	603.1

Note: Over time the coverage has changed and therefore the figures are not strictly comparable. The rule between 1963 and 1964 indicates a break in the series caused by a marked improvement in the coverage of private industry and commerce when an approximated 42,000 employees were added to this sector as a result of a survey of establishments in rural areas. In the analysis, the 1964-66 employment figures for Africans in that sector have hence been reduced by 40,000.

Source: Statistical Abstract 1967.

TABLE 5.4: Gross Domestic Product at Factor Cost by Major Economic Sectors, and Cost of Living Index, Nairobi, 1957–66

(million K£)

	1957	1958	1959	1960	1961	1962	1963	1964	1965	1966
Agriculture and Forestry[a]	33.5	34.6	35.6	40.0	38.7	40.0	44.4	48.0	44.4	50.9
Private Industry and Commerce	100.5	100.4	104.6	110.4	111.1	112.9	119.2	130.7	139.9	151.9
Government Sector	20.2	24.5	21.5	24.9	27.0	28.1	28.8	34.1	38.6	40.7
Gross Domestic Product	154.2	155.5	161.8	175.3	176.8	180.9	192.4	212.8	222.9	243.5
Cost of Living Index, Nairobi[b]	100.0	100.0	100.7	101.4	103.8	109.4	110.1	112.5	117.4	119.8

Source: Statistical Abstract 1967.

[a] Monetary economy only.
[b] Excluding rent.

The subscripts i, j, and k indicate ethnic group, economic sector and year of observation, respectively. The regression estimates are made for the parameters a, b, and c by ethnic group and sector. In the case of the government sector a dummy (I) is added which takes a value of zero for years before independence (1957–63) and a value of unity for years thereafter (1964–66).

The coefficients of the equations derived from these regressions are set out below, arranged by sector and ethnic group in twelve equations, of the general form (based on equation (5.4) above, but omitting all subscripts).

$$\log N = a + b \log(W/P) + c \log(\text{GDP}) + dI$$

where N = employment (in thousands),

W/P = nominal salaries (in K£) deflated by the Nairobi consumer price index to 1957 prices,

GDP/P = gross domestic product (in millions of K£) deflated by the Nairobi consumer price index to 1957 prices, and

I = independence dummy, for government sector, a) equations only; equals zero for 1957–63 and unity for 1964–66

t-values are given in parentheses and coefficients not significant at the 0.05 level of probability are marked*.

Regression Coefficients

Sectors, Equation Numbers and Ethnic Groups	a (intercept)	b (real wage)	c (GDP)	d (independence)	R^2
Agriculture					
(5.5) Africans	7.5062	−1.2301 (7.296)	0.6724 (2.856)		.93
(5.6) Asians	7.4541	0.1500* (0.764)	1.6712 (4.398)		.79
(5.7) Europeans	12.0392	−1.0008* (1.884)	−1.0269* (1.761)		.60
Private Industry and Commerce					
(5.8) Africans	5.2204	−0.7408 (9.465)	0.6648 (4.100)		.95
(5.9) Asians	1.0340	0.1257* (0.267)	0.3042* (0.948)		.50
(5.10) Europeans	9.9751	−1.4844 (3.075)	0.6341* (1.098)		.84
Government					
(5.11) Africans: no (I) term	3.7356	0.3500* (1.701)	−0.1182* (0.371)		.77
(5.11a) (I) included	4.7610	0.0980* (0.533)	−0.0802* (0.334)	0.1382 (2.528)	.89
(5.12) Asians: no (I) term	14.8484	−2.1438 (4.181)	0.3688* (1.121)		.88

Regression Coefficients *(continued)*

Sectors, Equation Numbers and Ethnic Groups	a (intercept)	b (real wage)	c (GDP)	d (independence)	R^2
(5.12a) (I) included	6.2136	−0.7924* (1.472)	0.3932* (1.823)	−0.3303 (3.212)	.96
(5.13) Europeans: no (I) term	9.7945	−1.5780 (3.002)	−0.2354* (0.394)		.82
(5.13a) (I) included	6.2400	−0.3386* (0.738)	−0.5304 (0.901)	−0.4002 (2.437)	.91

The regression estimates relating African employment to average salaries and gross domestic sectoral product yield significant coefficients for both independent variables in both commercial agriculture and private industry and commerce. The salary and GDP variables explain 93 percent of the variance of African employment in agriculture and 95 percent of the variance in private industry and commerce. As expected, demand is more price elastic for agricultural workers than for industrial workers, probably because of differences in schooling: African industrial workers have, on average, about four years of schooling compared to perhaps one for those in commercial agriculture.

The coefficients of sectoral GDP are almost exactly equal for Africans in agriculture and in private industry and commerce. For a one percent increase in sectoral GDP, African employment increases by 0.67 percent, salaries being held constant. This implies that if there were no labor transfers, real sectoral GDP would have to grow at 4.5 percent per annum for these two sectors.[5] If sectoral GDP does not grow at 4.5 percent per annum but the population growth rate remains at the 3 percent level, the two sectors will not be absorbing a proportional share of the labor; other sectors, such as the government or subsistence agriculture, would have to take an increasing proportion of the labor force if unemployment rates were to remain at the same level.[6] GDP in both sectors grew only about 3 percent

---

[5] If population grows at 3 percent annually, and the percentage of population that enters agriculture and private industry does not change, employment in the two sectors would also grow at 3 percent per annum.

[6] This rather pessimistic conclusion is supported by the findings of a study on employment and output in a number of selected African industries: C. R. Frank, Jr., "Urban Unemployment and Economic Growth in Africa," *Oxford Economic Papers*, Vol. 20, No. 2 (July 1968), pp. 250–274. The author's regressions of output growth on employment growth, based on time series covering an average of 15 years, show that substantial increases in output are necessary in order to compensate for the negative impact of the intercept term in the equations. The "breakeven growth," or growth in output required to keep employment from falling, ranges from 1.7 percent for Nigeria's tin industry to 6.7 percent for the East African Railways.

per annum in real terms during the ten-year period, so that each sector could have taken an additional 2 percent annually into its labor force had salaries remained constant. Since average salaries in real terms have also been increasing, African employment in the two sectors has remained essentially unchanged between 1957 and 1966.

The estimated parameters for Asians and Europeans (equations 5.6, 5.7, 5.9, 5.10, 5.12 and 5.13) are considerably less consistent than those for Africans. The former reflect changes in employment which stem from factors other than salary increments or changes in sectoral GDP. Thus the coefficients of determination (R^2) are considerably lower for Asians and Europeans than for Africans.[7] In the four equations relating to non-African private sector employment (5.6, 5.7, 5.9 and 5.10) there are only two estimated coefficients which are statistically significant at the 95 percent level, namely the real sectoral GDP coefficient for Asians in agriculture, and the real salaries coefficient for Europeans in private industry and commerce.

Demand Projections and Equilibrium Estimates for Africans with Primary Schooling

Using the demand estimates for African labor above we undertake two types of analyses of future labor conditions and educational requirements in Kenya. As an example of the first type of analysis we project the equilibrium, full-employment supply and wages of urban male Africans with 3 to 5 years of schooling. This is done under the assumptions that the supply of this level of labor is a function of the rate of return to schooling and that the desired equilibrium social rate of return to investment in 3 to 5 years of schooling in urban areas is 10 percent. In the second type of analysis we assume that the supply of labor is determined exogenously by the output of the school system, and that that output is not responsive to wage changes. Given the exogenously determined supply of labor with primary schooling, we find the level of real wages which will result in full employment of those with primary schooling. Alternatively, we estimate the level of unemployment at that schooling level if real wages do not change. To complete the illustration, we perform the same two analyses for secondary and university level training. Our results are summarized in Tables 5.6 and 5.7.

Parameters were estimated for data covering total employment of Asians and Europeans in all sectors (excluding subsistence agriculture), overall average salaries, and total GDP. The results were no more informative than the equations just mentioned.

TABLE 5.5: Projections of Demand for Teachers, 1974[a]

Formal Schooling Level of Teachers	Primary	Secondary	Total
Graduate	144[b]	3,645[e]	3,789
Secondary	9,863[c]	2,938[f]	12,801
Primary	49,590[d]	—	49,590
Total	59,597	6,583	66,180

[a] No estimate is included for the number of teachers needed for teacher training. For example, about 80 percent of the teachers with full secondary education teaching in primary schools in 1967 had two years of teacher training beyond their formal schooling. More than two-thirds of the teachers with primary education had two years of additional training. The teacher projections, therefore, would appear to be underestimates of the likely 1974 totals.

[b] The number of university trained teachers per thousand students in primary school is assumed to remain constant at 0.10. This probably biases upward the estimate of graduate teachers in primary schools in 1974.

[c] The number of teachers with full secondary education per thousand students in primary schools is assumed to rise at the same rate in 1967–74 as it averaged in 1960–67. The ratio would thus reach 6.84 in 1974.

[d] The number of primary school trained teachers, in keeping with the 1960–67 trends of an increase in total teachers per thousand students and a decrease in education of teachers per thousand students, is assumed to rise at the same rate in 1967–74 as in 1960–67. The ratio would therefore be 34.39 in 1974.

[e] The ratio of graduate teachers per thousand students in secondary school is assumed to remain constant at 24.14 between 1967 and 1974. This probably overestimates the number of graduate teachers per thousand secondary school students.

[f] The ratio of teachers with full secondary education in secondary schools is assumed to continue to rise at the same rate as in 1960–67, bringing the ratio to 19.46 in 1974 and reversing the trend toward fewer teachers per student in secondary school.

Source: EC-173, Annex G.

TABLE 5.6: Growth Alternatives, 1968–74: Social Rate of Return, Wages and Employment for Two Labor Force Levels

Alternatives for Africans	(1) 1968 Social Rate of Return to Years 3–5 (*Percent*)	(2) Desired 1974 Equilibrium Social Rate to Years 3–5 (*Percent*)	(3) Change in Level 2 Labor Force Average Wage to Attain (2) (*Percent Change Over 1968 Wage*)	(4) 1974 Level 2 Average Wage (K£)	(5) Level 2 Employment Implied by (4) (*thousands*)
Using Unadjusted rates[a] to find W_1 and W_2					
Alternative 1[b]	16.4	10.0	−22.5	70.7	298.2
Alternative 2[c]	16.4	10.0	−35.0	47.2	402.3
Using Adjusted rates[a] to find W_1 and W_2					
Alternative 1	16.7	10.0	−23.0	69.3	302.6
Alternative 2	16.7	10.0	−35.5	45.8	411.3

[a] For socio-economic characteristics.
[b] Level 1 Labor Force does not grow 1968–1974.
[c] Level 1 Labor Force grows by approximately 3 percent annually 1968–74.

TABLE 5.7: Growth Alternatives, 1968–74: Wages and Employment for Africans with Primary and Secondary School and University Training

Africans in 1974	Assumed Real Wage, K£/Year 1974 (1957 prices)	Net Addition to Total Available Labor Force 1968–74	Total Employment 1974	New Jobs 1968–74	New Unemployment 1974	Unfilled Jobs 1974
With Primary School Training[a]						
Monetary sector, agri., ind. and comm.	78		502,000			
Primary school teachers	136		50,000			
Government (non-teachers)	no change, 1968–74		180,000			
Total		1,700,000[e]	732,000	340,000	500,000[d]	
With Secondary School Training[b]						
Excluding teachers						
If real wage does not change	400	} 280,000	102,000			
If full employment is desired	65	7,000[e]	293,000			
Teachers	same relative wages as in past		13,000	7,000		
Total		287,000		{ 96,000 / 287,000 }		
With University Training[b]						
Excluding teachers						
If real wage does not change	800	} 3,800	7,300	6,300		
If full employment is desired	1,890	2,000	4,800	3,800		
Teachers		5,800	2,100	2,000		
Total				{ 8,300 / 5,800 }		2,500

[a] Assumes growth of 7.5 percent in private industry and government.
[b] Assumes growth of 6.0 percent in private sector.
[c] Includes females.
[d] Assumes 50 percent of those who receive primary education do not enter available labor force.
[e] Assumed equal to total new employment plus replacement.

Equilibrium Supply of Labor, Rate of Return to Schooling Equal to 10 Percent

In the estimated equations, employment of African men is a function of the real wages (W/P) and real output (GDP/P) in the sector in which they work. We will use equations (5.5), which covers Africans in agriculture, and (5.8), which covers Africans in private industry and commerce. In applying these equations to make labor projections in line with growth estimates for these two sectors of the Kenyan economy, we retain the assumptions introduced in the previous section to justify the use of ethnic-sector groups as proxies for education categories. That is, we assume that equation (5.5)—demand for male African labor in monetary agriculture—represents the demand function for male Africans with 0 to 2 years of schooling, and that equation (5.8)—the demand for Africans in private industry and commerce—can be used to estimate demand for male urban Africans with 3 to 5 years of schooling. We will henceforth call the lower education group schooling level one, and the higher, schooling level two. No demand estimates are undertaken for Asians and Europeans because of the poor regression results for these two ethnic groups.

Our first step in using equation (5.8) to make an employment projection for the higher of the two education levels (3 to 5 years of schooling) requires that we fix the value of GDP in private industry and commerce in 1974, so that we may then deal with possible combinations of real wages and employment in this sector in 1974. For this purpose, we give equation (5.8) the following form.[8]

$$\log N_{2(1974)} = 2.2671 - 0.7408 \log (W/P)_{2(1974)} + 0.6648 \log GDP_{1(1974)} \quad (5.14)$$

The subscript refers to schooling level two (3 to 5 years of schooling).

We project GDP on the basis of annual growth rates. The real rate of growth of the total monetary sector during 1963–67 averaged about 5.9 percent, and that of monetary agriculture, 2.1 percent.[9] The growth of the latter over the longer period 1956–64 was 4.0 percent in current prices, and about 3.6 percent in real terms. While the planned rates of growth for the period 1964–70 of 7.1 percent[10] overall and 6.2 percent for monetary agriculture would appear too high in the light of the foregoing figures, the 2.1 percent growth rate in agriculture reflects particularly adverse conditions during 1964–67. We use the somewhat high figure of 7.0 percent for

---

[8] For convenience's sake, the intercept term in equation (5.8) has been changed from natural to decimal log.

[9] *Economic Survey*, 1968, p. 7, shows GDP growth in current market prices equal to 7.6 percent per annum between 1963–67. Prices increased by about 11 percent during this period, reducing the rate of growth to 5.9 percent in real terms.

[10] *Kenya Development Plan, 1964–70*, Nairobi, 1964, Table 1, p. 83.

the whole monetary economy, 4.0 percent for monetary agriculture, 7.1 percent for private industry and commerce, and 7.5 percent in private industry and government together.

The assumed 7.1 percent growth rate of GDP in private industry and commerce yields a 1974 GDP of K£235.9 million (in 1957 prices):

$$GDP_{1974} = 118.8 \, (1.071)^{10}$$
$$= 235.9 \text{ million K£}$$

Substituting this value of GDP_{1974}, equation (5.14) becomes:

$$\log N_{2(1974)} = 3.8445 - 0.7408 \log (W/P)_2.$$

This last equation shows the employment level in private industry and commerce as a function of the development of real wages in that sector, under the assumption of a 7.1 percent annual real growth in sectoral output. It is possible to immediately derive from it, for example, the salary implications of a given employment target, or the employment consequences of a certain salary policy. Under certain simplifying assumptions, and in combination with the age-income profiles discussed in Chapter III, this kind of equation enables us to determine how much the equilibrium employment level of persons with a given level of education changes with a certain increase or decrease in the rate of return to investment in that level of education.

Let us assume that after taking into due account the risk, non-pecuniary benefits, and externalities (i.e. effects which extend beyond the individual investor) the "desirable" social pecuniary rate of return to formal schooling, is found to be 10 percent per year, and that this is an equilibrium rate applying to all levels of education. The question can then be posed: what future output of the school system meets this condition?

The solution can be derived using the formula below. We are limiting the reasoning to the two skill levels which correspond to the two schooling levels for which we have demand functions: level (1) has 0 to 2 years of schooling, level (2) has 3 to 5 years. We assume that the difference in wages between two skill levels of labor yields the benefits of investing in additional schooling. The shift of wages between 1968 and 1974 is assumed to be constant over the whole age-earnings profile of each skill level.[11]

We start with the general equation which relates the equilibrium value of the internal rate of return (r_2) to costs (C_i) and benefits (b_i) associated with the investment:

$$\sum_{i=1}^{S'} \frac{C_i}{(1+r_2)^i} = \sum_{i=S'+1}^{n} \frac{W_2 - W_1}{(1+r_2)^i} = \sum_{i=S'+1}^{n} \frac{b_i}{(1+r_2)^i} \qquad (5.15)$$

---

[11] The base year for calculating wage shifts is 1968, to conform with data from our Labor Force Survey.

If we assume that the cost and benefit streams shift over time because of a shift in the age earnings profiles, the relation becomes:

$$0 = -\sum_{i=1}^{S'} \frac{C_i + \Delta W_{1t}}{(1+r_2)^i} + \sum_{i=S'+1}^{n} \frac{b_i + \Delta W_{2t} - \Delta W_{1t}}{(1+r_2)^i} \quad (5.16)$$

where C_i and b_i = the expected costs and benefits, respectively, of taking additional years of schooling needed to move from skill level 1 to level 2, each level being defined in years of schooling (earnings foregone are assumed to equal 0 in primary school, so $\Delta W_{1t} = 0$ for $1 \leq i \leq S'$ (see Annex F).

ΔW_{1t} = the shift in the age-income profile of skill level 1 in time period t, assumed constant over the entire age range, $(S' + 1) \leq i \leq n$.

ΔW_{2t} = the corresponding shift in the age-income profile of skill level 2 in time period t.

r_2 = the rate of return to the additional investment in schooling required to move from skill level 1 to skill level 2.

S' = the number of years of schooling (3) required to move from level 1 to level 2.

In order to find the number of school leavers from a certain level necessary to fulfill the condition $r_2 = 0.10$ in, say, 1974, we must determine the changes in W_1 and W_2 between 1968 and 1974 which meet this condition. In order to reach a single solution, a further assumption fixing the wage change for one of the two groups has to be made; we choose to work with W_1. To fix a solution for W_1, we assume that the substitution pattern represented by equation (5.5) for agricultural employment holds for the group with 0 to 2 years of schooling, just as we assumed that equation (5.8) represents the demand for the group with 3 to 5 years of schooling. Analogously to our restatement of equation (5.8) as equation (5.14), equation (5.5) becomes:[12]

$$\log N_{1(1974)} = 3.2598 - 1.2301 \log (W/P)_{1(1974)} + 0.6724 \log (\text{GDP})_{1(1974)} \quad (5.17)$$

Continuing the analogous treatment, we apply the 4.0 percent growth rate for agricultural GDP to the 1964 GDP[13] of 41.72 million K£ and arrive

---
[12] As before, the intercept of equation (5.5) has been converted from natural to decimal log.
[13] This is the last year of the old income series on which our time series analysis was based.

at a sectoral product of 61.83 million K£ in 1974 (in 1957 prices). Equation (5.17) thus becomes

$$\log N_{1(1974)} = 3.2598 - 1.2301 \log(W/P)_{1(1974)} + 1.2044$$
$$= 4.4642 - 1.2301 \log(W/P)_{1(1974)}$$

Using this form of the equation, the average real wages of workers with the lowest skill level can be determined under numerous plausible assumptions about the likely development of employment and wages of this group. We consider only two:

a) Agricultural wage employment does not increase until the target year (1974);
b) It increases at the same rate as the population (2.9 percent a year), or, what amounts to roughly the same thing, it increases to an extent which leaves the real income level of that group unaffected, i.e. according to (5.5) and our assumption for the growth of agricultural GDP, at 0.6724×4.0 percent = 2.7 percent annually.

While the first case resembles most closely the previous ten years (see Table 5.3),[14] the other alternative is probably more acceptable from the point of view of social policy and employment.

Using equation (5.17), the average real wages (W_1) of workers with the lowest skill level can be determined for each of the two alternatives:

a) $W_{1(1974)} = $ K£55.8
b) $W_{1(1974)} = $ K£45.3.

The corresponding wage changes over the six-year period 1968–74, would hence be:[15]

a) $\Delta W_{1('68-'74)} = $ K£10.5
b) $\Delta W_{1('68-'74)} = $ K£0.0

This represents a 23 percent increase in real wages over the 1968 wage under the first assumption, and a zero percent increase under the second, where there is a 2.7 percent annual increase in the labor force in skill level (1). We can now apply these percentages to the average observed monthly

---

[14] The real annual wage for level (1) (agriculture) was 45.3 K£ (1957 prices) in 1964. We assume this real wage remains constant through 1968. Real wages in agriculture did not change between 1964 and 1966.

[15] In order to mesh the base year of ΔW_1 with the year of the Labor Force Survey, 1968 was chosen as the base. Therefore, the computed ΔW_1 is calculated by taking the difference between $(W/P)_{1974}$ and $(W/P)_{1968}$, assuming, for the moment, that the latter equals real wages for Africans in wage agriculture in 1964 (1957 prices).

income of the urban labor force with 0 to 2 years of education (Table 3.3). We then find an absolute change in wages between 1968 and 1974:

a) $\Delta W_{1('68-'74)}$ = 320 Ksh/month times 0.23 = K£44.4/year
b) $\Delta W_{1('68-'74)}$ = K£0.

Using the data on the costs and benefits of investing in Standards III, IV, and V (3 to 5 years of primary school) from Table 3.2, column one (Unadjusted age-income profiles), as values for C_i and b_i in equation (5.16), letting $r_2 = 0.10$, and taking the 1968–74 wage change values from above, we get the following alternative solutions for the absolute change in wages between 1968 and 1974 for the higher skill level:[16]

a) $\Delta W_2 = \dfrac{-840.9}{6.77} + 44.4$
$= -124.2 + 44.4$
$= -\text{K£}79.8/\text{year}$
b) $\Delta W_2 = -124.2 + 0$
$= -\text{K£}124.2/\text{year}.$

Thus, under the assumption of a constant level (1) employment figure, by 1974 wages of level (2) skills (W_2) would have to fall by K£79.8, or 22.5 percent of mean income (see Table 3.3) in order to reduce to 10 percent per annum the unadjusted social rate of return to investing in the third, fourth and fifth years of schooling for urban male Africans. This rate was 16.4 percent per annum in 1968. Similarly, in the second alternative where level (1) employment increases between 1968 and 1974, W_2 must fall by K£124.2, or 35 percent of mean income, for r_2 to equal 10 percent in 1974.

In order to estimate from equation (5.14) the increase in level (2) employment which these decreases in real income represent, we apply the percentage decreases to average wages of Africans in private industry and commerce. In 1964, the average wage (in 1957 prices) in private industry and commerce for Africans was K£112.3 annually. Employment in 1964 (corrected to the 1963 measurement of employment) was 129,200. Assume that the real wage decrease described in the previous paragraph can be extrapolated linearly to 1964. Thus the 22.5 percent decrease in wages between 1968 and 1974 becomes a 37 percent decrease between 1964 and 1974, and the 35 percent decrease becomes a 58 percent decrease between 1964 and 1974.

For the two alternatives these translate into (1957 prices):

a) $\Delta W_2 = -41.6\text{K£}/\text{year}$ and
b) $\Delta W_2 = -65.1\text{K£}$ year,

---

[16] See Annex F for complete solution for ΔW_2.

and (5.14) becomes, for the two alternatives:

a) $\log N_{2(1974)} = 3.8445 - 0.7408 \log(70.7)$
$= 2.4745$
$N_{2(1974)} = 298{,}200$

and

b) $\log N_{2(1974)} = 3.8445 - 0.7408 \log(47.2)$
$N_{2(1974)} = 402{,}300$

These figures indicate that if the social rate of return to investment in incomplete primary schooling were to attain 10 percent per annum, real incomes of those with 3 to 5 years of schooling would have to fall and employment would increase sharply.

If the social costs and benefits adjusted for socio-economic variables (column (2) of Table 3.2) are used instead of the unadjusted profiles, ΔW_2 and N_2 are essentially unchanged. Since the social rate of return to the third, fourth, and fifth years of schooling is almost the same when calculated on the basis of adjusted rather than unadjusted income streams (16.7 versus 16.4 percent), the real wage reduction necessary to bring the rate to 10 percent is only slightly greater. By the same token, employment of those with 3 to 5 years of schooling is also about the same.

Employment and Wage Changes, Labor Supply Exogenously Determined

Earlier, the discussion of employment and real wages in the monetary economy assumed that the future supply of manpower with different educational qualifications is a function of future wages and rates of return. In this section, supply projections (see Table 5.1), are used as the point of departure, and the wage implications of alternative employment targets for primary school trained labor are analyzed.

According to the supply projections, there will be a gross increase of 1.7 million in the supply of labor with 1 to 7 years of schooling between 1966 and 1974. African employment in the monetary sector of agriculture and private industry and commerce totalled 377,400 in 1966. The average education of this group is probably very close to the average education of the African male population, i.e. between 2.0 and 2.5 years of schooling.

If we also assume a working life of 33 years, i.e. an annual depreciation of 3 percent in the labor stock, the residual stock in 1974 is 286,800—a decrease of 90,600. Therefore, if it is desired to employ all new entrants into the monetary sector at this level, more than 1.6 million new jobs will be needed. Even under the extreme assumption that wage employment will be sought by males only, the increase in the labor supply of approximately 0.8 million cannot be absorbed in the monetary sector by any plausible combination of increased output and decreased wages, as the preceding section makes clear.

A more realistic employment assumption for the 1966–74 period is that only about 25 percent of males with various amounts of primary education find work in the monetary sector (both agriculture and private industry and commerce). There may be reasons why males with less schooling may be employed in agriculture, where physical ability probably counts for more than additional schooling, but probably the majority of males employed will have completed primary education. The remaining available men with 7 or fewer years of schooling are either voluntarily or involuntarily unemployed, or find work in the subsistence sector. If the rate of growth of output in the private monetary sector is set equal to 6 percent, (weighted average of 4.0 and 7.1 percent) and the male labor force employed in 1974 equal to about 500,000, we find that average real wages in 1974 (1957 prices) would have to be K£78 for those in the primary schooling category (1 to 7 years) who are employed.[17] Average real wages of Africans in agriculture and private industry and commerce in 1966 (1957 prices) equaled K£76, so in the eight-year period 1966–74, real wages of the 1 to 7 years of schooling group would have to remain essentially constant to allow even 20 percent of the newly available male labor force with 1 to 7 years of schooling to find employment in the private monetary sector.

An additional 50,000 or so individuals with primary schooling—almost all KPE certificate holders—might be able to find employment as primary school teachers after suitable professional preparation, at an average yearly salary of about K£170 in 1967 prices[18] or K£136 in 1957 prices, assuming that the structure of real wages of the variously qualified teachers does not

---

[17] The equation used to determine this figure is derived by totalling 1966 wages, employment, and GDP for the monetary agriculture, private industry, and commerce sectors together (K£76.1, 377,400, and K£190.2 million), and substituting into the equation below, in which the price and income elasticities of employment are assumed to be -1.0 and 0.67, respectively. These figures are unweighted averages of the elasticities in the private monetary sector of the economy as given in equations (5.5) and (5.8). A priori reasoning suggests that the price elasticity of the two relevant categories of labor (0 to 2 years, 3 to 5 years of schooling) would be lower than that for either taken alone. For simplicity's sake, however, a combined elasticity of unity is used here:

$$\text{Log}(377.4) = A - 1.0 \log(76.1) + 0.67 \log(190.2)$$

Solving for A yields a constant term equal to 2.9311, so

$$\text{Log } N_{1974} = 2.9311 - 1.0 \log(W/P)_{1974} + 0.67 \log \text{GDP}_{1974}.$$

[18] The average salary we use here is an average of the salaries given for the P3, P4, and KPE categories of primary teachers in Table 2.5, each weighted according to its share in the total number of P3, P4, and KPE teachers in 1967. Projections of teacher requirements are given in Table 5.5.

shift and that teachers with only primary schooling are not completely phased out of teaching. This means that about 550,000 Africans with 7 or fewer years of schooling will be employed in commercial agriculture, private industry and commerce, and as primary school teachers, if real wages in the former two stay constant and real wages of primary school teachers relative to more highly trained teachers stay about the same as in 1967. The estimate also assumes that all Africans employed in commercial agriculture and private industry and commerce fall into the primary schooling category.

If we further assume that the GDP elasticity of employment in government of Africans with primary schooling equals unity, that the wage elasticity equals zero (i.e. that average government wages do not change), and that all high- and middle-level African manpower in the 1964 manpower survey data are employed by the government, then approximately 97,000 non-teaching Africans with primary schooling were employed by the government in 1964.[19] If we project this figure to 1974 by means of a 6 percent growth rate, the employment of those with complete or incomplete primary schooling in 1974 in government rises to 180,000 and total employment in all sectors rises to 730,000, of which 340,000 represent the addition to the labor force between 1966 and 1974, including replacement of retirees. Even if we assume that only one-half of those becoming available at this level (1.7 million) in the eight-year period wish to enter the monetary labor force (850,000), about one-half million people will not find jobs in the monetary segment of the economy unless real wages fall rather sharply, an unlikely occurrence.

Demand Projections and Equilibrium Estimates for Africans with Secondary Schooling

Equilibrium Supply of Labor, Rate of Return to Schooling Equal to 10 Percent

Turning from primary to secondary schooling, we ask what decrease in wages is required to reduce the latter's rate of return to 10 percent annually.

---

[19] The figure we use is a residual. Government employment totalled 173,700 in 1964. It is assumed that the 12,800 Asians and Europeans in public service in that year all had more than primary schooling. The 1964 manpower survey shows 70,800 high- and middle-level manpower in Kenya outside of agriculture. If we subtract from this figure the 12,800 non-Africans in public service plus the 10,100 Europeans and 25 percent of the 28,000 Asians in private industry and commerce, we arrive at 41,000 with more than primary schooling who are Africans. This is probably somewhat of an overestimate, since skilled manual labor and technical and semi-professional labor is all assumed to have more than primary schooling. If all 41,000 were employed by the government, this leaves about 120,000 Africans with 0 to 7 years of schooling employed by the government in 1964, 23,000 of which are primary school teachers, leaving 97,000 non-teachers.

According to the Labor Force Survey, average earnings in 1968 for employees with secondary schooling were about K£400 annually[20] and about K£240 annually for those with completed primary schooling (see Table 3.6, 7-All category). Costs are estimated from Tables 4.2 and 4.3. Using the simplified rate of return formula which assumes that the average income difference is a perpetuity and that cost is incurred at one point in time ($c = y/r$), we find that the social rate of return to 10.5 years of schooling, adjusted for socio-economic variables, is equal to:

$$r = \frac{y}{c} = \frac{400 - 240}{480} = 0.33 \qquad (5.18)$$

or 33 percent, in 1968. This is an overestimate of the rate of return, as can be seen from a comparison with the more detailed discount formula (equation (5.15)).

As the average real income of persons with secondary education tends to fall toward the full employment equilibrium of K£65 (see below), there may be substitution of secondary school leavers for persons with only primary education. This would tend to hold up the wages of secondary-trained persons and lower the wages of primary leavers. If average real wages of primary school leavers fall by, say, 25 percent, to K£180 annually, income foregone would be decreased by 25 percent to K£135 and total costs to about K£435. This would mean that in order to lower the rate of return on investment in secondary schooling to 10 percent, real wages of Africans with secondary education should fall to about K£223 annually. As we show below, even at this real wage, a considerable number of persons with secondary schooling could still remain unemployed.

Since no suitable estimates are available for the relationships between the employment of African school leavers from post-primary levels, their wages, and the growth of sectoral output (especially in the non-agricultural sectors), an attempt is made here to approximate these relationships for employees with secondary school training and to assess from them (i) the employment effect of a constant wage assumption, and (ii) the wage effect of a full employment assumption between 1968 and 1974.

We can reasonably expect that the wage elasticity of employment of both secondary school and university leavers is lower than that of primary leavers, and the GDP elasticity higher (as discussed on p. 102.). We make

---

[20] The K£400 figure is arrived at by assuming the average level of schooling in the 8 to 13 group to be 10.5 years—which is also the average in the sample—and the average salary of those with 10.5 years of schooling as Ksh 660 monthly, a figure which lies between half and three quarters of the way between the average salary of those with nine years of schooling (505.2 Ksh) and that of the eleven-year schooling group (763.5 Ksh). See last line of Table 3.6.

the assumptions (probably realistic) that the wage elasticity of employment for those with secondary school education equals -0.5 and that the GDP elasticity of employment for this group is 1.5. Our purpose here is to demonstrate this particular line of approach to the problem of demand projections for different labor categories. Thus,

$$\log N_s = A - 0.5 \log(W/P) + 1.5 \log \text{GDP}_{(P+G)}. \qquad (5.19)$$

We start from a 1964 figure for GDP outside agriculture (i.e. private industry, commerce, and government) of K£146.5 million in 1957 prices, (see Table 5.4), and an average income of African employees with secondary schooling of about K£400 annually in 1968 (see above), which corresponds to about K£320 in 1957 prices.[21] If real wages are assumed constant between 1964 and 1968, 1964 wages in 1957 prices are K£320.

To solve for A in equation (5.19) we need estimates of secondary level employment in 1964. The 1964 manpower survey suggests that there were about 41,000 Africans with middle and higher levels of schooling (see footnote 19). In 1961 there were about 1,000 Africans in Kenya who had university training.[22] If we presume that another 500 Africans underwent university training between 1961–1964 (see Table 2.4), we arrive at a very crude estimate of 1,300 Africans (excluding 300 teachers—again a rough estimate) with university training in 1964, and of 40,000 Africans with some secondary education.

In the same year there were 4,800 teachers with some secondary training teaching in primary schools ($P_2 + P_1 + S_1 + \text{CSC} + \text{HSC}$ teachers) of whom a maximum of about 4,000 may have been Africans; about 25 percent of the 500 secondary school teachers with secondary training in 1964 were Africans. The total secondary-trained African teaching force in 1964 was thus of the order of 4,000, which leaves 36,000 secondary-trained Africans in jobs other than teaching. Using the GDP, wage and employment figures for 1964, we can solve for A in equation (5.19):

$$A = -0.4401$$

Applying the 7.5 percent target growth rate for GDP in private industry and government combined of the 1966–70 Development Plan leads to a 1974 sectoral product of K£293.3 million (in 1957 prices). Consequently, (5.19) becomes:

$$\log N_{S(1974)} = -0.4401 - 0.5 \log(W/P) + 1.5 \log(293.3)$$

Assuming that real wages do not change between 1968 and 1974 (K£320

---

[21] The cost of living index (1957 = 100) was approximately 125 in 1968 and 112.5 in 1964. See Table 5.4.

[22] Guy Hunter, *Education for a Developing Region*, (London: George Allen & Unwin, 1963), p. 58.

in 1957 prices), secondary-trained employment in non-teaching jobs estimated from equation (5.19) would be slightly over 100,000 in 1974. In addition, Table 5.5 shows that 13,000 secondary school trained teachers would be employed in 1974 if relative wages of teachers were to remain about the same as in the period 1960-67.[23] About 11,500 of them would be Africans. Total employment of Africans with secondary schooling is thus estimated to be about 114,000 if real wages remained the same.

Employment and Wage Changes, Labor Supply Exogenously Determined

We now look at the output from secondary schools. According to Table 5.1, about 280,000 individuals from all ethnic groups with any amount of secondary schooling will become available for employment between 1965 and 1974. The 1964 manpower survey shows 64,500 employees in the high- and middle-level manpower category who are below the professional and top management level. If we assume that they all have at least secondary schooling and that 2.5 percent retire annually from the labor force, a stock of 48,400 will remain in 1974. The total available labor force with secondary schooling in 1974 will thus be 328,000.

Assuming that employment of non-Africans with secondary schooling in public service and private industry and commerce will remain constant at 30,000 between 1964 and 1974 (which is probably an overestimate) and subtracting this figure from the total available labor force, gives us a stock of secondary-trained African males of about 300,000.

We projected that 13,000 secondary school trained teachers will be employed in secondary and primary school in 1974. If we assume that 2.5 percent of the 1967 teaching force of 7,000 will retire each year, then 1,400 will have left the profession by 1974 and 7,400 new teachers (1974 projections minus the remainder of the 1967 stock) will be needed, all of whom, it is assumed, will be Africans. Subtracting this figure from the above total of 300,000 leaves about 293,000 persons for whom jobs outside teaching would have to be found in order to secure full employment of secondary school trained Africans in 1974.

Under the elasticity assumption on which equation (5.19) is based, real annual wages of Africans with secondary education will have to fall to K£65 (in 1957 prices) to assure full employment. This wage would be lower than average real wages of employees with primary schooling if real wages of the latter did not fall. We would consequently expect that employers would substitute labor with secondary schooling for labor with primary schooling if relative wages of the former fall. Total 1974 primary school employment in non-agricultural sectors, however, will be only 530,000,

---

[23] This figure does not include teachers used for teacher training.

even if we assume that the figure of 200,000 employed in monetary agriculture in 1966 will remain constant until 1974. Full employment of the secondary school output of the years 1968–74 would mean that a substantial portion of primary school employment outside agriculture would have to be replaced by secondary school trained labor.

Alternatively, if real salaries of Africans with secondary schooling stayed constant at K£320 (at 1957 prices), only 102,000 of the 293,000 seeking employment outside teaching could be accommodated under the assumed conditions. Clearly, our elasticity assumptions may be wrong. However, to guarantee full employment for this category of labor under the hypotheses of constant real wages and a wage elasticity of 0.5, GDP elasticity would have to be about 2.0 (i.e. for every one percent increase in GDP, secondary employment would rise by 2 percent—a fairly high ratio). If wage elasticity were claimed to be higher, GDP elasticity would be lower to reach full employment.

Demand Projections and Equilibrium Estimates for Africans with University Training

Equilibrium Supply of Labor, Rate of Return to Schooling Equal to 10 Percent

To determine the change in wages needed to reach a rate of return of 10 percent annually for investment in higher education, we can make the same type of estimate as we do for secondary schooling. Assuming the average amount of schooling of university-trained people to be 15 years, the average cost of those two years of university education to be K£3,400, and the average difference in salaries between Africans with and without these two years of schooling to be K£340 annually (K£1,000 minus K£660, see Tables 5.6 and 5.7), the estimated rate of return following the perpetuity formula is 10 percent. No change in wages is thus necessary to reach the target rate of return.

To project the demand for labor with university training, we assume that the wage elasticity of employment for university-trained persons is equal to that of those with secondary schooling, −0.5, and that the income elasticity of employment is 2.5, a figure higher than the corresponding elasticity for secondary level employment. As in the equations for the primary and secondary level labor, the estimate of the demand function for university-trained persons does not include an approximation for the elasticity of substitution with labor from lower education categories (which may be relatively high). The data available do not even give a clue as to the order of magnitude for this elasticity. The simplified demand equation for those with university training, is then as follows:

$$\log N_u = A' - 0.5 \log (W/P) + 2.5 \log \text{GDP}_{(P+G)} \qquad (5.20)$$

As in equation (5.19), 1964 GDP outside agriculture equals K£146.5 million, and the average 1968 income of employees with university education, about K£800[24] (both in 1957 prices). Assuming that real salaries have not changed appreciably between 1964 and 1968, the 1968 figure can be used for the 1964 demand equation.

We estimated above that there were about 1,300 Africans with university training outside of teaching in 1964. Using the employment, real earnings, and GDP figures for that year, we can solve for A' in equation (5.20):

$$A' = -3.8491$$

Introducing the 7.5 percent target growth of GDP in private industry and government, equation (5.20) becomes:

$$\log N_{u(1974)} = -3.8491 - 0.5 \log(W/P) + 2.5 \log(293.3)$$

What will the demand for university trained labor be if we assume that real wages do not change between 1968 and 1974 (i.e. remain constant at K£800 in 1957 prices)? Employment in non-teaching jobs, estimated from equation (5.20), would be 7,300 in 1974. In addition, Table 5.6 shows a total demand by the school system for about 3,800 graduate teachers in 1974. If we assume that 50 of the 200 or so African graduate teachers in Kenya in 1964 will have retired by 1974, new demand for all graduate teachers will be about 3,700. If the non-African graduate teaching force remained at the 1967 level of about 1,700, this would leave about 2,000 new teaching positions for African graduates (out of a total of 2,100). If real wages remained constant and the structure of wages for teachers behaved as assumed in Table 5.6, total demand for university-trained Africans would equal 9,400 in 1974.

Employment and Wage Changes, Labor Supply Exogenously Determined

According to the Manpower Survey of 1964, 6,300 employees had university training. Fifteen hundred of these were Africans: 200 teachers and 1,300 other employees. If the employment of non-Africans with university training remained constant until 1974, 4,800 non-Africans would be employed in that year.

According to the supply projections of Table 5.1, about 7,800 university-trained persons will meanwhile become available, a high percentage of whom will be Africans. Assume that the latter's share were 75 percent, and

---

[24] The average income in 1968 of those with university training (K£1,000) is taken as a rough average of the mean salary of Africans in the sample with 13 and those with 17 years of school (see Tables 3.10 and 2.11).

that the 25 percent of non-Africans replaced leaving or retiring non-Africans in the labor force. In 1974, there would thus be 5,800 Africans with university training available for the labor force. Since we estimated in the previous paragraph that some 2,000 Africans would be employed as teachers, the remaining 3,800 African graduates would be available for non-teaching jobs. Adding the 1,100 or so university-trained Africans remaining from the 1968 stock outside teaching (1,300 minus 200 retirees between 1968 and 1974, assuming a 40 year working life), we arrive at a total of 4,800.

We estimated above, however, that the demand for university-trained Africans outside teaching (if their real wages remained constant) would be 7,300 in 1974—a fact which, given the supply figure of 4,800, implies a substantial shortage at this level in 1974. In order to reach equilibrium at an employment level of 4,800, real wages of Africans would have to rise to K£1,890 (in 1957 prices), or to almost twice the present level.[25]

Like the secondary school demand estimates for graduates, the university approximations are very sensitive to changes in the GDP elasticity of employment. Thus, an assumption of a 2.0 GDP elasticity and a 0.5 wage elasticity for university-trained persons yields an employment figure of 5,200 in non-teaching jobs at constant average wages, a much lower figure than the 7,300 estimate with a GDP elasticity of 2.5. Similarly, a 2.0 assumption would imply a rise in real wages from K£800 to K£943 in order to balance supply with demand outside the teaching profession.

Unlike the secondary school demand estimates, the university approximation is very sensitive to the projections of teacher demand, and thus indirectly very sensitive to the projection of enrollments in secondary education. If the figure of 151,000 pupils in 1974—on which the teacher demand estimate in Table 5.6 rests—were on the low side, the wages of university-trained teachers would tend to rise even more sharply between 1968 and 1974. If, for example, the rate of growth of secondary school enrollments in 1967–74 equaled the rate observed from 1960–67, there would be about 300,000 secondary school students enrolled in 1974; the demand for graduate teachers, given the assumptions of Table 5.6, would equal almost 7,500 in that year, of whom 5,800 would be Africans. This means that only 1,000 Africans would be available for non-teaching jobs. Even

---

[25] It should be noted, however, that the teacher projections we use are implicitly based on current relative wages, conceding only small increases or decreases in relative wages. However, if wages in the non-teacher labor market rose by very much, either graduate teacher wages would also rise, inducing schools to lower the graduate teacher per student ratio, or teachers would leave teaching to take advantage of relatively higher wages in the non-teaching jobs. In the long run, this would tend to reduce wages outside teaching.

with a GDP elasticity of demand for university-trained persons equal to 2.0, average annual wages of that group would have to rise to unrealistic levels of about K£23,000 to balance demand and supply.

Results and Conclusions

The methodology developed for educational planning in this study projects alternative future wage and employment patterns by using as a base both estimates of current wages of labor with different amounts of formal schooling and current rates of return to investment in additional schooling. Two types of estimates are made:

a) The calculation of equilibrium supply of labor with different amounts of schooling, assuming that the supply is a function of rates of return to schooling, and that the desired level of rates of return to all levels of schooling is 10 percent; and

b) Estimates of the real wage level consistent with full employment in 1974 for a given school output between 1968 and 1974, assuming that the supply of skills is independent of the rates of return, and alternatively, estimates of surpluses or shortages of labor of different educational qualifications given a certain level of real wages. (This approach resembles customary manpower requirements calculations.)

The results of these estimates, while admittedly crude, illustrate the sensitiveness of projections of demand for the outputs of a school system to changes in wages. If wages are not flexible, rapidly increasing output from schools can leave large numbers of educated persons without employment. Even if wages are flexible, declines in real wages may have to be unrealistically large in order to achieve full employment. Unemployment of trained manpower could, under such circumstances, be an inescapable result of the rapid expansion of an education system in a developing country.

As an illustration of a flexible wage planning model, our estimates for Kenya show that most of those Africans taking primary schooling in the next five years will by necessity remain either unemployed or in subsistence farming even if a rapid fall in real wages were to come about. The rapid growth of the number of Africans with secondary schooling between 1968 and 1974 would tend either to lower considerably their real income or to create substantial unemployment among secondary school leavers. Because of the large increase in secondary school enrollment and the resulting strong demand for university-trained Africans to fill teaching posts, it seems possible that there will be upward pressure on the wages of Africans with university training during this or an even longer period.

As a result of the downward pressure on the wages of secondary school leavers and the upward pressure on wages of university graduates, there is likely to be an increased recruitment of labor with secondary schooling both into jobs normally held by those with university training (especially teaching posts) and, as we have noted before, into jobs now held by those with primary schooling. In other words, the demand and supply situation would lead to an upgrading of many industry jobs requiring a fairly low level of training, and a downgrading of other jobs (presumably largely in the public sector) requiring a high level of training. Thus, the effects of the downward pressure on secondary wages may be partly dampened by the effects of a further downward pressure on primary school leavers' wages, on the one hand, and of an easing of the upward pressure on wages of university graduates on the other.

This downward pressure on the wages of those with primary schooling will tend to reduce even further the present low rates of return to that level, giving it, from the point of view of society, essentially the character of a "merit want" beyond purely economic justification. The rate of return to secondary schooling would initially fall, but the fall would be checked by the substitution process described above, which would both check the fall in job opportunities and lower the alternative income that could be secured by leaving school at the end of the primary cycle.

After 1974 a continued rapid growth in secondary school outputs might result in a sharp decline in the corresponding wages and possibly also in substantial unemployment at this level, causing the return to investment to decline sharply. At a later stage this decline might be reinforced by the increased supply of university graduates and a reversal of the substitution process described above. The rate of return to investment in university training, however, is not likely to fall even after 1974 if our forecast of a marked shortage of university-trained persons by that year is correct. Only if the universities' output were to catch up with and surpass the future demand for this category would the rate of return to university training fall.

Whatever the outcome of these speculations, it should be clear from this study that the state of our knowledge about the functioning of labor markets is most unsatisfactory. The theoretical framework we have used here is not matched by an adequate amount of information, and we are thus unable to test, reformulate, and improve our tools. It thus appears that the procurement of relevant data should rank high among the tasks of education and manpower economists.

VI

OUTCOME OF THE STUDY

In looking back on the preceding chapters, the authors cannot help wondering whether the range of topics covered in this study has not been so broad that the major results become difficult to see clearly and to relate one to another. For the benefit of those readers whose main interest is in the practical usefulness rather than the methodological details of the cost-benefit approach, our experience has been put into a more concise form in this concluding chapter.

The Specific Results

Rates of Return to Education in Kenya

To recapitulate the line of our analysis, we set out by assuming that additional education is associated with additional lifetime earnings, but that a number of intervening variables complicate this relationship. These variables can be grouped into three clusters: one relating to socio-economic background, the second to occupation, and the third to ability effects assumed to be manifested in examination results. We then attempt to disentangle these forces by means of a multiple regression analysis of data collected in Kenya in 1968 and to subject the initial earnings estimates to a series of successive corrections (Chapter III).

The next step is to combine cost data with the earnings profiles we obtain for urban African males by age and education group to obtain net lifetime earnings streams, and to calculate internal rates of return to a series of schooling packages (Chapter IV). The series we consider are: incomplete primary education (up to 4 years), completion of primary (5 to 7 years), incomplete secondary (8 to 9 years), completion of secondary (10 to 11 years), higher secondary (12 to 13 years), and university education (14 to 17 years). The private rates of return are corrected for taxes, socio-economic factors, and examination performance. The social rates are corrected for mortality, socio-economic factors, examination performance, union membership, public employment, and KPE certificate effect.

The initial unadjusted rates for urban African males suggest that from the viewpoint of a private investor, completion of primary and of secondary education are by far the most profitable choices (with rates of more than 50 percent), whereas the rates for all other packages are of the order of 25 percent (24–27 percent). The tax adjustments lead to some reduction of the rates for completion of secondary education and for post-secondary education (15–20 percent), but it is only after all the corrections listed above have been made that profound changes in the ranking of the private rates of return occur. Incomplete primary and completion of secondary come out on top with rates of return of 30 percent, and completion of primary and incomplete secondary are on the bottom with rates of the order of 10 percent (9–13 percent); higher secondary and university education have an intermediate position in the 20 percent range (20–33 percent).

The picture is somewhat different for the social rates of return. At the outset the ranking is similar, with completion of primary and of secondary education showing a lead over the rest (34–38 percent) and the rates of return to university education trailing behind all other rates (9 percent). The adjustment for mortality has virtually no effect on the rates (less than one percent), but the corrections for mortality, socio-economic variables, and examination scores together give the completion of secondary education a clear lead over incomplete primary and higher secondary (about 25 vs. 15 percent), whereas rates for the other education categories vary between about 5 and 10 percent. After further adjustments for examination certificate and public employment effects, complete secondary education (with about a 20 percent return) appears to be the most profitable educational alternative. It is followed by a group of three with a 15 percent return (incomplete and completion of primary and higher secondary education); the returns to university and incomplete secondary education are in the 5–10 percent range.

The considerable absolute changes in profitability which occur as a result of the corrections for non-educational determinants of earnings, and which in some cases affect the ranking of the whole set of education options, should serve as a warning against too straightforward an interpretation of uncorrected rates of return. While one should not expect similar analyses in other developing countries to come up with exact copies of our results, the relative impact of the various types of corrections and the variation from one educational level to another may well follow similar patterns. On the other hand, the differences in private and social profitability derive from the varying degree of public subsidization of schooling and, to a lesser extent, from progressive taxation of earnings. In other words, these differences depend on quite specific fiscal arrangements in a given country rather than on broader socio-economic or cultural patterns which might apply to a larger region.

Since the above-mentioned rates for primary education refer to the few fortunate school leavers who succeed in finding urban jobs, they convey a somewhat optimistic picture. A further correction is therefore in order. We make an attempt to derive rate-of-return estimates from rural income data and assess the effect of unemployment, for both our two lowest educational options (Chapter IV).[1] The combined rural–urban social rates corrected for unemployment are substantially lower (14 vs. 16 and 11 vs. 38 percent) than those for the urban survey group alone (unadjusted except for age), in spite of several positive biases in our estimates of the rural component. Further downward adjustments would occur if educated females, whose earnings and employment probabilities are consistently lower than those for similarly educated males, were included in the analysis.

In Chapter IV, we restrict our analysis of the profitability of education to a comparison among various alternative packages. This outlook would be adequate if we were interested only in finding out how best to allocate a given total education budget over the various levels and branches of education.[2] (The corresponding issue from an individual's point of view would be whether to have one son continue secondary education, or send two daughters to primary school, for example.) If we want rather to assess investment in education relative to investment in various types of physical capital, we need some benchmark rates of return from other sectors of the economy. Table 6.1 provides us with a set of such figures.

It can be argued that all these rates of return to investment in physical capital are suitable yardsticks for evaluating the social rates of return to investment in education. However, they are probably a poor means of

---

[1] The other education groups presently show only negligible unemployment and rural employment, with the exception of the incomplete secondary education category, whose prospects appear to be deteriorating rapidly.

[2] Since in the short run we are faced with given numbers of teachers, pupils, facilities, etc., there is little room for budgetary maneuvering. The question of optimum resource allocation has thus either to be posed from a long-term viewpoint, or to be applied to additional rather than total budget appropriations.

TABLE 6.1: Rates of Return to Investment in Physical Capital

Field of Investment	Average Rate of Return (percent)
Thirty-one major companies dealt in on the Nairobi stock exchange[a]	
Yield p.a. on ordinary shares	9.1
Earnings on net assets	11.1
Net profit on ordinary capital	17.1
Gross profit on ordinary capital	35.4
Seven World Bank projects totalling $40 million	>15
Various agricultural projects	
Smallholder tea development	50
Agricultural administration and extension	
Nyeri District	40
Elgeyo-Marakwet District	35
Central Nyanza District	12
Mwea-Tebere irrigation scheme	22
Perkerra irrigation scheme	11
Low density resettlement	6–9[b]
New settlement on rain-fed land	4

[a] Figures refer to 1966/67.
[b] 6 percent = 70 percent fulfillment of targets, 9 percent = 90 percent fulfillment.
Sources: *Nairobi Stock Exchange Official Yearbook 1968*, Nairobi, 1968; C. H. Ruthenberg, *African Agricultural Production Policy in Kenya, 1952–1965*, Berlin–Heidelberg, 1966; various World Bank documents.

orientation as far as private investors are concerned. The only item which from the individual's point of view may be a meaningful alternative is investment in industrial stocks. Again this in all likelihood applies only to a few of those parents who live in Nairobi or the main urban areas, and to educational investment decisions beyond the primary level. For the great majority of parents the above figures are clearly irrelevant.

What then are comparable investments? Since the great majority of parents are from rural areas, the most likely alternative to spending on school fees is small-scale investment on the farm. The monthly salary of one farm worker who may be needed to cope with peak labor requirements is roughly equivalent to the annual primary school fees for one child (K£3). Other possible investments would be in improved seeds, fertilizers, or pesticides. Many projects, such as the purchase of livestock or major land improvements, would be beyond the range of primary school fees but may be comparable to the annual fee-level in Harambee schools (K£25–50). There is no doubt that these agricultural investments would result in sizeable benefits, though lower than those to stocks or other investments.

However, this assumes that capital markets and other investment outlets are equally available to everyone. In fact, different kinds of investment may be open to persons with different amounts of schooling, not because of the schooling, but because they are physically or socially remote from the country's economic mainstream. The average rate of return to alternative investments may be lower for less educated people, and education may be one of the most available and obvious investments for individuals. In this case, individual decisions about further schooling would be determined by the rates of return to those investments that are within the realm of the group the individual belongs to, not by the relationship of the rates to each other or to those for a universal, abstract set of alternative investments.

We advance the tentative conclusion that an average Kenyan family, particularly a rural one, may not be selecting the "best" investment when it sends its children to primary school, though this depends on the available alternative investments. Even if we concede that the overall rate of return to investments on small farms may be as low as say, 3–5 percent, this still might compare favorably with the fully corrected urban-rural set of private rates for different amounts of primary education, in view of the upward biases built into these rates and given the prospect of a further deterioration of employment opportunities for the two lowest education categories (see pp. 133–134).

There are various possible explanations for this behavior which may apply alternatively or in conjunction with each other. First, families may have lacked information and may be investing in primary education on the basis of rates of return which were obtained in the immediate post-independence period (1963–64) when private rates of return to finishing primary school were substantially higher than at present.

Second, families may have unrealistic expectations of their children's chances of proceeding as far as the CSC or HSC level or of finding wage employment. While the lack of realism about the possible educational achievement will probably persist, false expectations about employment possibilities should be of a temporary nature given the continuous feedback of labor market information from the cities to the villages, particularly through returning unsuccessful job-seekers. Even families which do have a clear view of the potential gains from education and of the odds against realizing them may be unaware that a great part of the advantage they observe educated persons to enjoy should be credited to socio-economic advantages which they themselves do not necessarily share, and not to education.

Third, families may be more or less aware of all the odds, but, with what has been called in another context the "energy of despair"[3] may take on a gamble which seems worthwhile, considering the absolute size of the potential rewards against both the background of their own poverty and the

---

[3] P. C. W. Gutkind, "African Responses to Urban Wage Employment," *International Labour Review*, No. 87 (February 1968), pp. 135–166.

relative smallness of the sum that is at stake.[4] Fourth, they may already have carried out all preferable investments of comparable size (e.g. those which require as little as K£3 per year, if the alternative is primary education), and, being unable to tackle a large-scale profitable project, choose to invest in the schooling of their children.

Finally, most rural families may have come to accept primary education for their children as desirable regardless of the economic advantages which result from it. This attitude may or may not be reinforced by an implicit association of education and general progress or by an element of social competition in rural communities.

Turning our attention from the private to the public investor in education, we are given to similar doubts. The rapid decrease in the social rates of return to investment in primary education from 1960 to 1966 suggests that the present volume of primary schooling—two-thirds of which is financed by public authorities—cannot be justified on economic grounds alone unless delayed income effects (via reduced fertility or improved health standards, for example) or non-economic benefits (such as the promotion of national unity) are taken into account. If the net external benefits to primary schooling are not considered significant, the relatively low private rates to investment at that level indicate that primary schooling should be considered as a consumption good.

One possible response to this situation is for the government to aim at a shift in the distribution of financial burdens between the public and private sectors by increasing fees. This would not only make public funds available for more profitable investments, and, in the long run, provide revenues which could be channeled into education, but also possibly increase production[5] and somewhat reduce the private demand for education. This in turn would tend to increase, albeit imperceptibly, its profitability.[6] Whether such a policy would be politically and socially feasible in present-day Kenya is an open question, however, and one beyond the scope of this study.[7]

Regardless of the pattern of financing chosen, the moderate rates of

---

[4] This attitude would have its parallel in the behavior of, say, European families who play the football pools or buy lottery tickets.

[5] It might be argued that subsistence farms are operating below capacity, and that the availability of a highly desirable consumption good such as primary schooling may encourage the rural family to increase its farm output for the express purpose of paying for the good. Thus, increased consumption may actually be met by an increase in output, rather than inducing a shift from savings into consumption.

[6] The latter effect may also come about by an autonomous reduction in the demand for education. The emerging of such a cobweb effect cannot be ruled out completely, if indeed the demand is dominated by economic considerations.

[7] A necessary complement of a (restrictive) fee policy is a scholarship policy aiming at the fostering of superior individual talent.

return to investment in primary schooling and the high probability of still lower rates to both primary and secondary schooling in the near future (see below) indicate that considerable resources (whether private or public) are being put to a use which seems to provide little yield in immediate economic development. However, instead of making the "evident" conclusion of channeling resources away from education, one might examine the structure, curriculum, technology, and objectives of the education sector in the context of the economic system as a whole, with a view towards making the former more relevant to the latter's needs. While these issues are beyond the scope of this study, they nevertheless appear to be in urgent need of research.

Future Alternatives: The Employment Outlook for Educated Manpower in Kenya

The analysis in Chapters III and IV is in terms of the present situation. Since the interest of education planners lies in future deviations, Chapter V presents labor market projections to 1974.

The assessment of the future demand for educated manpower starts with a regression analysis of time series on employment of the country's three main ethnic groups (Africans, Asians, Europeans) in the three major sectors of the monetary economy (commercial agriculture, industry and services, and government).[8] Employment in each sector is analyzed as a function of average real wages and output in the sector. Two of the demand equations for ethnic/sector groups which we obtain—those for Africans in agriculture and Africans in private industry and commerce—are then put to use to project demand for the two education groups with which we feel they correspond, namely, Africans with 1 to 2 years of schooling, and Africans with 3 to 5 years, respectively. Equations of similar form are constructed for higher levels of education (secondary school and university) on the assumption that demand for higher levels of skill is characterized by a relatively low wage elasticity and a rather high output elasticity. Given a certain real rate of sectoral growth, we examine:

a) The employment implications of a certain salary policy;
b) The salary implications of a certain employment policy; and
c) The employment and salary conditions which would lead to a certain (desired) level of the rate of return to education.

---

[8] We mention in passing an attempt to develop Cobb-Douglas production functions with the various kinds of labor subject to a constant elasticity of substitution condition. Unfortunately, the implementation of this apparently acceptable theoretical approach is foiled by data shortcomings (see EC-173, Chapter IX, Section 3).

The results can be summed up as follows. The output of the primary school system over the projection period cannot be absorbed by the private monetary sector except under extremely implausible assumptions of a radical reduction of real wages and/or of a real annual output growth much higher than the already optimistic 7.1 percent we adopt from the country's Development Plan. Unless the government sector provides large numbers of new jobs, the majority of primary school leavers will have to stay in the small-farm sector or remain completely unemployed.

There will be a strong downward pressure on the earnings of secondary-trained people as more and more of them start looking for jobs; the full employment wage level for this group would be below the present average earnings of employees with primary education.

The wages of university-trained people will remain high and be subject to further upward pressure, partly because of continued Africanization of high-level jobs, and partly because of the large number of university-trained secondary teachers needed.

There is likely to be a two-sided substitution process of secondary school leavers for the two other categories, relieving somewhat the upward pressure on wages for the highest manpower category, but aggravating the employment situation at the lower end of the scale.

The General Lesson

Manpower Requirements Approach: The Alternative to Cost-Benefit Analysis

Present efforts being made in comprehensive educational planning to go beyond the education sector and its peculiar planning problems (such as projecting enrollments or financial needs) and to deal with the broader issues of formation and utilization of human capital, rely entirely on the so-called manpower requirements approach.[9]

There are many reasons for the early popularity of this approach among

---

[9] Apart from the cost-benefit approach followed in this study (which to our knowledge has not been used before as a basis for educational planning) or some variation of this approach such as a linear programming model to determine school input needs, there exists one other widely advocated alternative to the manpower requirements technique. In this approach social demand for education is taken as the criterion for making educational investment decisions. The underlying political concept is that the role of the government is to meet, as rapidly as possible, the demand for the different kinds and levels of fee-free schooling. This implicitly assumes that the social returns to all levels of education are high and persistent. It is difficult however to consider this social demand approach as comprehensive educational planning. For a detailed methodological discussion, see M. Blaug, "A Cost-Benefit Approach to Educational Planning in Developing Countries," IBRD Economics Department, Staff Study EC-157, December 20, 1967.

educational planners, but its main appeal probably derives from the misleading impression of straightforwardness, simplicity, and exactness which it conveys. The results obtained can be immediately understood by administrators, policy-makers and the public in general: we are told that certain investments in the various segments of the education system are necessary to provide a given number of people with the qualifications necessary to bring forth a gross domestic product of a given size and composition by some target year. Furthermore, the data required may be obtained relatively easily, since the basic information for the initial manpower inventory is often collected in the course of a general population census. Thirdly, in developing countries the acquisition of skills, their allocation over the economy, their contribution to production, and the interactions of these processes may be less flexible than in industrialized countries. Such a situation favors the application of the manpower requirements approach, the very rationale of which is the implicit assumption of such rigidity.

Conceptual Difficulties with Cost-Benefit Analysis

Compared to the manpower requirements approach, the application of cost-benefit techniques leads to seemingly vague results. This has probably been one of the major reasons why these techniques have never found theoretical recognition, let alone practical acceptance, among education and manpower planners. Another inhibiting force may have been an a priori reluctance, particularly among non-economists, to submit educational investments to any test which involves a comparison with investments in other sectors. Thirdly, data requirements are more difficult to meet, a fact which consciously or otherwise may influence the attitude of an educational planner towards this approach. Finally, the manpower requirements approach is likely to find more favor from a political point of view, because of what might be called its innate expansionist quality. Even a bold educational growth policy can be plausibly justified in this way, something which the more restrictive nature of the cost-benefit approach would not permit without falling back on a second line of defense, namely, that of indirect or non-economic benefits.

It is thus hardly surprising that a good number of arguments have been provided, and are still being put forward, against the use of cost-benefit analysis in educational planning.[10] They are discussed in the first chapter

---

[10] It may be noted in passing that many of these objections, and other more serious ones, apply to the manpower requirements approach as well, although on the whole they seem to be either silently ignored or dealt with much more generously. However, such a duplication of shortcomings is hardly a satisfactory counterargument.

of this study and need not be repeated in detail. It will suffice to name them here and to recapitulate briefly the way in which we try to take account of them.

The argument of ability or other income-relevant factors. It is shown that under certain circumstances the impact of ability and other income-relevant factors can be more important than that of education. It is possible, however, to deal with these influences in a reasonably satisfactory way. The variables can conveniently be aggregated into three groups: the first encompassing socio-economic variables such as tribe or parental education, the second, job-related variables (occupation, length of work experience, etc.), and the third, personal traits like ability in a specific or general sense.

In this study an assessment has been made of the impact of each of these variables or group of variables through multiple regression analysis and the earnings streams corrected accordingly; the last group of variables could be dealt with only by introducing the proxy measure of examination performance. It is questionable, however, whether the very complex phenomenon of ability can be measured at all satisfactorily by means of any one single effort such as an ad hoc survey without extended experimentation and observation. This exercise as a whole, apart from performing the prime task of separating the influence of education from that of other income-relevant factors, can shed light on, for example, the possibilities and limitations of a policy of equal educational opportunities.

The argument of systematic earnings biases. The three kinds of distortions usually mentioned in this context are those related to the size of the firm, union membership, and affiliation with the public service. The influence of these variables as a group, wherever it is significant, can be assessed and corrected for in exactly the same way as for the above-mentioned three groups of variables. They can conveniently be attributed to the cluster of job-related variables and do not constitute a problem sui generis.

It is worthwhile, however, to discuss in somewhat more detail the case of salaries in the government sector. The public sector is usually the largest single employer in both developing and developed countries, so that a significant (usually positive) divergence of its salaries from the corresponding salaries in the private sector is cause for concern. The problem is not so much one of identification but of interpretation: are the "true" rates of return those realized in the private sector (in which case private sector earnings might serve as a yardstick for both educational investments and eventual salary reforms in the public sector), or should a weighted average of the two categories be used? The answer to this question depends a good deal on whether one views the inter-sectoral earnings biases as a transitory or permanent feature of the labor market in a given country. If they are believed transitory, budgetary and social pressure will lead to an adjustment of civil service salaries; if permanent, it may be necessary to offer attractive salaries to expatriate manpower (e.g., teachers), and to respect the strong political powers of civil servants.

If these differences have indeed prevailed over a considerable period, an endogenous explanation may exist. The public sector subsample of our Labor Force Survey, which unfortunately is non-random and thus cannot yield conclusive results, appears at the CSC and HSC[11] levels to encompass a much larger share of certificate holders from schools which are considered, both by common consent and on the grounds of examination results, the country's best. If the statistical significance of this difference could be established, it could be argued that one is really dealing with two different groups of school leavers, as the elite schools (in the academic sense) might have provided quite a different experience and conveyed a different set of attitudes than those of the other secondary schools.[12] In this case it would be justified to regard the two groups of schools as separate systems, one opening access to better paid civil service positions, the other to private sector jobs, and each with its own rates of return.

The argument of spillover effects or externalities. As has been pointed out earlier in the study, the spillover effects of education may appear in many areas of an individual's and a society's life. These are occasionally straightforward, but more often than not rather elusive. While it is certainly not always possible to express them in monetary terms, if only for want of adequate data, it should be feasible to trace and quantify them in some form or other.

The main reason why we neglect externalities in this study is that this subject justifies a major study in itself. The extreme complexity of the issue may be illustrated by two examples. We have mentioned that the Labor Force Survey data as well as the 1966 Census figures show a negative association between educational achievement of adults and the number of children they have. It is an open question whether a causal relationship is at work or not. Table 6.2 justifies this caution. While the figures do not come as a surprise, they should dispel the illusion that spillover effects are easily discernible phenomena.

On the whole, we feel that claims of spillover benefits should be viewed with some reservation. A first sound rule in interpreting them is to determine whether symmetry of external benefits and external costs (dis-benefits) is maintained. In other words, increased national cohesion should not be credited to education without also taking account of the possible dis-

---

[11] The following argument would not be very convincing for HSC holders alone, since secondary schools with senior classes are almost by definition above average.

[12] That is, above and beyond differences which are reflected in the examination scores and which have been otherwise accounted for in the analysis.

TABLE 6.2: Attitudes of East African Pupils toward Family Planning, 1965-66
(percent)

Subpopulations	Rank[a]	Positive Answers	Ambivalent Answers	Negative Answers	Total Number of Respondents
Male primary pupils	24.5	15.2	60.1	24.7	1150
Male secondary pupils	12.5	19.0	60.2	20.7	469
Female primary pupils	22	15.8	59.1	25.1	708
Female secondary pupils	5	22.4	54.9	22.7	321
Primary pupils under 15	19	17.3	59.2	23.5	676
Primary pupils age 15 and over	27	14.4	60.0	25.6	1182
Secondary pupils under 15	1	29.4	54.9	15.7	51
Secondary pupils age 15 and over	7	19.7	58.4	21.9	739
Respondents in Kenya	12.5	19.0	57.5	23.5	952
Respondents in Tanzania	29	13.2	60.4	26.4	975
Respondents in Uganda	10.5	19.1	59.9	21.0	721
Primary pupils in Kenya	19	17.3	57.9	24.8	560
Secondary pupils in Kenya	6	21.4	56.9	21.7	392
Primary pupils in Tanzania	30	13.1	59.5	27.4	751
Secondary pupils in Tanzania	28	13.8	63.4	22.8	224
Primary pupils in Uganda	21	16.8	61.8	21.4	547
Secondary pupils in Uganda	2	26.4	54.0	19.6	174
Kikuyu males	4	22.5	56.0	21.5	200
Kikuyu females	3	26.0	50.7	23.3	142
Ganda males	15	18.5	59.7	21.8	427
Ganda females	8	19.3	62.0	18.7	171
Luo males	24.5	15.2	63.0	21.8	302
Luo females	9	19.2	53.9	26.9	167
Sukuma males	32	8.7	64.0	27.3	231
Sukuma females	31	12.0	64.9	23.1	208
Rural areas	26	14.6	60.1	25.3	708
Semi-urban areas	17	17.4	58.8	23.8	1479
Urban areas	10.5	19.1	59.0	21.9	461
Catholics	23	15.7	62.2	22.1	1257
Protestants	14	18.8	58.8	22.4	383
Muslim	16	18.4	55.3	26.3	315
Others	19	17.3	55.9	26.8	693

[a] Percent positive answers (in descending order).
Source: A. von Molnos, *Attitudes towards Family Planning in East Africa*, Munich, 1968 (IFO-Institut fur Wirtschaftsforschung, Afrika-Studien, Nr. 26), pp. 161–172.

integrating influence of large numbers of unemployed school leavers with frustrated expectations. Or, to use a more remote example: the increased familiarity with modern life of a country's law-abiding majority of citizens ought to be confronted with the increased sophistication of its law-breaking minority.

Secondly, externality arguments should normally not be used, either within the education system or between it and other sectors of the economy, to invent a ranking which has been arrived at by applying purely economic (income) criteria, in view of the implicit (or, as in Kenya, explicit)[13] priority of economic criteria in many developing countries.

This is not to deny that there may be occasional exceptions to this rule,

---

[13] Chapter I, pp. 6–7.

but they can probably be dealt with in more expeditious ways. If, for example, a government is pledged to the achievement of universal free primary education, it may as well regard its decision as a basic political choice, rather than looking for real or imaginary externalities to justify it after the event.

The argument of non-marginality. While we contend that the study shows how the above-mentioned arguments can be dealt with, we are not sure whether it answers the last and most important objection. As has been pointed out time and again, a single set of rate-of-return figures says a great deal about current conditions in the market for skills, the demand and supply of educated labor, and hence, the most rewarding directions for educational expenditure under present conditions. However, it tells us little as to what level expenditure on various kinds of education would have to be made before the rate of return would equal that of the next profitable segment of the educational system. The obvious way out of this dilemma is to link the differential earnings of cohorts of school leavers to their differential education costs over a period of years. From there one might choose some form of extrapolation to describe the likely future development of rates of return to schooling under ceteris paribus assumptions.

Unfortunately the data problem in most countries, regardless of level of economic development, virtually excludes the reconstruction of past rates of return to education. This can be particularly disturbing when dealing with educational systems which are rapidly expanding from a small initial volume, and in a situation where there is a premium on speed rather than precision.[14] In this study, we use a substitute for the time series of rates of return, based on the fact that employment probabilities and their changes over time (in this case 1960–66) have a very much greater impact on rates of return to primary education than any plausible change in nominal wages. Projections based on such estimates are probably prone to substantial errors, but so are almost any macro-economic estimates; judging from past experience, manpower requirements projections are just as prone to error.

The substitute we use is nevertheless not totally satisfactory, and during the course of the study a number of more sophisticated projections of rates of return are attempted; they are reported on in Chapter V. It is obvious that any attempt to refine rate-of-return calculations beyond the stage of straightforward extrapolation of time series requires the introduction of demand functions for various categories of educated manpower. The de-

---

[14] One should caution against exaggerated notions of what constitutes an acceptable trade-off between speed and precision. With a few exceptions, the complexity of the process of human resources development and the severe punishment for major policy errors should rule out "instant" answers.

mand function we tried is of the Cobb-Douglas type, with the aggregate labor term replaced by three broad manpower categories (distinguished by the amount of education received); manpower is supposed to enter the production process under conditions of constant elasticity of substitution.

This attempt is largely unsuccessful, and this is thought to be due to data shortcomings (the data basis consisted of a rather heterogeneous cross-section of firms). However, even if the information available were more adequate, the aggregation of all skills into only three categories might prove too much of a simplification, whereas an increase in the number of manpower categories would obviously render the data collecting and analytical problems more difficult.

We also deal with the estimation of employment figures corresponding to certain combinations of wages and rates of return, and the wage implications of certain combinations of employment figures and rates of return. This is a somewhat modified realization of M. Blaug's[15] proposal to determine the wage levels for a given category of educated manpower at which the profitability ranking order with the next higher and next lower categories becomes reversed. Our treatment of the unemployment issue is actually one step beyond the original concept. However, since the analysis again is based on woefully inadequate data, it cannot be more than an abstract demonstration of the technique.

Practical Difficulties

The most important data element in the rate-of-return calculation is an age-education-earnings cross-classification of the economically active population. Since in most countries this information is not readily available, data collection through a sample survey becomes necessary. Once the decision to undertake such a survey is made, little extra effort is required to include questions about socio-economic, job-related, and other income-relevant factors, data which are necessary for the various types of corrections of the earnings profiles by age and education group. Cost considerations do not negate this approach: our experience in Kenya implies that the necessary field work can be done in a very short time with a relatively small staff. The analysis of the data becomes more expeditious once a certain routine has been established.

However, a number of impediments remain. First of all, in most developing countries it is quite difficult to obtain data on unemployment, underemployment, and subsistence sector employment. Moreover, these three categories are not easy to define precisely in a predominantly rural

---

[15] Blaug, *A Cost-Benefit Approach to Educational Planning in Developing Countries*.

society. Very often the best one can hope for is a fairly precise picture of employment and earnings in the monetary sector, and a more or less fragmented view of subsistence farming. There are basic conceptual difficulties as well. While the difficulties of measuring underemployment can be overcome if hourly earnings and number of hours worked over a given period are known, the problem of how to allocate value added in subsistence agriculture to the various factors of production is extremely difficult. Even if the inputs of tools and other equipment were negligible, there remain the tasks of imputing rent for the land, of obtaining data on the employment of non-family workers, and of allocating the remainder of farm income in a plausible way among the family members.

The urban–rural discrepancies make themselves felt in yet another way. If the rates of return to education are strikingly different for these two segments of the population, and moreover, if access to urban jobs is found to be confined to those who have grown up in an urban environment, the appropriate orientation for educational investment in rural areas would be the rural rates of return, not a weighted urban–rural average.

The rather global nature of rate-of-return calculations may also be criticized. While we could measure the impact on earnings of attending different branches of secondary education, or different types (public and private) of primary and secondary schools, we do not carry out a rate-of-return analysis for these segments of the educational system, since the sub-samples are too small to yield significant results. However, merely by sufficiently enlarging the survey population we could take a greater number of educational options into account without any additional difficulties.

A different kind of problem arises if the costs and benefits of a new educational subsystem without precedent are to be assessed. The establishment of a new faculty or a comprehensive secondary school system are examples. While the cost development can be reasonably well anticipated with the help of budget figures, the future benefits are certainly less clear. Nevertheless, earnings data for, say, expatriate personnel with comparable qualifications may give an indication of the benefits that can be expected from such a project.

Finally, there is the question of how to deal with individual expenditure items within the educational budget. This is of particular importance for agencies which are concentrating on investment expenditure—particularly on school buildings or on providing teachers. It is easy to see that an evaluation of alternative expenditure patterns for an educational unit (an individual school, for example) is beyond the scope of a global rate-of-return analysis. The specific answer at this level of disaggregation depends on specific knowledge of what is going on inside a school.

There remains the question of how to interpret the experience of this study from the viewpoint of those who have to make large-scale decisions on the financing of education. The technique demonstrated in Chapters III and IV is effective chiefly because it can rank any number of educational "packages" according to economic attractiveness, allowing for the influence of exogenous factors which are superimposed on, and which tend to blur the relationships between, education and earnings. This ranking is expressed in terms of internal rates of return, i.e. in a form which makes the results comparable to similar profitability assessments in other fields of economic activity.

The first and decisive advantage is, then, that using the cost-benefit approach to educational planning permits us to put expenditure in this sector on an equal footing with expenditure in other fields. While such a standardization of evaluation criteria is clearly not an end in itself, there can be no doubt as to its desirability when viewing education in a wider context of economic and social activities.

With all its present shortcomings, the rate-of-return approach to educational investment planning has to be considered an essential addition to the arsenal of techniques. The practical difficulties encountered in this first application should not be held against its more widespread use; rather, they should serve as an argument to persuade member countries to include the relevant data for a rate-of-return analysis in their regular education and labor market statistics.

It should also have become clear that by its very nature cost-benefit analysis does not easily lend itself to the evaluation of individual education projects. Such evaluation requires a combination of the rate-of-return (Chapter IV) and education process (Annex A) analyses. In other words the rate-of-return approach is most adequate in situations which call for a broad and comprehensive view, such as general sector surveys or other inquiries which precede the formulation of educational policies. As the decision-making process moves from the general to a more specific level, the approach has to be supplemented by other analytical elements. Its usefulness does not end there, however. Valuable insights into questions such as that of the distribution of financial responsibilities for education between the public and private sectors[16] may be gained by comparisons of private and social rates of return. Thus, this approach can help in a number of ways to put educational planning on a more rational basis.

---

[16] For a promising step in this direction, see D. C. Rogers, "Student Loan Programs and the Returns to Investment in Higher Levels of Education in Kenya," Teachers College, Columbia University, New York, March 1969. (To be published in *Economic Development and Cultural Change*, 1971.)

ANNEX A

THE DETERMINANTS OF EXAMINATION PERFORMANCE AND RATES OF RETURN TO SCHOOL INPUTS

An Exploratory Analysis

The Quality of School Output

Chapters III and IV focused on the influence of non-schooling factors on earnings and the calculation of average present rates of return to different levels of schooling, adjusted for these influences. Such rates give an idea at which levels within the schooling system investment gives the highest returns. Such an analysis assumes implicitly that from a purely technological point of view an optimum is achieved, i.e. that the various factors of production are combined in the most efficient way. In contrast, we examine in this Annex the influence of some school factors on the quality of school output, and calculate rates of return to schooling inputs.

The quality of output is equated with students' examination performance: if average examination performance in one school is higher than in another, the quality of output of the first is considered to be higher than that of the second. It would be more accurate to measure the quality of schooling by estimating the change in students' performance over the schooling period or parts of it rather than the absolute level of examination performance at one point in time. Also, examination scores do not necessarily reflect the training which students receive in discipline, consciousness of time, and hierarchical interactions, or other changes in attitude brought about through education. Because such training improves productivity and contributes to an increase in national income, it is very important in an industrializing society. However, our data do not permit us to take any of these factors into account in our estimates of schooling quality.

The concern with quality of schooling arises for two reasons. First, we would like to be able to project the quality of the supply of educated labor through time in absolute terms on the basis of assumptions about schooling inputs, and to use this component in supply projections similar to those of Chapter V. Second, we want to explore the relationship between expenditure on schooling inputs and the quality of schooling output. While it is commonly held that increasing expenditure per student on schooling inputs, especially teacher expenditure per pupil, raises the quality of school output, this hypothesis has never been tested in the context of developing countries, and rarely in industrialized countries.[1]

The question of the effect of expenditure per pupil on school output is important not only for the efficient allocation of school budgets this year and next, but also for the long-range planning of a school system. Recent studies have shown that a student's performance on an examination is highly correlated with his socio-economic background; thus, his background may be largely responsible for his success or failure.[2] Furthermore, it is probable that new students attracted during a period of rapid educational expansion in a developing country come from less favored socio-economic backgrounds than the pre-expansion students. The earliest students are likely to be the more gifted children and the children from families who are keen on education. As schools increase their enrollments the school population is likely to include growing numbers of pupils who are either less gifted or come from families less interested in education.

Thus, in the short run a rapid expansion of enrollments is likely to lead to a decrease in the average absolute quality of output as measured by examination performance, everything else, particularly the "schooling intensity" (the amount of school inputs per pupil) being equal. Only in the long run will the gradual increase in the average education of the population and the concomitant socio-economic change reverse this development. The time-path of quality of school output may be illustrated by the following figure.

The quality of output (Q_t), which is assumed to be approximated by

---

[1] J. Burkhead, T. G. Fox, and J. W. Holland, *Input and Output in Large-City High Schools* (Syracuse, N.W.: Syracuse University Press, 1967); Thomas Ribich, *Education and Poverty* (Washington, D.C.: Brookings Institution, 1968).

[2] J. Coleman *et al.*, *Educational Opportunity*, U.S. Office of Education, Washington, D.C.; Government Printing Office, 1967; Thorsten Husen, "Talent, Opportunity and Career: a 26-Year Follow-up," *School Review*, 76 (2), June 1968, pp. 190–209; D. Wolfle, "National Resources of Ability," in *Ability and Educational Opportunity*, A. H. Hasey (ed.), Paris: OECD, 1961.

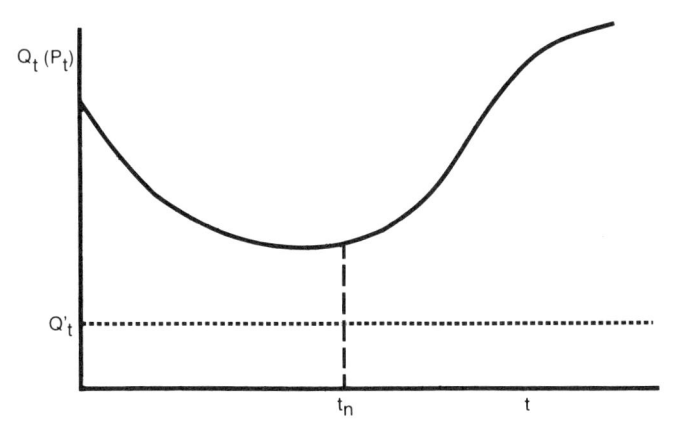

FIGURE A.1: TIME-PATH OF SCHOOL OUTPUT QUALITY AS A FUNCTION OF EXAMINATION PERFORMANCE

examination performance (P_t), follows a U-shaped course over time. At point t_n, the temporary negative effect of the rapid expansion of enrollments is offset by the positive effect of increased parental education.[3] In the figure, the value added by schooling (Q'_t) is considered constant. This need not be the case; if the quality of graduates who become teachers, the most important determinant of school output, follows a path similar to that of the quality of all graduates (Q_t), then the latter will in turn be influenced by the change in the former, and Q_t will follow a parabolic path similar to that of $Q_t(P_t)$.

An adult literacy campaign, the widespread introduction of television, or rapid migration into the cities might shift the curve upward. Nevertheless, it seems more effective and relevant to influence $Q_t(P_t)$, i.e. to improve examination results by working directly with schooling inputs. Including these inputs as variables, we express the curve of Figure A.1 in the following equation.

$$P_t = a + b \sum_{i=1}^{k} X_i + c \left(\frac{S}{P}\right)_{t_o} + d \left[\frac{\frac{S}{P_{t_o}}}{\frac{S}{P_{t_o-j}}}\right] + e \left(\frac{H}{P}\right)_{t_o} \quad (A.1)$$

---

[3] More elaborately, P_t could be expressed as a function of, say, the rates of increase in the percentage of the school age population enrolled, and in the average education level of the parental population. We might expect the age-specific enrollment ratio to be positively correlated with the average parental education, but the change in the ratio would tend to be negatively correlated.

where P_t = examination performance;
t = time in years;
j = interval at which the expansion of enrollments is measured;[4]
X_i = the annual schooling inputs over a period of K years;
$\frac{S}{P}$ = enrollment level in the area observed;
$\frac{H}{P}$ = average education, or "stock of schooling," per capita of the population in the same area (measured in this study by average male education);
and a, b, c, d, e = parameters.

Our intent is to estimate examination performance as a function of the above variables with cross-section data. Because information on enrollment rates over time and on socio-economic background of pupils is unavailable, we have to represent S/P and H/P by proxies which are available only at the county level. The proxy for change in secondary enrollment rates is the share of secondary school students in the total county population in 1967.[5] The proxy for the "stock of schooling" is the average amount of education (in years) of males and females over 30 (used as separate variables) in 1962 in the county where the secondary school is located.[6] Since the primary school examination results and schooling input data could be collected for only two counties, the use of the proxy variables is restricted to the analysis of secondary examination results (CSC and HSC). However, since no systematic or significant results emerged, for all intents and purposes our analysis is limited to the first two terms of equation (A.1): that is, the effect on examination results of various schooling inputs and rates of return to increasing them, largely uncorrected for enrollment ratios, and the socio-economic composition of the student population.

Although the actual analysis is thus inevitably a second-best compromise,[7] it nevertheless yields a good many worthwhile results, some of

---

[4] The choice of this interval is largely arbitrary. For data convenience, it could be geared to the frequency with which other socio-economic indicators such as census results become available. It could also be linked to the length of educational cycles. In the present study, the interval 1962–67 was chosen.

[5] This implies that the number of secondary school students in 1962 (the year t_o–5) was negligibly small, not an unreasonable assumption for most counties, given the almost eightfold increase in the total number of African secondary pupils in that period. It also assumes similar age structures in different counties.

[6] We assume that a school's catchment area is by and large restricted to its county, a plausible simplification if one ignores Kenya's dozen or so extra-provincial schools which recruit country-wide.

[7] The most serious effect of omitting socio-economic background as a variable is the bias it causes in the estimates of the coefficient b.

which are in contradiction to widely accepted premises of educational policy. For example, the analysis makes clear that simply increasing expenditure per pupil cannot be relied on to raise examination performance, and that the impact of the different expenditure components (teachers' salaries, boarding facilities, etc.) must be examined. While we are far from suggesting that concrete action be taken on such a narrow factual basis, we feel strongly about the necessity of a thorough educational process analysis preceding any major reallocation of resources, whether from other public activities to education, from one educational subsystem to another, or within a subsystem between groups of inputs. Also, while we are unable to estimate the coefficients c and d in the above equation, and therefore cannot project a quality component into the supply projections used previously, we believe the model to be adequate and verifiable given more detailed data.

Primary Education

The Kenya Preliminary Exam (KPE)

The KPE was introduced in 1967, superseding the examinations that had formerly concluded the Primary and Intermediate courses in African, Asian and European schools. A centralized examination designed, supervised and evaluated by the Ministry of Education, it consists of a battery of 240 questions in three subject groups,[8] 90 of which form an English language test, whereas 50 refer to mathematics and 100 to general subjects. The maximum score in each subject group is 100 points, giving a theoretical total range of 0–300 points.[9] This score has replaced the fail-pass-qualify classification used until 1966 (only a qualify could make a student acceptable to secondary school).

Not only is the KPE the leaving examination after seven years of primary schooling, but performance in it constitutes the main, if not the only, criterion for admission to secondary education in maintained and assisted schools. Only in a few marginal cases do secondary schools resort to additional inquiries (personal interviews, information from the former headmaster, etc.) to assess an applicant's aptitude. In the last few years the KPE's role as a selection screen has gained an ever-increasing importance,

---

[8] The following description refers to the 1967 examination (See: Ministry of Education, Kenya Preliminary Examination 1967, English, Mathematics and General Papers).

[9] These extreme scores are of course very unlikely to occur. Since all but five composition tests are multiple choice questions involving four alternatives, a completely random answering and a failure in the composition text would already yield on average a total of 71 points. On the other hand, it is obvious that the theoretical maximum is not attained either, given the relative difficulty of the examination. (In 1967 the best performances were in the neighborhood of 270 points.)

as secondary education has become a virtual pre-condition for urban wage employment. Due to the educational system's lack of flexibility and its vertical orientation, the KPE is a once-and-for-all decision that entails a good deal of individual hardship, no provision being made for late academic development, strongly biased ability profiles and the like.

Since permission to repeat Standard VII and KPE depends on the availability of school places and is usually not given, unsuccessful candidates often display considerable determination and ingenuity to circumvent the official policy—a popular device being to change one's name and repeat Standard VII in a more remote school. A recent study has shown that out of a sample of 834 pupils who sat KPE in 1964 in Central Nyanza, Embu, Kericho and Kitui districts, 68, or more than 8 percent, were still repeating in 1967 (the corresponding 1966 and 1965 figures being 37 and 16 percent, respectively). More than half of the 1965 repeaters had obtained a KPE pass in the previous year and obviously stayed in school in the hope of improving their score to the point where they would be acceptable to a secondary school. Similar results were obtained in a sample of 203 KPE candidates (1964) in four schools in the Tetu location of Nyeri district. There is evidence that repeaters had a better chance of qualifying for entrance into secondary schools than first-time candidates.[10]

The Data and Their Limitations

The 1967 KPE register provides a unique source of data, giving information for every individual candidate on the following characteristics: sex, age, number of previous examination attempts, total KPE score, score in each of the three subject groups, previous ranking in the class, and the candidate's first, second, and third choice of a secondary school in case he or she would qualify. However, the register does not give information on the socio-economic background of candidates.

Once the KPE score is accepted as a reliable indicator of scholastic achievement, the question arises of how the score is influenced by certain educational policy measures if all extra-educational factors are kept equal. Ideally, this question should be approached on the basis of completely disaggregated data, i.e. at the level of the individual pupil. The 1967 KPE results does contain individuals' results by subject group, but time and personnel constraints did not permit compilation and analysis of data in

---

[10] L. Brownstein, "Preliminary Results of a Survey of 1964 KPE Candidates in Embu, Kitui, Kericho and Nyanza" (mimeo), Institute for Development Studies, University College, Nairobi, 1967. J. Anderson, "The Adolescent in the Rural Community," in *Education, Employment and Rural Development*, J. R. Sheffield (ed.) (Nairobi: East African Publishing House, 1967), pp. 420–421.

this degree of detail. Furthermore, information reflecting environmental influences on the individual pupil and other extra-educational data are available at the county level at best (and even there mostly in the form of rough estimates), so that matching these two kinds of data would have been unfeasible, particularly since data were taken from schools in only two counties.

For these reasons the information is aggregated and analyzed at the level of the individual school. Only the first four data items are used: percent of girls among a school's candidates, average age, percent of repeaters, and average total KPE score. The data basis is a 20 percent random sample of all primary schools in Muranga and Meru Counties that presented KPE candidates in 1967, totaling 89 schools with 3,405 candidates, or roughly 2½ percent of the national total. Although these two countries, situated in the Central and Eastern Provinces north of Nairobi, have a number of socio-economic features in common, there are sufficient differences between them to make them adequately representative of many of Kenya's rural areas.

This information is supplemented by school data contained in the budgets of the two county councils, including enrollments in each standard, number of classes, number of teachers in each category, and total teachers' salaries, all at the level of the individual school.

On the whole the data appear to be fairly reliable, with the exception of the share of repeaters and possibly also the average age of candidates.[11] In the case of Meru County, in particular, the understatements on repeaters must be of major proportions (only 11 out of 41 schools reported any repeaters at all, against 46 out of 48 in Muranga).[12] No allowance can be made for this bias, which might explain why the percentage of repeaters is not a significant explanator of a school's average examination performance. On the other hand, average age of candidates is a significant variable.

Regression Analysis Results

Initially, we designate teachers' salaries per pupil (E_t/S) as the sole determinant of average KPE scores. (t-values of the coefficients are in parentheses.)

---

[11] The data on the average age of candidates appear to be less subject to misreporting, an impression which is borne out by the virtual absence of correlation between the share of repeaters and the average age of candidates ($R^2 = 0.002$).

[12] In a 10 percent random sample of all primary schools conducted by the Ministry of Education in 1967, this tendency showed even more strongly. The percentage of repeaters in Standard VII was 14.1 percent for the whole county, 1.7 percent for Meru and 14.5 percent for Muranga (3.7 percent and 16.6 percent, respectively, in our sample).

$$\text{KPE} = 150.312 + \underset{(0.187)}{0.152\, E_t/S} \qquad R^2 = 0.004 \qquad (A.2)$$

Both the *t*-value and *F*-value are insignificant, and expenditure per pupil appears to have a negligible impact on average KPE scores.

In an effort to obtain better results we disaggregate the teachers' salaries variable into its two major components, average teacher salaries (E_t/T) and teacher-pupil ratio (T/S). The latter does not seem to have an effect,[13] but the former does.

$$\text{KPE} = 136.146 + \underset{(2.35)}{0.079\,(E_t/T)} \qquad R^2 = 0.06 \qquad (A.3)$$

In seeking to understand the reason why teacher salaries seem to affect examination score, we examine the three factors which influence the average teacher salary: performance-related bonuses, the average formal qualification of the teaching staff, and its average seniority. In Kenya, there are no bonus incentives, except for headmasters' administrative allowances which are not related to teaching performance. Formal qualification undoubtedly has a strong influence on the school salary bill. The starting salary for the most highly qualified teachers (P1) is more than four times that of an unqualified teacher without KPE. However, the composition of the teaching staff does not turn out to be a good explanator of KPE score. In no case does the share of a specific category of teachers in a school's teaching force constitute a variable with a significant *t*-value, nor was the *F*-value for the whole equation significant.

The seniority of the teaching staff cannot be assessed directly from the available data. However, we are able to satisfactorily correct the school salary bill for seniority. We calculate two hypothetical salary bills, E_t^* and E_t^{**}. To find E_t^{**}, we multiply the number of teachers in each category by the corresponding initial salaries and sum the products for each school.[14] E_t^* is derived in the same way, except that it is based on the average salary for each category observed in the two counties for which we have data. We then formulate two equations analogous to (A.3).

---

[13] Inclusion of T/S as an independent variable caused the *F*-value of the equation to become insignificant. Regressing partial teacher-pupil ratios for the different grades of teachers (P1, P2, P3, P4 and unqualified teachers) on KPE scores resulted in negative and insignificant regression coefficients for the P2, P3 and unqualified teachers.

[14] Since seniority increases are about the same in relative terms for all categories (except for unqualified teachers, whose salaries remain constant), this procedure implies that increases in teaching experience are positively related to the level of professional qualification, which does not seem unrealistic. For evidence from a developed country, see K. Richmond, *Culture and General Education* (London: Methuen & Co., Ltd., 1963).

$$\text{KPE} = 144.152 + 0.039\ E_t^*/T \qquad R^2 = 0.006 \qquad (A.4)$$
$$\phantom{\text{KPE} = 144.152 +\ }(0.56)$$
$$\text{KPE} = 144.432 + 0.045\ E_t^{**}/T \qquad R^2 = 0.005 \qquad (A.5)$$
$$\phantom{\text{KPE} = 144.432 +\ }(0.48)$$

A comparison of (A.3) and (A.4) shows the full impact of seniority on exam results, whereas a comparison of (A.3) and (A.5) brings out the effect of the deviations from average seniority. In both cases, the inclusion of seniority makes the difference between obtaining insignificant and significant t- and F-values at the 0.05 level, though the absolute size of the fraction of variance removed is rather small. Thus, seniority seems to be a better predictor of examination performance than is the formal qualification of the teaching staff.

However, one should not jump to the conclusion that the effect of seniority is solely due to the accumulated teaching experience of senior teachers. The positive association of KPE results and seniority may reflect the beneficial effects of having a stable staff, since the older, more senior teachers are less likely than younger ones to be transferred to other schools, regardless of qualifications. Furthermore, the deep-rooted respect for older persons in African societies may add to the classroom effectiveness of the more senior teachers, particularly in rural areas where traditional values have been conserved. Finally, the senior teacher has probably come to terms with the prospect of spending his life in a rural environment, whereas the novice, particularly if he is more qualified, may experience a feeling of futility which is bound to affect his work.

The next equation includes E_t/T and three additional variables related to the size and composition of the school's student body: number of pupils (S), share of KPE candidates (K/S), and average age of KPE candidates (A).

$$\text{KPE} = 212.325 + 0.090\ E_t/T - 0.048\ S - 59.250\ K/S - 3.943\ A$$
$$\phantom{\text{KPE} = 212.325 +\ }(2.64)(2.82)(1.67)(1.87)$$
$$R^2 = 0.173 \qquad\qquad\qquad\qquad\qquad\qquad\qquad\qquad (A.6)$$

These results are difficult to interpret. The t-values for the first two regression coefficients are significant at the 0.01 level, and those for the last two at the 0.10 level. The combined explanatory power of the four variables is only moderate—roughly 17 percent of the variation in examination score—which is hardly surprising given that we have no data on many educational variables (teacher turnover, commuting distances, equipment standards, etc.) nor on the still larger number of socio-economic factors.

The negative correlation of size of school and KPE results seems to fit into our description of the educational growth process in the beginning of this chapter. The first pupils in a new school are likely to be the most gifted children and the children from families who are keen on education.[15] As the school increases its catchment area both in width (by attracting pupils from more remote homes) and in depth (by enrolling more pupils within the school district), not only the size of the school increases. The school population is also likely to include growing numbers of pupils who are either less gifted or who have longer commuting distances, families less interested in education, or more limited financial resources. Consequently the average examination scores are likely to decrease as school size increases. However, increasing total inputs into the teaching process and/or improvement in the input mix may bring about an increase in examination scores.

There are two possible explanations for the negative correlation of the share of candidates in the school's student body (K/S) and the KPE results. First, in a school which screens its pupils severely during early standards, the surviving KPE candidates are likely to perform better than those in a school with casual screening. Second, a low K/S could indicate that the candidates are those more favored, fewer children who started school prior to a recent rapid enrollment expansion. The average age of candidates is also negatively correlated with average KPE score, since older students are more likely to have repeated a standard, to be KPE repeaters, or to have temporarily dropped out of school.

As we mentioned when discussing the data, the percentage of repeaters is not a significant explanator of examination scores. Neither is the percentage of girls among candidates, possibly as a result of the conflict during a girl's education between negative attitudes on the part of society and positive ability and motivation on the part of the individual.

In summary, we have regressed eight variables on KPE score. Four are not significant: percentage of repeaters and share of girls among candidates, teacher-pupil ratio, and teachers' salaries per pupil. Four are significant: number of pupils in school, share of KPE candidates in school, average age of candidates, and average teacher salaries.

The Rates of Return to Additional Inputs

In this section we illustrate how the returns to additional expenditure on teacher's salaries can be assessed. For many reasons, which are enumerated

---

[15] One might object that the most important factor in a family's decision to send the children to school is ability to pay the school fees. However, since family income levels are closely related to the education of the main income earner, the families whose head earns more and is better able to pay school fees are also the families whose head is better educated and most likely to be keen on educating his children.

at the end of the section, we emphasize that this section is meant to be purely demonstrative. We choose average teacher salaries as our variable because, of the variables we were able to regress on KPE, it is the only one which is both significant and a meaningful policy variable. Thus, the costs are the increase in spending on teacher salaries, and the benefits are the additional earnings a student can expect when his examination score is higher.[16]

We showed in Chapter IV that the average salaries of African males with 6–8 years of education employed in the urban sector varied considerably with scholastic achievement.[17] The average monthly salary for persons who failed the KPE was Ksh 342; for those who passed, Ksh 439, and for those who qualified for secondary education without actually entering Form I, Ksh 468. The data we have for the KPE–average teacher salaries relationship (equation (A.6)) is in terms of continuous examination scores rather than the fail-pass-qualify categories (the latter were discontinued in 1966), and so we have to devise hypothetical border scores. Using the cut-off point for admission actually in use by government-maintained and assisted secondary schools in 1967 (about 180 points)[18] and assuming the average score of those who passed or did better to be 195 points,[19] we have determined an average qualifying score which will be associated, on the average, with the mean monthly earnings figure of Ksh 468.

If we further suppose a symmetric normal distribution of scores around the mean (both theoretical and actual) of 150 points,[20] and the equidistance

---

[16] The analysis covers only those benefits to additional teachers' salaries which appear once the examination is taken. Benefits which have accrued earlier, for example, through a reduction of repetition and dropout rates or through better earnings prospects for those who do drop out before the examination are omitted.

[17] To mesh these data with the results of an education process analysis in rural schools is of course an unsatisfactory procedure. However, the rural income data did not contain any income differentiation by examination results. We deem the procedure nonetheless admissible in the context of an analysis which serves for demonstration purposes.

[18] There was some regional variation in the average qualifying score of 183 points, depending on the relative scarcity of secondary school places. The score was thus lower in Coastal Province and higher in Central Province.

[19] Based on the detailed results of the 1960 JSLE in Uganda, an examination similar to the KPE and applied to a school population with very much the same amount and kind of schooling as their counterparts in Kenya. (Source: II. C. A. Somerset, *Predicting Success in School Certificate*, Nairobi: East African Publishing House, 1968, Table III). The reader who feels uneasy about this procedure might note that even a substantial allowance for errors (through a series of alternative calculations for the 180 and 210 points scores and the corresponding sub-average values) would change the results only marginally.

[20] The average performance in the 89 schools of our sample was 151.3 points.

of the upper and lower cut-off points from the mean, we arrive at average scores of 105 points for the fail category and 150 points for the pass category. Applying linear interpolation, a one-point increase in score below the pass score is associated with a Ksh 2.16 increase in average monthly earnings; above the pass score the increase is only Ksh 0.67 for each additional point.

A K£1 increase in average teachers' salaries is associated with an average increase of 0.09 examination points, according to equation (A.6) (other variables remaining equal). For a group of 38 candidates, the school average in the sample, such an input increase would result in a total increase of 3.4 examination points for the school. Repeating the additional outlay over the eight-year period of primary schooling (the extra year accounts for repeating Standards) amounts to an additional outlay of Ksh 160 in teachers' salaries; the additional monthly earnings of the student associated with this increase will be Ksh 7.34 for a school with an average score below the pass, and Ksh 2.28 for a school scoring above the pass. Taking the latter figures as perpetuities, we arrive at rates of return of 4.6 percent (7.34/160) and 1.4 percent (2.28/160), respectively. If we assume that pupils who attain the qualifying scores are also able to complete the primary course in the nominal time of seven years, the latter figure becomes 1.6 percent (2.28/140).

These results have been obtained by making a number of simplifying assumptions. First, it is supposed that average monthly earnings increase continuously rather than discretely when moving from the fail through the pass to the qualify category. Second, we assume the average examination score in the qualify category could not be lower than 195 points. However, those who qualify but do not continue their education might be marginal qualifiers. Correcting for this type of error would have only a limited absolute impact, resulting in rates of 2.1 and 6.9 instead of 1.4 and 4.6 percent, respectively, if the "borderline" score of 180 points and the corresponding lower one of 120 were chosen (see above).

Third, we assume that increased expenditure on teachers' salaries would move a school's mean KPE score upward without changing the shape of the distribution of individual scores, although this measure could have an asymmetric effect by helping the below-average pupils more than the above-average, or vice versa. Even if this assumption holds, the distribution of the scores around the mean, which we approximate by a symmetric normal distribution, would result in an underestimation of the returns in above-average schools and an overestimation of returns in below-average schools. In the schools whose average score was above a pass, for example, both above- and below-average candidates would be credited with a salary gain of Ksh 0.67 even though the below-average candidates would actually realize a gain of Ksh 2.16. Without knowing the actual shape of the distribution, it is impossible to assess the dimension of this error.

Fourth, our treatment of the differential earnings as perpetuities implies some overstatement of the rates of return. Fifth, an additional upward bias results from taking the average salaries for the three categories regardless of age, given the fairly low average age observed in the labor sample— 27.3, 28.2 and 28.6 for the qualify, pass and fail categories, respectively—and the fact that salary curves tend to flatten out with increasing age. Sixth, the sample is assumed to be representative of rural Kenya though it is relatively small. As has been pointed out, Meru and Muranga are distinct socio-economic entities. Since a dummy variable identifying the county proved to be insignificant in one of the subsidiary variants of the analysis, the validity of the results may not be as restricted geographically as it would appear at first sight.

The most serious objection is that urban wage differentials have been used to represent benefits, though we showed in Chapter IV that a weighted average of wage differentials in available forms of profitable employment is a more appropriate measure of benefits. If we were to make this correction, which includes an allowance for unemployment, the rates of return would be reduced to a negligible figure. Thus, while the markedly low rate of return to increasing teachers' salaries once a school has reached an average score of pass or better suggests that salaries should be raised in schools with below pass scores, such a measure could fail to produce the above income effects because these schools may be in areas where wage employment outside agriculture is rare.

The fact that most of our simplifying assumptions tend to give an upward bias to these rates of return casts an unfavorable light on the rates, which are already very low. Though a more thorough and extensive inquiry would be necessary to consolidate these results, it would seem that increasing average teacher salaries while improving students' performance on the KPE, would be a rather uneconomic measure of general income policy.

Recalling our analysis in the previous section of the components of teacher salaries per pupil, it seems doubtful that it would be economically profitable to upgrade teachers on a large scale even if some cost increases could be absorbed by an increase in the pupil-teacher ratio, which appears to have little effect on KPE score. In that analysis, the composition of a school's teaching staff by formal qualification explained little of the variation in KPE scores, while seniority was a more potent explanator. In the absence of performance-related salary components and of geographic differentials in salaries, it is not possible to determine whether efficiency-tied or autonomous salary increases would lead to better KPE scores and higher quality of schooling output.

Secondary Education

The CSC and HSC Exams

As was explained in Chapter II, the Cambridge School Certificate examination (CSC) is administered at the end of Form IV, after four years of secondary schooling under the auspices of the University of Cambridge Local Examinations Syndicate. Only a small proportion of those entering the CSC examination continue their education in Form V or in teacher training colleges (S1 courses). The CSC is thus the main entrance requirement for most of the medium-level clerical and administrative occupations. The number of schools which present candidates for this examination has increased sharply, in line with the general expansion of the secondary school system, from 42 in 1956 (only 13 of which were African schools) to 144 in 1966. Those schools which also have an upper secondary cycle (Forms V and VI) leading to the Higher School Certificate examination (HSC) constitute a nucleus of first-rate schools whose pupils perform consistently better than the average, partly because many of them are "extra-provincial" schools, which recruit their pupils from all over the country.

Data and Assumptions

The data on the first four years (Forms) of secondary education leading to the Cambridge School Certificate examination (CSC) cover 133 schools, of which 115 reported the composition of the teaching staff and expenditure on non-teacher inputs in 1966.[21] These 115 schools form the basis of the regression analysis. The available statistics include individual school data, reported by the schools, on:

a) The number of students taking the CSC examination and their breakdown by results (Division I, Division II, Division III, GCE (0), Fail);

b) The number of teachers by grade of qualification;

c) Non-teacher current expenditure; and

d) The number of students in the school by sex and form of attendance (boarders/non-boarders).

There are also data on:

e) The average education of adult males and females in the county where the school is located (associated with each school for the purposes of the analysis).[22] In the case of entirely African schools the

---

[21] Ministry of Education.
[22] Ministry of Economic Planning and Development, Statistics Division: *Kenya Population Census, 1962*; Vol. III of *African Population*, Nairobi, 1966.

average education is estimated for the African population in the county. In the case of mixed schools or predominantly Asian or European schools, the average education of Asians and Europeans in the whole country from the 1962 census is combined with the average education of Africans in the county on the basis of the percentage of Asians, Europeans and Africans in the school.[23]

f) A dummy variable indicating the presence or absence of a Higher School Certificate cycle (Forms V and VI) at the school;

g) The number of CSC students per one thousand population in the county where the school is located. This figure is estimated by summing all pupils in Forms I–IV in the 133 CSC cycle schools by county and then dividing the sums by the total population in each county.

In both (e) and (g), the administrative division existing at the time of the 1962 census has been followed.

In order to be able to use the data to estimate relationships, the various CSC exam scores have to be quantified. It is assumed that failure of the CSC equals 1.0, Division I pass equals 3.5, Division II pass equals 1.75, Division III equals 1.25, and GCE equals 1.5.[24] The number of candidates by school achieving each level is multiplied by these indices. The sum of these products is divided by the total number of candidates to give an average score for each school. The mean score for all schools is 1.82, or an average Division II result.

Data on teacher expenditure do not cover all the schools, hence estimates are made on the basis of the number of teachers at each level of qualification and the average salary for that level.[25] Overseas term teachers[26] are

---

[23] Ministry of Education. This information was available for Forms V and VI only; where necessary, adjustments for Form IV enrollments have been made on the basis of the 1967 individual CSC results as published in the *East African Standard*, February 13–14, 1968.

[24] These are the reciprocal values of the midpoints of the theoretical ranges of the various CSC scores (Division I, Division II, etc.), multiplied by 100 and divided by the value obtained for the Fail category; the GCE coefficient of 1.5 has been fixed arbitrarily. Later adjustments allowing for an uneven distribution of examination performance within each of the ranges on the basis of the 1966 CSC results in Uganda (i.e. of a country whose education system resembled closely that of Kenya, with an identical examination taken by a school population with by and large the same characteristics), did not produce, with the exception of Division I, significantly different weights (1.0, 1.24, 1.65, and 2.56 for failure, Division III, Division II, and Division I passes, respectively).

[25] Since most local teachers are of below average seniority, this estimate probably has an upward bias.

[26] Defined as teachers who have overseas leave and passage privileges, regardless of the scheme under which they are provided.

assumed to cost K£1740 in addition to the average pay of a Kenyan citizen or local term teacher.[27] Annex Table A.3 shows the salary ranges for the teaching force in Kenya.

Since many schools have both CSC and HSC cycles but their teachers are not identified by cycle taught, some sort of allocation has to be made. On the basis of information given by the Ministry of Education, it is assumed that only graduate teachers teach in the HSC cycle (Forms 5 and 6) and about 1.5 times as many graduate teachers per student are employed in teaching HSC as CSC students. The number of graduate teachers in the CSC cycle can therefore be estimated as follows:

$$\frac{\text{Graduate Teachers}}{\text{in Forms I through IV}} = \frac{\text{Total Graduate Teachers}}{1 + \frac{\text{Students in Forms V and VI}}{1.5 \text{ (Students in Forms I-IV)}}} \quad (A.7)$$

The number of graduate teachers in the CSC cycle estimated in this way is added to the total number of teachers at lower levels of qualification reported by the schools.

In addition to overall teacher expenditure per pupil, a measure of graduate teacher input is used as a variable in the regression equations. The graduate equivalent number of teachers per pupil is estimated by weighting each teacher reported by the ratio of his salary (as approximated by the average salary paid to his level of qualification) to the average salary of a graduate teacher. The weighting scheme assumes that relative salaries reflect the relative efficiency of teachers and that the graduate equivalent teacher/pupil ratio is a much more meaningful figure than the simple teacher/pupil ratio.

Regression Analysis Results

CSC, all schools. The hypothesis tested for the CSC cycle is that examination performance is positively related to total expenditure per student, non-teacher expenditure per student, and teacher expenditure per student, holding other variables, such as school size, constant. In addition, we assume that examination performance is positively related to average education of adult males and females in the county (these are proxies for the propensity of families to have their children educated) and that performance is negatively related to the relative frequency of CSC students in the county (i.e. the percentage of the 15–19 year age group enrolled in secondary schools having a Form IV), when adult male and female education are held constant. This means that we expect average examination performance on a

---

[27] Estimated on the basis of data published in United Kingdom, Ministry of Overseas Development, Statistics Division, *British Government Economic Aid, Statistics of Aid to Developing Countries, 1962 to June 1967*, London, 1968.

standard examination to rise as parents' education rises because of non-schooling inputs in the home, and we expect it to fall as the number of students attending secondary school increases as a percentage of the total population (this assumes a constant age distribution from county to county and a strictly performance-oriented selection of secondary school pupils).

The cross-section regression results estimating these relationships are the following:[28]

$$\text{CSC} = 1.6788 + \underset{(2.134)}{0.0016\,(E/S)} \qquad R^2 = 0.039 \quad (A.8)$$

$$\log \text{CSC} = 0.0669 + \underset{(3.410)}{0.1012 \log S} + \underset{(2.713)}{0.0947\,B}$$
$$+ \underset{(0.335)}{0.0114 \log(E/S)} \qquad R^2 = 0.145 \quad (A.9)$$

$$\log \text{CSC} = 0.0183 + \underset{(2.154)}{0.0811 \log S} + \underset{(2.787)}{0.1117\,B} + \underset{(0.236)}{0.0081 \log(E/S)}$$
$$+ \underset{(0.866)}{0.0088\,H/P} \qquad R^2 = 0.151 \quad (A.10)$$

$$\log \text{CSC} = 0.2747 + \underset{(1.445)}{0.0584 \log S} + \underset{(2.162)}{0.0902\,B} - \underset{(0.318)}{0.0114 \log(E/S)}$$
$$+ \underset{(0.816)}{0.0093\,H/P} + \underset{(1.824)}{0.0792\,C} - \underset{(0.556)}{0.0008\,(S/P)}$$
$$R^2 = 0.178 \quad (A.11)$$

$$\log \text{CSC} = 0.1501 + \underset{(2.028)}{0.0686 \log S} + \underset{(2.393)}{0.0785\,B} + \underset{(1.920)}{0.0776\,C}$$
$$R^2 = 0.172 \quad (A.12)$$

where CSC = average examination performance in points for each school;
E/S = total expenditure per CSC student in K£, net of boarding expenditure;
S = number of students in Forms I–IV;
B = percent boarders in Forms I–IV;
H/P = average male education in years in the district where the school is located;
C = dummy variable for whether or not the school has an HSC cycle;
S/P = number of CSC pupils per thousand inhabitants in the district where the school is located; and
log = natural logarithm.

---

[28] Figures in parentheses refer to *t*-values.

Other variables, such as the percentage of female students in each school, the percentage of overseas term teachers, non-teacher expenditure per pupil, teacher expenditure per pupil, and the percent of total expenditure on teachers were also run but were either highly correlated with the variables shown or contributed very little to the regression estimate.

The results show that if expenditure per student is the only variable used to explain examination performance, it is significantly related to performance, but covers only a small part (4 percent) of the variation in examination score. The linear relationship (equation (A.8)) also indicates that it would cost (or save) K£6 per student to raise (or lower) examination scores by one percentage point, everything else being equal.

As we move down to equation (A.9), however, it is clear that expenditure per pupil is not a significant variable when school size and the percentage of boarders in the school are held constant. If expenditure per pupil (net of boarding expenditure) and the percentage of boarders do not vary, the size of the school (as measured by the number of pupils), is positively related to examination score with an elasticity of 0.1, i.e. if the number of students in the school is increased by ten percent, examination performance is increased by one percent. The average number of pupils in the CSC cycle is 258, or 64.5 per Form. Similarly, holding school size and expenditure constant, increasing the percentage of boarders by 10 percentage points increases average examination score by one percent, or close to .02 points. However, all three variables explain only about 15 percent of the variation in examination score.

Equation (A.12) indicates that analyzing schools on the basis of whether they do or do not have an HSC cycle reduces the coefficients of school size and percentage of boarders considerably. This reflects the larger size and higher share of boarders in schools with an HSC cycle. The average size of HSC schools is 387 students, 70 percent of whom are boarders, whereas non-HSC schools average 196 pupils and 50 percent boarders. HSC schools also spend more per pupil in the CSC cycle (K£113 compared to K£70 in non-HSC schools, per year). The result is a difference of 8 percent or about 14 points in average examination score between the two types of schools, holding size of school and percentage of boarders constant. The coefficient of (C) changes little when expenditure per pupil, male education, and CSC pupils per thousand population are also held constant (see equation (A.11)). This indicates that CSC schools with HSC cycles attract a type of pupil that does better even when a number of other variables that affect examination score are held constant.

CSC, schools grouped by education level in school's county. In an effort to explain a larger fraction of the variance in examination scores, the group of 115 schools was divided into three sub-groups based on average male education in the school's county, namely:

a) Schools in counties with average male education of less than or equal to 1.9 years, which typify most of the poorer areas of the country;
b) Schools in counties with average male education between 2.0 and 3.5 years, which includes all other areas; and,
c) Schools with both African and non-African students, the latter group being recruited from a population with an average educational level more than twice as high as the highest district average for the African population.

As could be expected from the statistically insignificant coefficient for male education in equations (A.10) and (A.11), differences in average examination score between the three groups of schools are not large: the first group has an average score of 1.74, and the other two, 1.85 and 1.80, respectively.[29] The average values of the other main variables are shown in Annex Table A.1.

The results of the regression estimates within groups are as follows.

Group 1: 35 schools in districts with an average education of adult African males in 1962 of 1.9 years or less:

$$\log \text{CSC} = 0.3554 + 0.0404 \log S - 0.1140\,G + 0.1960\,B$$
$$(0.571) \qquad (1.702) \qquad (2.847)$$
$$- 0.063 \log(E/S) + 0.0540\,(S/P)$$
$$(1.000) \qquad (2.437)$$
$$R^2 = 0.328 \quad (\text{A.13})$$

$$\log \text{CSC} = 0.6278 + 0.0119 \log S - 0.0997\,G + 0.2080\,B$$
$$(0.172) \qquad (1.554) \qquad (3.366)$$
$$- 0.1281 \log(E_n/S) + 0.0433\,(S/P)$$
$$(2.006) \qquad (2.091)$$
$$R^2 = 0.389 \quad (\text{A.14})$$

Group 2: 50 schools in districts with an average education of adult African males in 1962 of 2.0–3.5 years:

$$\log \text{CSC} = 0.9511 + 0.1940 \log S + 0.0317\,B + 9.4890\,(T/S)$$
$$(2.452) \qquad (0.589) \qquad (2.336)$$
$$- 0.4389 \log(E/S) - 0.0007\,(S/P)$$
$$(2.085) \qquad (0.242)$$
$$R^2 = 0.231 \quad (\text{A.15})$$

$$\text{CSC} = 1.760 + 0.3933\,C \qquad R^2 = 0.201 \quad (\text{A.16})$$
$$(3.472)$$

---

[29] This probably means that average male education in a given area is a poor proxy for the average education of those families whose children go to secondary schools.

ANNEX TABLE A.1: Average Value (Mean) of Main Variables Used in Examination Performance Regressions, CSC and HSC Cycles, 1966

	Mean Score	Non-Teacher Expenditure/Pupil (K£)	Teacher Expenditure/Pupil (K£)	Total Expenditure/Pupil (K£)	Percent Overseas Teachers	Percent Boarders	Number of Students	Number of Candidates
CSC: All Schools	1.82	20.5	66.6	87.1	42	54	258	48
Group 1: adult male population with average of 1.9 years of education or less (less prosperous and less populous rural counties)	1.74	21.8	67.3	89.1	42	76	178	32
Group 2: adult male population with average of 2-3 years of education (more prosperous and populous rural, and African urban counties)	1.85	19.8	64.7	84.6	44	58	219	39
Group 3: adult male population with average of 3.6 years of education or more (mixed urban schools)	1.80	18.7	66.6	85.2	38	21	431	80
HSC: All Schools	2.66	30.9	143.8	174.6	67	69	65	24

	Percent of Schools with HSC Cycle	Av. Male Education in District (years)	CSC Pupils/10³ Population in Dist.	Graduate Teacher Equivalent Per Pupil (number)
CSC: All Schools	23	3.27	11.0	0.054
Group 1	8	1.52	2.4	0.054
Group 2	24	2.50	8.3	0.052
Group 3	38	6.56	26.4	0.054
HSC: All Schools	—	2.85	—	0.060

Source: Calculated from Ministry of Education data.

Group 3: 30 multi-ethnic or minority schools drawing their pupils from a population with an average education of adult males in 1962 of 3.6 years or more:

$$\text{CSC} = 1.606 + 0.0023\,(E/S) \qquad R^2 = 0.170 \quad \text{(A.17)}$$
$$\phantom{\text{CSC} = 1.606 + }(2.478)$$

$$\log \text{CSC} = 0.5117 + 0.1304\,B + 0.1484\,(OT) \qquad R^2 = 0.322 \quad \text{(A.18)}$$
$$\phantom{\log \text{CSC} = 0.5117 + }(2.404)(2.108)$$

$$\log \text{CSC} = -0.0673 + 0.0862 \log S + 0.0076\,G + 0.1844\,B$$
$$\phantom{\log \text{CSC} = -0.0673 + }(1.524)(0.157)(2.727)$$
$$+\ 0.0263 \log (E/S) - 0.0002\,(S/P)$$
$$(0.584)(0.107)$$
$$R^2 = .320 \quad \text{(A.19)}$$

where CSC, E/S, S, B, S/P, C, H/P, and log are defined as for equations (A.8–A.12) and

G = percentage girl students;
T/S = school's teacher–student ratio;
OT = overseas term teachers as percent of total teachers; and
E_n/S = non-teacher expenditure per CSC candidate in K£ (net of boarding expenditure).

This division into three groups does yield higher coefficients of determination (R^2). The coefficients of the percentage of boarders are significant in the lowest and highest groups and almost equal with the same independent variables held constant (equations (A.13) and (A.19)). An increase in the percentage of boarders in both cases raises the examination score more than in the aggregate CSC regression estimate. A ten percentage point rise in boarders raises the examination score by about four percentage points. Table A.1 shows the average number of boarders in the two groups of schools to be at opposite ends of the spectrum. The contribution which boarding facilities make to efficiency may be expected to vary with the density of population and the average income level. Group 1 schools are mostly in thinly populated, poor areas. Even if half their pupils were boarding, the contribution that an additional boarding place might make in enabling suitable pupils within the catchment areas to attend might be no less than that of the first boarding place in an urban area. The 58 percent level in the middle group of schools, located mostly in urban or densely populated rural areas, may represent a comparatively higher level of boarding[30] than the other two, and the substantially smaller regression

---

[30] If we assume a scale of boarding intensity, starting with the minimum proportion needed for a school to function in its area and ending at the maximum that

coefficient for boarders may reflect diminishing marginal returns to additional boarders.

When other variables are held constant, the coefficients of expenditure per pupil and school size are significant only for Group 2 where the coefficient of expenditure per pupil is negative, but the coefficient of teachers per pupil is positive. Teacher expenditure per pupil as a percentage of total expenditure is, however, so highly correlated with overall expenditure per pupil as to create an obvious collinearity problem, and the teacher pupil ratio is merely indicative of teacher expenditures.[31] The meaning of the separate coefficients is therefore not clear. When expenditure per pupil is the only variable used, its coefficient is significant and it explains 17 percent of the variation in examination scores in multi-ethnic or minority schools. Even so, for every £10 increase in total expenditure per pupil (representing about 12 percent of average per pupil expenditure in that group), average examination scores would go up only by two percentage points.

In Group 1 (1.9 years of average male education or less), non-teacher expenditure is negatively and significantly related to examination score, and the number of CSC pupils per thousand population positively. The latter effect is interesting, since it suggests that for this group of schools which are in counties with very low secondary school enrollment ratios, increasing the number of CSC pupils might result in some sort of external economy in the exam performance of other pupils. The enrollment ratio S/P is not a significant variable in the other groups.

The schools were also divided into those with and without HSC cycles. Within the latter there was little change in the aggregate results; in the group of schools with the HSC cycle the results of the regression were very similar to those for the HSC exam itself, except that the coefficient of determination (R^2) was regularly lower.

HSC, all schools. Examination scores on the Higher School Certificate

---

makes any further contribution to efficiency, the 76 percent average of boarders in the Group 1 (rural, less populated) counties might mean no higher "effective intensity" than the 21 percent average in ethnically mixed schools which are all in urban areas.

[31] The positive correlation of the teacher–pupil ratio and total expenditure per pupil might be expected to eliminate the significance of the coefficients in equation (A.15). However, if this equation is estimated without including T/S, we find the following results.

$$\log \text{CSC} = -0.3205 + 0.1484 \log S + 0.0301 B + 0.0278 \log E/S$$
$$(1.846) \qquad (0.404) \qquad (0.402)$$
$$-0.0010 \log (S/P) \qquad\qquad\qquad R^2 = 0.136$$
$$(0.324) \qquad\qquad\qquad\qquad\qquad\qquad\qquad (A.20)$$

Thus the correlation between T/S and E/S leads to a more significant coefficient for E/S and a significant coefficient for T/S.

are differentiated by number of passes in principal and subsidiary subjects. The weighting used here assigned a 5.0 to five principal subjects passed, 4.0 to four principal subjects passed, down to zero for no principal subjects passed. With these weights, the regression estimate yields the following relation between inputs and examination score:

$$\log \text{HSC} = -1.2470 + \underset{(2.456)}{0.2614 \log S} + \underset{(2.006)}{0.6455\, B} - \underset{(2.001)}{0.2399\, (E/S)}$$
$$+ \underset{(1.827)}{1.4998\, E_t/E} + \underset{(3.631)}{0.5198 \log H/P}$$
$$R^2 = 0.548 \quad \text{(A.21)}$$

where $S, B, E/S, H/P$, and log are defined as for equations (A.8–A.12), and

HSC = school's average exam performance;
E_t/E = school's expenditure on teacher salaries as percentage of school's total expenditure.

The HSC cycle averages a much smaller number of pupils per Form (32.5) and a much higher annual expenditure per pupil (K£175) than the CSC cycle, mostly due to much higher expenditure per pupil on teachers. As in Group 2 of the CSC schools, the coefficient of expenditure per pupil is negative and the coefficient of the percentage of expenditure on teachers' salaries is positive but not significant at the five percent level. As in the overall CSC estimate, the coefficient of the percentage of boarders in the school is positive. In this case the coefficient of adult male education in the county where the school is located is significant; it is positive and shows an elasticity of 0.5: for every one percent increase in adult male education in the school's county there would be a 0.5 percent increase in examination score. These variables together explain 55 percent of the variation in examination score in the 33 schools observed.

Rates of Return to Additional Inputs

From the Labor Force Sample Survey and the age-education-earnings analysis derived from it, we have found relationships between examination performance at the CSC level and earnings (see Chapters III and IV). Given the estimates of the contribution of various inputs to exam score, it is possible to assess the returns of additional inputs into the education process. The rates are summarized in Annex Table A.2.

The additional income associated with an increase in examination score is derived from the mean incomes of secondary school leavers with different results on their terminal examination. We estimate income differences between those with different scores on the CSC examination (Division I, Division II, Division III, GCE, fail) from two regression equations. The

ANNEX TABLE A.2: Rates of Return to Additional per Pupil Expenditure

(1) Significant Variable	(2) Increase in (1)	(3) Exam score Increase Associated with (2) (in points)	(4) Additional Income Associated with (3)	(5) Annual Rate of Return to (2) (percent)
Level of Schooling (Examination)				
Primary (KPE: score range 0–300 150 points = pass)				
Schools with average score above pass	Average teacher salaries	160 Ksh (20 Ksh/yr.)	3.4	0.67 Ksh/mo.	1.4
Schools with average score below pass	Average teacher salaries	160 Ksh (20 Ksh/yr.)	3.4	2.16 Ksh/mo.	4.6
Secondary (CSC: score range 1.00–3.50)				
Schools with average score of 1.75 or below	Total expenditure per pupil	K£125 (K£31.25/yr.)	.05	K£7–8/yr.	5.6–6.4
	Teacher salaries per pupil	K£105.2 (K£26.3/yr.)	.05	K£7–8/yr.	6.7–7.6
	Percent boarders	24 percentage points: K£ in social cost per pupil	.05	K£7–8/yr.	140–160
Schools with average score above 1.75	Total expenditure per pupil	K£125 (K£31.25/yr.)	.05	K£0.3–0.6/yr.	0.25–0.5
	Teacher salaries per pupil	K£105.2 (K£26.3/yr.)	.05	K£0.3–0.6/yr.	0.3–0.6
	Percent boarders	24 percentage points: K£5 in social cost per pupil	.05	K£0.3–0.6/yr.	6–12

first estimates income differences by relating earnings of urban African males to examination score, no other variables held constant. The second relates earnings to examination score with age variables held constant, thus correcting for differences in age distribution. The results are as follows:

	No Other Variables Constant	Age Variables Constant
	(Ksh/month)	
Income difference between scoring Division II and Division I pass (1.75 − 3.50 points on CSC examination)	20	34
Income difference between scoring Division III and Division II pass (1.25 − 1.75 points on CSC examination)	133	120

If there were more observations in this subgroup of the Labor Force Survey, significant coefficients for examination score could be obtained when correcting for socio-economic background as well. With an even larger number of observations in the sample group, we could make examination score a parameter, as in the case of the primary schooling analysis.

Increasing percentage of boarders. The average cost per boarder derived from the school data is K£25.8 annually. In order to determine the additional private and social costs of boarding, however, the average expenditure of a secondary school student while living at home must be subtracted from the costs at school. From a survey taken in Nairobi in July 1963, the average expenditure of an adult equivalent member of an average size middle income family on food plus recreation plus household operation is Ksh 66.3/month. Housing expenditure was not included because it is probably not reduced when a young adult leaves home and goes to a boarding school. For a nine-month school year (in 1966 prices) this comes to K£31.7/school year. A similar survey of the former Central Province in 1963/64 yields average adult expenditures of K£5.5 (in 1966 prices) on food, beverages, and services in rural areas per school year and of K£24 (in 1966 prices) in eight Central Province towns.[32] Taking the simple average of these expenditures as an approximation of the deductible component in family expenditure yields K£20/school year. Net secondary school boarding costs are thus about K£6/year.

Holding the HSC dummy, size of school (S) and total non-boarding expenditure per pupil (E/S) constant, equation (A.11) yields a coefficient of

---

[32] Ministry of Economic Planning and Development, *Economic Survey of Central Province, 1963/64*, Nairobi, 1968.

B equal to 0.0902. To increase an average CSC score of 1.82 by 5 percentage points to 1.87, for example, would require an increase in the percentage of boarders of 24 percentage points. Since the average percentage of boarders in CSC schools is 54, this represents an increase by nearly one-half (44 percent). The number of boarders averages 122 per school, so a 44 percent increase means 54 more boarders per school, at a net increase in total social cost of K£324 per year and per school, or K£1,296 for Forms I through IV. Since the average number of students per CSC school is 258, the average increase in the social cost per student as a result of the additional boarders is K£5 for the four-year cycle.

On the benefit side, the increase of five percentage points in examination score on the range between an average Division II (1.75 points) and an average Division I score (3.50 points) results in an addition of (5/175) times 20–34 shillings/month = 0.5–1.0 Ksh/month to the average salary of urban African males. If this salary increase of K£0.3–0.6 per year is taken as a perpetuity, the rate of return which equates the additional earnings to the additional cost of boarding ranges from $r = \frac{0.3}{5}$, or 6 percent per annum, to $r = \frac{0.6}{5} = 12$ percent per annum. The increase of five percentage points in examination score between an average Division III (1.25 points) and an average Division II score (1.75 points) results in an addition of 5/50 times 120–133 Ksh/month, or K£7–8 a year. If this increase is taken as a perpetuity the rate of return ranges from 140–160 percent per annum.

Increasing total expenditure. The relationship between examination score and total expenditure per pupil estimated for the entire set of observed CSC schools yields a slope of 0.0016 (equation [A.8]). For every K£6.25 increase in expenditure per pupil per year the average examination score is expected to rise by one percentage point. The estimated relationship does not include any other variables. A five percentage point increase in examination score, from the observed mean of 1.82 to 1.87, would require K£31.25 additional expenditure per pupil per year, or K£125 for the four-year CSC cycle—a substantial increase over the observed expenditure of K£84.7. Nevertheless, a five point increase in examination score between Division II (1.75) and Division I (3.50) results in a maximum increase in earnings of (5/175) times Ksh 20–34 monthly, or K£0.3–K£0.6 annually.

Assuming again that the additional income is a perpetuity, the rate of return can be estimated as:

$$r = \frac{0.3}{125} = 0.0025,$$
$$r = \frac{0.6}{125} = 0.005.$$

The 0.25–0.5 percent rate of return calculated in this way is an upward biased estimate, since income differences from higher examination scores are lower in the early working years and higher later. The rate of return is higher to additional expenditures made at lower average examination score levels because the income difference for those scoring a Division II pass and those scoring a Division III or GCE pass is greater than that between Division I and Division II. Since both Divisions I and II are clearly above average passes on the CSC, it is a plausible result that the income difference between those who obtain a poor pass or who fail (Division III, GCE, and fail) and those in the Division I/Division II group would be greater than the differences within the latter category.

If the estimated income differences are taken from the regression results when age variables are included, a five point increase in examination score from, say, 1.70 to 1.75, adds K£7 annually to the average income of African males. If the differences are taken from the regression results relating income only to examination score, the increase in K£8 annually. The rates of return to additional schooling expenditure over the four-year CSC cycle (K£125) are 5.6 and 6.4 percent, respectively. Both estimates are biased upward because of the smaller differences in income in earlier years of working life.

Further calculation shows that in CSC schools with mixed ethnic student bodies (Group 3, average education of adult males in 1962 of 3.6 years or more), the total expenditure per pupil variable explains 17 percent of average examination score variation among individual schools. The rate of return to additional expenditure in that group is 0.35–0.7 percent for examination score increases between Division II and I, and between 8.0 and 9.2 percent for increases in the Division III to Division II range.[33] The rates are therefore higher than the aggregates of all CSC schools taken together. The coefficient of expenditure per pupil is not significant in the other two groups of CSC schools when expenditure per pupil is the only independent variable.

Increasing teachers' salaries. Since schooling costs are divided among teachers' salaries and other recurrent expenditures (net of boarding expenses), it is possible to estimate the rate of return to increasing expenditure in one or the other of these categories. When the two cost components are related separately and individually to examination score using all CSC schools, only the teachers' salaries component has a significant regression coefficient. The relationship is:

$$\text{CSC} = 1.6898 + 0.0019\,(E_t/S) \qquad R^2 = 0.038 \qquad (A.22)$$
$$(2.012)$$

---

[33] One implicit assumption is of course that there are no significant performance differences within these schools between pupils from the different ethnic groups.

ANNEX TABLE A.3: Salary Scales for the Teaching Service

(K£ per year)

Category	Old Scale[a]	New Scale[b]	Actual Average Salaries[e]
Unqualified without KPE	84	90	84
with KPE	96	103.4	96[f]
with KJSE	108	117	108
with CSC	240	252	240
with HSC			n.a.
one PP[d]	300	330	n.a.
two PP	350	366	n.a.
Qualified			
PH and ATI II without KPE	120–6–180[e]	135–6–177–9–231	179
P3 and ATI II with KPE	162–6–180–12–264	180–9–216–12–360	204
P2 and TI I	240–12–276–18–456	264–12–300–18–480	301
P1 and SATI	348–27–726	378–27–756	411
SI, AEO and T1	582–24–750–25–800–30–830–35–1110	684–27–981–30–1011–36–1119	582[g]
STI	1110–40–1230	1155–42–1239	n.a.
TM	750–25–800–35–1110–40–1350–50–1450	810–42–978–45–1158–48–1446	n.a.
Graduate Teacher	804–43–976–44–1108–46–1292	810–42–978–45–1158–48–1446–51–1548–54–1710	n.a.
AL II	804–43–976–44–1108–46–1292	810–42–978–45–1158–48–1302	n.a.
AL I	1154–46–1338–52–1442	1158–48–1446	n.a.
Lecturer	1494–52–1598–56–1710	1494–51–1548–54–1710	n.a.
Senior Lecturer	1839–75–1989	1839–75–1989	n.a.

[a] In force from April 1, 1964.
[b] As proposed in Sessional Paper No. 11 of 1967.
[c] All teachers employed in the primary schools of Kiambu and Nyeri counties in 1967.
[d] PP = principal pass.
[e] Read: K£120 increasing in steps of K£6 to K£180.
[f] Not included 17 teachers with K£102.
[g] One teacher only.

Note:
ATI = assistant technical instructor.
TI = techn. instructor.
SATI = senior techn. ass. instructor.
STI = senior techn. instructor.
TM = technical master.
AL = assistant lecturer.
AEO = assistant education offices.

Source: Ministry of Education and Ministry of Local Government.

where E_t/S is the school's expenditure on teacher salaries per pupil. According to (A.22), a five-point change in examination score would require K£26.3 additional expenditure annually on teachers' salaries, or K£105.2 for the four-year cycle. The rates of return are therefore 0.3–0.6/105.2, or $r = 0.003$–0.006, which is higher than the rate to increasing total expenditure.

If observations at the 13 years of schooling level had yielded significant relationships between examination score and income, it would have been possible to estimate similar rates of return to additional schooling inputs in Forms V and VI (higher secondary). Unfortunately, the small number of observations at that level (135 males, of whom only 36 were Africans) and the poor response to the HSC examination score question resulted in insignificant coefficients for the dummies indicating the number of principal subjects passed. It is therefore not possible to estimate rates of return to additional inputs at the higher secondary level.

Summary

Annex Table A.2 summarizes most of the rates of return calculated in this chapter. We state below the major results from the regression analysis.

Primary School:

a) The formal qualifications of the teaching force appear to have no significant effect on examination score, and the return to increasing average teachers' salaries is very low (less than 5 percent in a strongly upward-biased example).

b) The teacher-pupil ratio apparently has no impact on the examination performance, not even when disaggregated into partial ratios based on teacher qualifications.

c) The size of the school is negatively related to examination score, i.e. large schools have lower average scores on the KPE.

Secondary School:

a) Taken alone, expenditure per student is a variable with a positive and significant regression coefficient, but explains only a small part of exam score variation. The low regression coefficient implies that expenditure could theoretically be decreased by nearly one-half without decreasing examination score below an average Division II pass. Of course, the regression estimates are valid only for much smaller changes in expenditure, so a policy of large changes would entail a different kind of analysis.

b) Expenditure per student is not significant once size of school, percentage of boarders, and other variables are taken into account.

Our results fail to produce evidence that a straightforward increase in school expenditure will improve examination scores at the secondary level. Total expenditure per pupil is not used as a variable at the primary education level due to lack of data, but the results for teacher expenditure per pupil (which account for all but a small portion of total expenditure per pupil) suggest the same negative conclusion at the primary level. As we stated at the outset of this chapter, our results do not substantiate some widely held beliefs about how to improve the quality of schooling, but they are not sufficient in quantity and quality to form the basis for an alternate set of hypotheses. Their main value is in indicating the direction for future research and in showing how results could be incorporated into a cost-benefit analysis.

ANNEX B

SCOPE AND ORGANIZATION OF THE LABOR FORCE SAMPLE SURVEY

The need to conduct a special sample survey arose from the complete lack of the cross-classified data on earnings, age and education which are a pre-condition of rate-of-return analysis in education. The original design covered the following Divisions of the I.S.I.C.:[1] 1 (mining and quarrying), 2/3 (manufacturing), 4 (construction), 5 (electricity, gas, water and sanitary services), 6 (commerce), 7 (transport, storage and communication) and 82 through 84 (services except government). At a later stage a small non-random sample of the public sector was included as well. Thus the only economic activity that remained uncovered, in view of obvious organizational difficulties, was Division 0 (agriculture, forestry, hunting and fishing).

The sample was a double-stratified random sample of the country's firms, distinguishing among four size groups (under 15, 15 to 49, 50 to 99, 100 and more employees) and three locations (Nairobi, Mombasa, all other towns). In the light of time and manpower constraints, firms located in or around Nakuru (Rift Valley Province) were taken as representative of all firms not located in either Nairobi or Mombasa. For each size group and location a random sample of firms totalling 2.5 percent of the country's 1967 employment in these sectors was taken. The interviews, which we conducted with the help of a number of local assistants during the period January 24 to February 12, 1968, covered in principle each employee. There

[1] International Standard Industrial Classification of All Economic Activities, Statistical Papers, Series M, No. 4, Statistical Office of the United Nations, New York, April, 1956.

were only two exceptions to this rule: first, an incomplete coverage of the firm's management, due to the fact that executives were frequently absent for business or other reasons; second, the omission of employees working in a second shift in the few cases where this applied. While the first imperfection would tend to give a downward bias to the survey results, the second one is not likely to distort the data in any systematic way (the underlying assumption being that workers temporarily on the night shift do not have educational or other characteristics different from the rest of the firm's labor force).

The only intentional divergence from the original sample schedule was a reduced coverage of firms in the 1-14 group and of enterprises in the Nakuru area. In the case of the small firms it was felt that the amount of time involved in interviewing and incidental work (such as making preliminary arrangements, commuting to the firms, etc.) was quite disproportionate given the low (and probably decreasing) importance of these firms for manpower and educational planning. In the case of the Nakuru establishments, the reduced coverage was all but inevitable, since only one team-day could be made available for this segment of the survey.

A total of 4,290 employees working in 57 firms were interviewed, of whom 3,050 and 35, respectively, were from Nairobi, 802 and 14 from Mombasa, and 438 and 8 from Nakuru. Fifty-three questionnaires (slightly more than 1 percent) had to be rejected; most of these originated in one firm interviewed during the first days, and in this case one of the questions was misunderstood. It is worth mentioning that the cooperation of private firms was outstanding; participation was nearly complete (only one firm out of about 70 contacted did not wish to take part), and the general attitude was one of interest and enthusiasm, which was most encouraging in the difficult early stages of the survey.

Since the public sector accounts for half of non-agricultural employment, and for a still higher proportion of medium-level and highly skilled personnel, some coverage of this sector had been envisaged from the beginning. In view of time and personnel constraints and of the superior average qualification of civil servants, it was decided not to conduct interviews but to have questionnaires distributed among the employees of the participating government agencies which would then be collected centrally. The number of responses thus obtained was 558, all from persons stationed permanently or temporarily in Nairobi (of which 377 were from the Ministry of Economic Planning and Development and the Treasury, and 160 from a detachment of the Kenya Police).[2] The number of rejected questionnaires (52, or 9.3 per-

---

[2] The Nairobi staff of the Ministry of Education were approached as well, but for reasons at which we can only guess, the participation was negligibly small (21 questionnaires).

cent) was significantly higher than in the private sector, thus supporting the assumption that a questionnaire survey (at least one involving more than a few simple questions) should be conducted by personal interviews rather than indirectly.

The length of the questionnaire, which we suspect is beyond the optimum, as well as its structure, clearly reflect the experimental nature of the case study in general and the survey in particular.[3] Several questions were reformulated in the light of the first days' experience, giving due regard to local idiosyncrasies which had not yet come to our attention when the questionnaire was drafted in Washington.

CONFIDENTIAL　　　　　　　　　　　　Code No. of Firm or
　　　　　　　　　　　　　　　　　　　Government Agency

1968 Labor Force Survey Individual Questionnaire

1. Sex　　M_____　　　F_____

2(a). Of what country are you a citizen?
Kenya_____ Other East Africa_____ Other_____
　　　　　　　　　　　　Afr.　　Asn.　　Eur.

2(b). Ethnic origin　　_____　_____　_____

3. If African, what tribe? _____

4. Year of birth_____

5. How long have you lived in this town?_____ years
　　　　　　　　　　　　　　　　　　　　　　　months

6(a). What was the highest level of schooling you completed?
Primary:　　0–2_____　3–5_____　6–8_____
Type of Primary school: Government_____　Mission_____
Secondary:　　1–2_____　3–4_____　5–6_____
Type of Secondary school: Technical_____　General_____
　Government_____　Mission_____　Harambee_____
Teacher Training: Incomplete_____　Complete_____
University: Incomplete_____　Complete_____
Location: Kenya_____ Other East Africa_____ Abroad_____
Faculty: _____　Subject: _____

6(b). What exams did you attempt?　CEE_____　KPE_____
KASSE_____　KJSE_____　CSC_____　GCE_____　HSC_____

7(a). Where did you go to primary school? _____

---

[3] For a replica of the questionnaire, see attachment to this Annex.

8. What was your grade in: CEE (fail, pass)_____
                                KPE (fail, pass, qualify) _____
9. What was your grade in GCE_____, CSC (Div. I, II, III)_____, or HSC_____?
10. In what year did you leave school?_____
11. In what year did you start paid work?_____
12. What is (was) your father's occupation?_____
13. Does (did) your father know how to read and write? Yes_____ No_____
14. Does (did) your mother know how to read and write? Yes_____ No_____
15. How many years of schooling did he or she have? Father_____ Mother_____
16. What is your present occupation? _____
17. What were your previous occupations? _____
18. How long have you been with this firm? _____years
                                                                   months
19(a). Are you married?   Yes_____   No_____
19(b). How many children do you have?_____
20. Are you at present following an education program? Yes_____ No_____ If so, what kind?_____
21. Have you had any on-the-job training or been in a special training program?   Yes_____ No_____
    If so, what kind?_____
22. What is your name? _____

TO BE FILLED IN WITH EMPLOYER'S ASSISTANCE

Gross Cash Wages (before tax) Shs._____(per day, week, month, year)
Is housing provided?   Yes_____   No_____
Cash Value of housing or rent allowance Shs._____(per week, month, year)
Food   Shs._____
Other Shs._____   for_____ (per week, month, year)
       Shs._____   for_____ (per week, month, year)
       Shs._____   for_____ (per week, month, year)

ANNEX C

REGRESSION ANALYSIS, INCOME AND EDUCATION OF AFRICAN MALES: SCHOOLING AS A VARIABLE

Besides estimating age-earnings profiles for each year of schooling, it is useful for us to know the effect on earnings of schooling as a variable—rather than as a parameter—and how that relationship changes with the addition of other variables. Although this exercise has the disadvantage of leaving out the interaction effect between schooling and other factors,[1] it does show the approximate trade-off between taking additional schooling and having the characteristic described by some other variable. The analysis also tells us how well these variables explain variation in earnings of a particular sex-ethnic group (African males).

The sample of urban African males with 11 years of schooling or less is analyzed in its entirety with schooling employed as a variable, along with other variables, to explain variations in the earnings of that group. The results of this analysis show the differences in average earnings of urban African male wage-earners due to schooling, age, tribe, parents' literacy, father's occupation, size of employing firm, industry, occupation, and other variables. We assume that the non-schooling characteristics of African males will vary as the amount of schooling increases. No adjustment is made for changes in the other variables associated with changes in the amount of schooling. When we regress years of schooling on monthly earn-

---

[1] That is, the effect of being in a certain schooling group *and* having a certain tribal affiliation, or living in a certain city, etc. The parametric estimation within schooling category, in the text of Chapter III, does account for interaction effects.

ANNEX TABLE C.1: Regression Coefficients of Schooling and Independent Dummy Variables, Dependent Variable: Monthly Earnings, African Males, 1968, Schooling from 0–11 Years

		Number and Name of Independent Variables	Coefficients Equation 1	Coefficients Equation 2	Coefficients Equation 3	Coefficients Equation 4	Coefficients Equation 5	Means of Variables
Age	85	Years of Schooling	25.3	36.2	31.5	18.8	12.3	0.512
	5	Age ≤14		−328.8*	−342.1*	−217.0*	−202.9*	0.001
	6	Age 15–16		−492.8*	−466.1*	−224.4*	−177.8*	0.000
	7	Age 17–19		−278.9	−292.5	−234.3	−209.4	0.019
	8	Age 20–24		−204.4	−211.7	−183.3	−182.2	0.176
	9	Age 25–29		−101.4	−110.6	−89.7	−87.1	0.216
	10	Age 30–34		−32.6	−35.5	−30.7	−25.8	0.210
	12	Age 45–54		−3.2*	2.4*	7.2*	5.6*	0.100
	13	Age 55+		17.1*	20.2	−6.1	−3.1	0.026
Literacy	21	Father illit.			109.4	118.9*	80.2*	0.690
	22	Father lit.			152.6	146.5	107.2*	0.291
	24	Mother illit.			−84.7	−47.5	−40.9	0.872
	26	Mother no ans.			75.0	117.4	76.6*	0.016
Tribe	27	Kikuyu			−75.3	−54.9	−52.4	0.316
	28	Kamba			−69.3	−54.5	−52.5	0.207
	29	Luhya			−92.1	−56.6	−45.4	0.171
	30	Coastal			−79.3	−84.5	−95.6	0.067
	31	Luo			−80.0	−34.1	−22.3*	0.127
	32	Kalenjin			−33.5*	−48.5*	−42.5*	0.013
Father's Occupation	68	Farmer			31.7	17.0*	12.4*	0.499
	69	Prof. 1			12.6*	24.9*	76.5*	0.029
	70	Prof. 2			37.9*	−30.7*	−17.9*	0.104
	71	Techn.			28.3*	59.8*	80.2*	0.059
	72	Foreman			32.2*	−1.6*	−4.0*	0.108
	73	Admin.			49.6*	17.2*	2.9*	0.101
	74	Clerk			66.5	30.0*	25.4*	0.132
	75	Skill.			78.5	55.7	58.8	0.146
	76	Semi-skill.			25.3*	27.1*	30.4	0.236
Firm Location and Size	14	Nairobi				27.4*	28.8*	0.754
	15	Mombasa				65.3	69.5	0.162
	2	Public sector				94.4	8.0*	0.096
	17	Firm size 1–14				−75.5	−76.2*	0.006

178

	18	Firm size 15–49		−50.1	−50.6	0.095
	20	Firm size 100+		−15.3*	−18.4*	0.655
Occupation	39	Farmer		−102.0*	−28.1*	0.000
	40	Prof. 1		109.6	99.5	0.012
	41	Prof. 2		209.5*	247.3*	0.001
	42	Technician		172.5	138.5	0.005
	43	Foreman		252.8	257.1	0.019
	44	Admin.		954.7	873.0	0.015
	45	Clerk		136.4	117.0	0.118
	46	Skill.		−1.3*	21.3*	0.138
	47	Semi-Skill.		−74.0	−55.1*	0.414
	49	Manufacturing		30.2*	28.8*	0.450
	50	Construction		3.0*	4.4*	0.070
	51	Commerce		27.6*	47.8	0.159
	52	Services		−2.1*	16.4*	0.137
	53	Union		113.2	122.8	0.695
Education	56	Primary public		−46.3	−12.2*	0.253
	57	Primary private		−49.6	−11.8	0.397
	78	Addl. educ.		72.2*	86.1*	0.137
	79	No addl. educ.		55.3*	70.5*	0.849
	81	Addl. training		75.1	−12.3*	0.164
	82	No addl. training		−8.6*	−96.2*	0.824
	60	Sec. public general			78.4	0.048
	61	Sec. public teacher training			278.7	0.002
	62	Sec. private technical			−64.7*	0.004
	63	Sec. private general			−56.5	0.032
	64	Sec. private teacher training			−175.7*	0.001
	65	Sec. Harambee			−110.9*	0.003
	66	Sec. not applicable			−33.9	0.619
	67	Sec. no answer			42.6	0.213
	34	CSC Division I			455.4	0.003
	35	CSC Division II			357.8	0.011
	36	CSC Division III			293.0	0.013
	37	CSC GCE			231.2	0.005
		R^2	0.09	0.16	0.19	0.37	0.42
		Intercept term	278.3	299.0	324.2	178.0	269.0
		Average earnings (Ksh/month)					392.4
		Average age (years)					32.9

* Not significant.

Source: Labor Force Sample Survey, January/February 1968

ings (in Ksh—Kenyan shillings), we find a coefficient of 25.3 for schooling. This means that if we know nothing more about two groups of African males than that their average schooling differs by one year, we would expect their average monthly incomes to differ by 25.3 Ksh. This first regression is represented in the Annex Table C.1 by "Coefficients, Equation 1."

We next relate both schooling and age together to earnings. By including the age variables in the regression estimate, we separate the effect of age on earnings from the schooling–earnings relationship, i.e. the relation of schooling to earnings is corrected for differences in the age distribution of individuals with different amounts of schooling (Equation 2). The age-corrected increase in earnings from additional schooling is 36.2 Ksh per month for each year of additional schooling, i.e. 43 percent more than the unadjusted figure. The reason for this increase in the coefficient is the lower average age of wage-earners with better education. Thus, correcting for age augments the earnings differentials due to additional schooling.

The next adjustment we make on the schooling–earnings relation is for socio-economic variables—father's occupation, tribe, and parents' literacy. The relation between these variables and earnings is separated from the schooling–earnings relationship. This adjustment reduces the schooling coefficient to 31.5 Ksh per month per additional year of schooling (Equation 3). The coefficient has now been corrected for all those non-schooling variables which are unconnected with formal education. The increase in wage-earners' age, and the added job experience that goes with it, is not part of formal schooling, and the effect of age on earnings is therefore separated from the schooling–earnings relation by holding age constant. Likewise, father's occupation, tribe, and literacy of parents are proxies for variables exogenous to schooling—such as influence on the job market, closeness or remoteness from the major centers of demand for manpower, and home training—and they are also corrected for.

The remaining two groups of non-schooling variables—occupation, size of firm, and sector of employment and secondary school examination score —are also brought into the regression (Equations 4 and 5). As we explain in Chapter V with reference to the earnings profiles corrected for the latter groups of variables, we consider the decrease in the schooling coefficient when these variables are held constant to be an overcorrection, because their values are linked to the amount of schooling.

ANNEX D

DERIVATION OF PROCEDURES FOR ESTIMATION OF ABSOLUTE EARNINGS FROM REGRESSION DATA

As stated in the text of Chapter III, the model we use in performing the regression of age, socio-economic, and occupational variables on income for each schooling group is of the form:

$$Y_i = B_o + \sum_j B_j X_{ij} + \sum_k C_k Z_{ik} + U_i \quad \begin{matrix} i = 1 \ldots n \\ j = 1 \ldots m \\ k = 1 \ldots l \end{matrix}$$

and the predictive equation may be expressed in the notation both of deviates (e.g. $X_{ij} - \bar{X}_j$) and of the original variables (X_{ij}, etc.):

Deviates

$$\hat{Y}_i = \bar{Y} + \sum_j b_j(X_{ij} - \bar{X}_j) + \sum_k c_k(Z_{ik} - \bar{Z}_k) \quad (1)$$

Original Variables

$$\hat{Y}_i = b_o + \sum_j b_j X_{ij} + \sum_k c_k Z_{ik}$$

where $b_o = \hat{B}_o$ X_{ij} = age variables
$b_j = \hat{B}_j$ Z_k = socio-economic, occupational variables
$c_k = \hat{C}_k$ $\bar{Y}, \bar{X}, \bar{Z}$ = means of X, Y, and Z within a schooling group

Our objective is to find for each schooling group of African males with 11 or fewer years of schooling a monthly income figure that has been adjusted to eliminate differences in earnings due to differences (within the schooling group or between schooling groups) in parents' literacy, father's occupation, or other characteristics which influence earnings. The computational procedure is derived below simultaneously in the deviate and original variable notations. The calculations in the text are in the deviate form; the original variables form is an equivalent alternative for the computation.

First, (1) is evaluated when $Z_{ik} = \bar{Z}_k$ for all i, that is, when the Z_{ik} are set equal to their mean values.

$$
\begin{array}{l|l}
\text{Deviates} & \text{Original Variables} \\
\hat{Y}_i\Big|_{Z_{ik} = \bar{Z}_k} = \bar{Y} + \sum_j b_j(X_{ij} - \bar{X}_j) & \hat{Y}_i\Big|_{Z_{ik} = \bar{Z}_k} = b_o + \sum_j b_j X_{ij} \\
\quad = \bar{Y} + \sum_j b_j X_{ij} - \sum_j b_j \bar{X}_j & \qquad\qquad + \sum_k c_k \bar{Z}_k
\end{array}
\qquad (2)
$$

Since the X_{ij} are zero-one variables, $X_j = 1$ for age j and zero otherwise. Restating (2) for the case $X = X_j$, we obtain:[1]

$$
\hat{Y}_i\Big|_{\substack{Z_{ik} = \bar{Z}_k \\ X = X_j}} = \bar{Y} + b_j - \sum_j b_j \bar{X}_j \quad \Big| \quad \hat{Y}_i\Big|_{\substack{Z_{ik} = \bar{Z}_k \\ X = X_j}} = b_o + b_j + \sum_k c_k \bar{Z}_k \quad (3)
$$

We now wish to adjust the Y_i to reflect the extent to which the particular schooling group varies from the whole sample (African males with 11 or fewer years of schooling) with respect to the distribution of socio-economic and other variables. We designate $\bar{Z}_k^*$ as the means for the whole sample of the socio-economic and occupational variables. Recalling that the $\bar{Z}_k$ are the means of these variables for the individual schooling groups, we add the adjustment D:

$$ D = \sum_k c_k(\bar{Z}_k^* - \bar{Z}_k) $$

---

[1] A look at (3) shows in a particularly clear way the relationship between the schooling group means in the deviate form (Y) and their relevant intercept terms in the original variables form (b_o). By setting equal the right hand terms of the two equations, we find:

$$ b_o = \bar{Y} - (\sum_j b_j \bar{X}_j + \sum_k c_k \bar{Z}_k) $$

which may be recognized as the usual formula for the least squares intercept or, regrouping:

$$ \bar{Y} = b_o + \sum_j b_j \bar{X}_j + \sum_k c_k \bar{Z}_k $$

and this gives:

$$\hat{Y}_i + D = \bar{Y} + b_j - \sum_j b_j \bar{X}_j + \sum_k c_k(\bar{Z}_k^* - \bar{Z}_k)$$

$$= \left[\bar{Y} - \sum_j b_j \bar{X}_j + \sum_k c_k \cdot (\bar{Z}_k^* - \bar{Z}_k) \right] + b_j$$

$$\hat{Y}_i + D = b_o + b_j + \sum_k c_k \bar{Z}_k + \sum_k c_k(\bar{Z}_k^* - \bar{Z}_k)$$

$$= \left[b_o + \sum_k c_k \bar{Z}_k^* \right] + b_j$$

(4)

The adjusted incomes are thus equivalent to those measured by the given regression equation where the Z variables are assumed to take on the sample mean values for all regressions. The expression (4) in deviate notation describes algebraically the computational procedure carried out in the Example in Chapter III, when the Z are the socio-economic variables only. It describes the procedures used to obtain the Table 3.7, when the Z are the socio-economic and occupational variables, but when only significant values of c_k are used.

ANNEX E

CORRECTION OF RURAL LANDHOLDER INCOMES FOR ACREAGE AND FAMILY SIZE DIFFERENTIALS BETWEEN AGE GROUPS AND BETWEEN EDUCATION LEVELS FOR GIVEN AGE GROUP

The correction is made in eight steps. The data are from *Economic Survey of Central Province*, Statistics Division of Ministry of Economic Planning and Development.[1]

Step 1. Farm size in acres (S) is estimated as a linear function of age of household head (A) within each schooling category.

Schooling Category	Equation	F	t	R^2
Illiterate	$S = -1.147 + 0.1460A$	0.01	0.01	0.03
Literate	$S = -1.645 + 0.1735A$	0.01	0.01	0.16
1–3	$S = -4.668 + 0.3048A$	0.01	0.01	0.21
4–8	$S = -3.667 + 0.3074A$	0.01	0.01	0.13
9 plus	$S = -8.242 + 0.4548A$	0.05	0.05	0.25

Step 2. Gross farm income in Ksh/yr. per acre (Y_f/S) is estimated as a hyperbolic function of farm size (S).

Schooling Category	Equation	F	t	R^2
Illiterate	$Y_f/S = 169.1 + 107.2/S$	0.01	0.01	0.10
Literate	$Y_f/S = 102.6 + 273.0/S$	0.01	0.01	0.35
1–3	$Y_f/S = 195.4 + 168.6/S$	0.01	0.01	0.24
4–8 9 plus	Neither the F nor the t-value is significant; we assume average farm income per acre to be 271.3 and 219.0 respectively for the two groups.			

[1] Data communicated by Benton F. Massell, Stanford Food Research Institute.

Step 3. Total cost of family labor besides household head is estimated by first calculating from the Central Province Survey the number of man-, woman-, and child-days worked annually on the farm as a function of farm size.[2] The data refer to three farm size groups (<4.00 acres, 4.00–7.99 acres, and ≥8.00 acres):

Acre	Man-days	Woman-days	Child-days
2.33	165	249	57
5.62	208	318	84
13.45	250	452	164

Family size (F) is estimated as a function of farm size (estimated from means, not as a linear regression).

Acres	Equation
$S \leq 2.33$	$F = 4.96 + 0.41\,(2.33 - S)$
$2.33 \leq S \leq 5.62$	$F = 4.96 + 0.41\,(S - 2.33)$
$5.62 \leq S \leq 13.45$	$F = 6.31 + 0.31\,(S - 5.62)$
$13.45 \leq S$	$F = 8.76 + 0.31\,S$

From these results and the average shares of adult males and females in the whole sample, we arrive at the number of men per family as a function of farm size. Assuming 21.8 percent adult males and 27.3 percent adult females regardless of family size, we arrive at 1.08 males for a farm of 2.33 acres, 1.38 males for a farm of 5.62 acres, and 1.91 males for a farm of 13.45 acres. The number of man-days of work by non-head of household males is thus 13 for 2.33 acres, 57 for 5.62 acres, and 119 for 13.45 acres. Weighting these man-days of work by 2.19 Ksh/day, and the woman- and child-days of work from above by 1.60 and 1.00 Ksh/day, respectively, we arrive at the total imputed labor cost of non-household head family labor as a function of farm size:

Acres	Total Imputed Family Labor Cost (Excluding Head of Household)	Cost per Acre	Land Rent per Acre	Total Cost per Acre
2.33	483.9	207.7	20	227.7
5.62	717.6	127.7	20	147.7
13.45	1147.8	85.3	20	105.3

To get total cost per acre at other farm sizes, we interpolate between these acreages, extrapolate below 2.33 acres, and assume that the cost of 105.3 Ksh/acre stays constant above 13.45 acres.

---

[2] The average cost of hired labor is only about 13 Ksh a year, and is generally restricted to larger farms. It is omitted from this analysis.

Step 4. The imputed farm income of the household head by age (Annex Table E.1, columns (b) is found by subtracting total cost per acre (Step 3) times the number of acres by age (Step 1) from family farm income as a function of education and age of household head (combined Steps 1 and 2; see table, columns (a)).

Step 5. The non-farm income of the family (Y_{nf}) is estimated as a function of age of household head (A) for schooling groups.

Schooling Category	Equation	F	t	R^2
Illiterate	$Y_{nf} = 518.7 + 5.596A$	0.05	0.01	0.01
Literate	$Y_{nf} = 755.1 + 16.06A$	n.s.	0.05	0.00
1–3	$Y_{nf} = -1963 + 88.45A$	0.01	0.01	0.11
4–8	$Y_{nf} = 295.2 + 66.40A$	0.05	0.05	0.04
9 plus	$Y_{nf} = 3066 + 32.89A$	n.s.	0.01	0.01

Although the F-levels of two equations are not statistically significant at the 5 percent level, the equations are used anyway as the best estimates of non-farm income as a function of age.

Step 6. The number of adult male and female family members as a function of age of household head is found by taking the relation between farm size and size of family (Step 3) and inserting it into the relation between farm size and age (Step 1). Again, 21.8 percent of the family is assumed to be adult males and 27.3 percent adult females. The Central Province Survey results show that 23.6 percent of adult males and 5 percent of adult females work off the farm, which implies that a female has about a 20 percent probability of working off the farm relative to adult males. Females also earn less than males—it is assumed that they earn 73 percent the wages of males (1.60/2.19). One adult farm female is thus equivalent to 0.146 adult farm males. Using these weights, we find the total male equivalents on farms grouped by age and schooling of head of household.

Age	0 Illit.	0 Lit.	1–3	4–8	9 plus
17	1.17	1.17	1.09	1.19	—
20	1.22	1.23	1.18	1.29	1.12
30	1.37	1.43	1.50	1.62	1.61
40	1.55	1.60	1.77	1.87	1.97
50	1.64	1.74	2.03	2.11	2.33
60	1.78	1.88	2.27	2.36	2.71

Step 7. Under the assumption that the members of the family (in male equivalents) are of the same non-farm wage-earning capacity as the head of household, we divide family non-farm income (Step 5)

ANNEX TABLE E.1: Gross Family Farm Income and Imputed Farm and Non-Farm Income of Household Head, by Age and Education, 1963–64

Age	Illiterate (a)	Illiterate (b)	Illiterate (c)	Literate (a)	Literate (b)	Literate (c)	1–3 (a)	1–3 (b)	1–3 (c)	4–8 (a)	4–8 (b)	4–8 (c)	9 plus (a)	9 plus (b)	9 plus (c)
17	334	−4	525	406	77	879	269	130	−422	423	39	1197	—	—	—
20	406	−20	517	460	23	875	448	93	−164	673	117	1258	186	−38	3325
30	653	−12	501	638	−67	865	1044	256	460	1508	674	1412	1183	357	2517
40	900	98	479	817	−10	874	1640	601	889	2341	1202	1259	2179	945	2174
50	1147	255	487	995	9	896	2236	956	1211	3174	1828	1147	3176	1654	1979
60	1394	302	480	1164	14	915	2832	1401	1472	4010	2458	1307	4172	2172	1823

Note: Column (a): Gross family farm income. Derived from Annex E, Steps 1 and 2. See Step 4. Column (b): Imputed farm income of household head. See Annex E, Step 4. Column (c): Imputed non-farm income of household head. See Annex E, Step 7.

by these equivalents (Step 6) to get the non-farm income of the head of household himself. The results are shown in Annex Table E.1, column (c).

Step 8. The total imputed income of heads of household by age and education corrected for acreage and family size differentials is the sum of columns (b) and (c), as shown in Table 3.15.

ANNEX F

SOLUTION FOR CHANGE IN WAGE LEVEL TWO FROM DISCOUNT FORMULA

We begin with equation (5.16):

$$0 = -\sum_{i=1}^{S'} \frac{C_i + W_{1t}}{(1 + r_2)^i} + \sum_{i=S'+1}^{n} \frac{b_i + \Delta W_{2t} - \Delta W_{1t}}{(1 + r_2)^i}$$

where C_i and b_i = The expected discounted costs and lifetime benefits, respectively, of taking the additional year of schooling needed to move from skill level 1 to level 2, each level being defined in years of schooling;

ΔW_{1t} = The change in real annual wages (income) of skill level 1 in time period t, to be assumed constant over the entire age range, $i = S' + 1$ to $i = n$.

ΔW_{2t} = The corresponding change in real annual income of skill level 2 in time period t;

r_2 = The rate of return to the additional investment in schooling required to move from skill level 1 to skill level 2;

and S' = The number of years of schooling required to move from level 1 to level 2.

Regrouping this equation, we find:

$$-\sum_{i=1}^{n} \frac{-C_i + b_i}{(1 + r_2)^i} = -\sum_{i=1}^{S'} \frac{\Delta W_{1t}}{(1 + r_2)^i} + \sum_{i=S'+1}^{n} \frac{\Delta W_{2t} - \Delta W_{1t}}{(1 + r_2)^i}$$

$$-\sum_{i=1}^{n}\frac{-C_i + b_i}{(1+r_2)^i} = -\Delta W_{1t}\sum_{i=1}^{S'}(1+r_2)^{-i}$$

$$+ (\Delta W_{2t} - \Delta W_{1t})\sum_{i=S'+1}^{n}(1+r_2)^{-i}$$

$$\Delta W_{2t} - \Delta W_{1t} = \frac{-\sum_{i=1}^{n}\frac{-C_i + b_i}{(1+r_2)^i} + \Delta W_{1t}\sum_{i=1}^{S'}(1+r_2)^{-i}}{\sum_{i=S'+1}^{n}(1+r_2)^{-i}}$$

$$\Delta W_{2t} = \frac{-\sum_{i=1}^{n}\frac{-C_i + b_i}{(1+r_2)^i} + \Delta W_1\sum_{i=1}^{S'}(1+r_2)^{-i} + \Delta W_{1t}}{\sum_{i=S'+1}^{n}(1+r_2)^{-i}}$$

When income foregone does not enter into the calculations, the equation and solution for W_2 are simplified.

$$0 = \sum_{i=1}^{n}\frac{-C_i + b_i}{(1+r_2)^i} + \sum_{i=S'+1}^{n}\frac{\Delta W_{2t} - \Delta W_{1t}}{(1+r_2)^i}$$

$$-\sum_{i=1}^{n}\frac{-C_i + b_i}{(1+r_2)^i} = (\Delta W_{2t} - \Delta W_{1t})\sum_{i=S'+1}^{n}\frac{1}{(1+r_2)^i}$$

$$\Delta W_{2t} = \frac{-\sum_{i=1}^{n}\frac{-C_i + b_i}{(1+r_2)^i}}{\sum_{i+S'+1}^{n}(1+r_2)^{-i}} + \Delta W_{1t}$$

SELECTED BIBLIOGRAPHY

BOOKS

Blaug, M., Layard, P. R. G., and Woodhall, M. *The Causes of Graduate Unemployment in India*. London: Allen Lane, 1969.

Bowles, S. *Planning Education for Economic Growth*. Cambridge, Mass.: Harvard University Press, 1969.

Burkhead, J., Fox, T. G., and Holland, J. W. *Input and Output in Large-City High Schools*. Syracuse, N.Y.: Syracuse University Press, 1967.

Coleman, J., et al. *Educational Opportunity*. U.S. Office of Education. Washington, D.C.: Government Printing Office, 1967.

Denison, E. F. *The Sources of Growth in the United States and the Alternatives Before Us*. New York: Committee for Economic Development, 1962.

Hunter, G. *Education for a Developing Region*. London: George Allen & Unwin, 1963.

Hyman, H. H., Levine, G. N., and Wright, C. R. *Inducing Social Change in Developing Communities, An International Survey of Expert Advice*. Geneva: U.N. Research Institute for Social Development, 1967.

Knight, J. B. *The Costing and Financing of Educational Development in Tanzania*. International Institute of Educational Planning. Paris: UNESCO, 1966.

Richmond, K. *Culture and General Education*. London: Methuen & Co., Ltd., 1963.

Ribich, T. *Education and Poverty*. Washington, D.C.: Brookings Institution, 1968.

Schultz, T. W. *The Economic Value of Education*. New York: Columbia University Press, 1963.

Soja, E. W. *The Geography of Modernization in Kenya*. Syracuse, N.Y.: Syracuse University Press, 1968.

Somerset, H. C. A. *Predicting Success in School Certificate.* Nairobi: East African Publishing House, 1968.

von Molnos, A. *Attitudes Towards Family Planning in East Africa.* African Study No. 26. Munich: IFO—Institut fuer Wirtschaftsforschung, 1968.

ARTICLES AND REPORTS

Anderson, J. "The Adolescent in the Rural Community." *Education, Employment and Rural Development,* J. R. Sheffield (ed.) Nairobi: East African Publishing House, 1967.

Becker, G. S. "Investment in Human Capital: A Theoretical Analyses." *Journal of Political Economy* (Supplement) Vol. LXX (October 1962).

Blaug, M. "A Cost-Benefit Approach to Educational Planning in Developing Countries." IBRD Economics Department Staff Study EC-157, December 1967.

Brownstein, L. "Preliminary Results of a Survey of 1964 KPE Candidates in Embu, Kitui, Kericho and Nyanza." (Mimeo.) Institute for Development Studies, University College. Nairobi, 1967.

Carnoy, M. "Earnings and Schooling in Mexico." *Economic Development and Cultural Change,* July 1967.

———. "Rates of Return to Schooling in Latin America." *Journal of Human Resources,* Vol. II, No. 3 (Summer 1967).

Foster, P. and Yost, L. "Population Growth and Rural Development in Buganda: A Simulation of a Micro-Socio-Economic System." Miscellaneous Publication No. 621, Agricultural Experiment Station. University of Maryland, College Park, Md., 1968.

Frank, C. R., Jr. "Urban Unemployment and Economic Growth in Africa." *Oxford Economic Papers* Vol. 20, No. 2 (July 1968).

Gutkind, P. C. W. "African Responses to Urban Wage Employment." *International Labour Review,* No. 87 (February 1968).

Husen, T. "Talent Opportunity and Career: A 26-Year Follow-Up." *School Review,* 76(2) (June 1968).

Rogers, D. C. "Student Loan Programs and the Returns to Investment in Higher Levels of Education in Kenya." (Mimeo.) Teachers College, Columbia University, New York, March 1969. (To be published in *Economic Development and Cultural Change,* 1971.)

Schultz, T. P. "Returns to Education in Bogota, Colombia." The Rand Corporation, Memorandum RM-J645-RC/AID, September 1968.

Selowsky, M. "The Effect of Unemployment and Growth on the Rate of Return to Education: The Case of Colombia." (Mimeo.) Harvard University, 1968.

Smyth, J. and Bennett, N. "Rates of Return on Investment in Education: A Tool for Short-Term Educational Planning, Illustrated with Uganda Data." *World Year Book of Education,* G. Bereday and J. Lanwergs. London: Evans Bros., Ltd., 1968.

Wolfle, D. "National Resources of Ability." *Ability and Educational Opportunity,* A. H. Halsey (ed.). Paris: OECD, 1961.

KENYAN AND U.K. GOVERNMENT PUBLICATIONS

Kenya

Education Commission Report. Nairobi, 1965.

African Socialism and Its Application to Planning in Kenya. Sessional Paper No. 10. Nairobi, 1965.

Ministry of Economic Planning and Development. *Economic Survey, 1968*. Nairobi, 1968.
———. *Economic Survey of Central Province, 1963–64*. Nairobi, 1964.
———. *Kenya Development Plan, 1964–70*. Nairobi, 1964.
———. *Kenya Population Census, 1962*. Nairobi, 1966.
Ministry of Education. *Triennial Survey, 1961–1963*. Nairobi, 1964.

U.K.

Ministry of Overseas Development. *British Government Economic Aid, Statistics of Aid to Developing Countries, 1962 to June 1967*. London, 1968.